Regulating lobbying: a global comparison

Manchester University Press

European Policy Research Unit Series

Series Editors: *Simon Bulmer, Peter Humphreys* and *Mick Moran*

The European Policy Research Unit Series aims to provide advanced textbooks and thematic studies of key public policy issues in Europe. They concentrate, in particular, on comparing patterns of national policy content, but pay due attention to the European Union dimension. The thematic studies are guided by the character of the policy issue under examination.

The European Policy Research Unit (EPRU) was set up in 1989 within the University of Manchester's Department of Government to promote research on European politics and public policy. The series is part of EPRU's effort to facilitate intellectual exchange and substantive debate on the key policy issues confronting the European states and the European Union.

Titles in the series also include:

Globalisation and policy-making in the European Union   Ian Bartle

The Europeanisation of Whitehall   Simon Bulmer and Martin Burch

The power of the centre: Central governments and the macro-implementation of EU public policy   Dionyssis G. Dimitrakopoulos

Creating a transatlantic marketplace   Michelle P. Egan (ed.)

The politics of health in Europe   Richard Freeman

Immigration and European integration (2nd edn)   Andrew Geddes

Agricultural policy in Europe   Alan Greer

The European Union and the regulation of media markets   Alison Harcourt

Mass media and media policy in Western Europe   Peter Humphreys

The politics of fisheries in the European Union   Christian Lequesne

The European Union and culture: Between economic regulation and European cultural policy   Annabelle Littoz-Monnet

Sports law and policy in the European Union   Richard Parrish

The Eurogroup   Uwe Puetter

EU pharmaceutical regulation   Govin Permanand

Regulatory quality in Europe: Concepts, measures and policy processes   Claudio M. Radaelli and Fabrizio de Francesco

Extending European cooperation   Alasdair R. Young

Regulatory politics in the enlarging European Union   Alasdair Young and Helen Wallace

Regulating lobbying: a global comparison

Raj Chari, John Hogan and Gary Murphy

Manchester University Press

Manchester and New York

distributed in the United States exclusively
by Palgrave Macmillan

Copyright © Raj Chari, John Hogan and Gary Murphy 2010

The right of Raj Chari, John Hogan and Gary Murphy to be identified as the authors of this work has been asserted by them in accordance with the Copyright, Designs and Patents Act 1988.

Published by Manchester University Press
Oxford Road, Manchester M13 9NR, UK
and Room 400, 175 Fifth Avenue, New York, NY 10010, USA
www.manchesteruniversitypress.co.uk

Distributed exclusively in the USA by
Palgrave Macmillan, 175 Fifth Avenue, New York,
NY 10010, USA

Distributed exclusively in Canada by
UBC Press, University of British Columbia, 2029 West Mall,
Vancouver, BC, Canada V6T 1Z2

British Library Cataloguing-in-Publication Data
A catalogue record for this book is available from the British Library

Library of Congress Cataloging-in-Publication Data applied for

ISBN 978 0 7190 7937 5 *hardback*

First published 2010

The publisher has no responsibility for the persistence or accuracy of URLs for any external or third-party internet websites referred to in this book, and does not guarantee that any content on such websites is, or will remain, accurate or appropriate.

Typeset by R. J. Footring Ltd, Derby
Printed by Lightning Source

Contents

Figures

Tables

Acknowledgements

First of all, we would like to thank the European Politics Research Unit book series editors: Simon Bulmer, Peter Humphreys and Michael Moran. We are particularly indebted to Mick Moran for his belief in this project right from the very beginning. Tony Mason of Manchester University Press and his team were a delight to work with and we are grateful for their efficiency throughout the process. The anonymous external reviewers also offered excellent constructive comments from which this book has benefited. We are also very grateful to Ralph Footring for his excellent copy-editing of the text and owe him a significant debt of gratitude.

We acknowledge the financial support of the Department of the Environment, Heritage and Local Government, Government of Ireland, and specifically thank Mary Tully and Eoin Corrigan for their encouragement throughout the initial phases of our research. The Irish Research Council for Humanities and Social Science also funded part of our research on lobbying regulation through its Research Development Initiative.

The participants of the Canadian Political Science Association meeting in Saskatoon in June 2007, the American Political Science Association panel on lobbying in Boston in August 2008 and in Toronto in September 2009, and the European Centre for Public Affairs annual meeting in Brussels in October 2008 also offered important comments from which this book has benefited. We specifically thank Frank Baumgartner, Christine Mahoney, Conor McGrath, Irina Michalowitz, Richard Sigurdson and Tom Spencer for their excellent insights.

The universities where we work, and our colleagues throughout the world, provided invaluable support and we are indebted to Ken Benoit, Billie Crosbie, Robert Elgie, José Elguero, José Folgado, Michael Gallagher, Craig Holman, Marty Hooper, Mike Howlett, Eugene Kennedy, Fiona Killard, Monte Krueger, Michael Marsh, Philomena Murray, Alfred E. Neuman, Paul O'Sullivan, George Pagoulatos, Declan Raftery, Jon Slapin, Duff Spafford and James Wickham.

We are especially grateful to those politicians, lobbyists and administrators who responded to our surveys and agreed to be interviewed in confidence. Their answers and honest views have made this less an academic exercise and more a discovery of knowledge.

As always, our families have been our backbone – through good times and bad. Amy, Aoife, Celia, Debbie, Isabel, Jack and Mandy: no words could be enough, so we won't even try.

Raj, John and Gary
Dublin and Madrid

Abbreviations

BC	British Columbia
CPI	Center for Public Integrity
DPOH	Designated public office holder
EP	European Parliament
EU	European Union
FDI	Foreign direct investment
FECA	Federal Election Campaign Act
FOI	Freedom of information
LLA	Law on Lobbying Activity (Lithuania)
MEP	Member of the European Parliament
MLA	Member of a legislative assembly
MP	Member of Parliament
NATO	North Atlantic Treaty Organization
NGO	Non-governmental organisation
PAC	Political action committee
PDC	Public Disclosure Commission
SEA	Single European Act
SEC	Securities and Exchange Commission

1

Outlining central questions and method of analysis

Introduction

Sparked by Arthur Bentley's seminal work *The Process of Government*, political scientists for over a century have examined the different pressures on government by highlighting the importance of 'group activities' (Bentley, 1908: 200–222). As Howlett and Ramesh (2003: 37–38) state, 'Bentley argued that different interests in society found their concrete manifestation in different groups consisting of different individuals with similar concerns'. Several scholars have since studied the role of interest groups (or lobby groups – we use the two terms interchangeably throughout the book) and offered telling insights with regard to what takes place when public policy is formulated. Of course, what goes on within the 'black box' of the policy-making process has been open to much debate. Pluralist scholars, such as Dahl (1961), considered that all groups had equal access to the process, regardless of resource constraints, and could influence policy equally. Neo-pluralists, such as Lindblom (1977), argued that some interest groups had disproportionate influence, as pluralism became corrupted, something which they believed, nevertheless, was reversible. Neo-Marxists, such as Miliband (1969), who did not share the neo-pluralists' view that disproportionate influence was simply an anomaly, contended that business interests were guaranteed a privileged place in policy making, given the importance of the capitalist economic system. Following these traditions, our own previous work has also examined the role of interest groups, analysing how they function and how they try to influence policy development in different political systems in Europe, whether the European Union (EU) or the member states (Chari and Cavatorta, 2002; Murphy, 2004; Trommer and Chari, 2006).

All of these studies have shown that, without doubt, the work carried out by interest groups is a central and legitimate part of the democratic process within all liberal democratic systems. Although the term has often had negative connotations, throughout the democratic world the work of lobbyists is essential when policy is formulated. Lobbyists are an accepted element within society, providing the necessary input and feedback into the

1

political system, thereby helping to develop the policy outputs which drive political and economic aspects of our daily lives.

However, because of issues surrounding the openness of the policy-making process, some countries have sought to regulate the activities of lobbyists. As Bertók (2008: 18) argues, 'when public concern is about the integrity of government decision making, measures to ensure transparency and accountability become essential'. Many democracies have attempted to do this by means of freedom of information legislation, while others have sought to regulate lobbyists through the decision-making process. In both cases, the focus is on transparency and accountability. The basic rationale behind implementing regulations is that the public should have some insight into, as well as oversight of, the mechanisms that draw lobbyists into the policy-making environment, in order to better understand how they influence policy outputs.

With this in mind, while this book finds a niche within the broader scholarship on interest groups, it offers an innovative approach to the literature because it is less preoccupied with private interests' role and actions when specific policies are made; instead, it is more concerned with comparing how lobby groups are formally regulated throughout the world and the impact this has had, something which is a significant, if not surprising, omission in the literature. Although some scholars, including ourselves, have focused on lobbying regulation in Canada, the US, the EU and Germany (Baumgartner and Leech, 2001; Chari *et al.*, 2007; Dyck, 2004; Greenwood, 2007; Ronit and Schneider, 1998; Rush, 1998; Stark, 1992; Wolpe and Levine, 1996; Zeller, 1958), no major work in political science has offered an in-depth, detailed analysis of this phenomenon from a global comparative perspective, including analysis of developments in North America, Europe and Asia, as well as Australia, continents which have all established lobbying laws, as discussed below. Nor has any project attempted fresh research examining why other jurisdictions have not developed lobbying laws, despite the fact that their neighbours have pursued such initiatives.

Before outlining the main questions that guide the book, we first consider what is meant by the terms 'lobby groups' and 'lobbying', as well as the concept of regulation of such groups. We then offer a theoretical discussion of why regulating lobbyists is important, while also presenting a balanced view of why some scholars have considered it to have drawbacks. Following this, in order to set up our main research questions, we examine the international trends with regard to regulating lobbyists, as this allows us to contextualise the development of such regulations: which jurisdictions have adopted lobbying legislation, and when? After outlining the main questions addressed in the book, we then turn to a discussion of the methods of analysis used in the study. We close the chapter by highlighting the structure of the book.

What is a lobby group and what is lobbying? And what is meant by 'regulation of lobbyists'?

Providing a working definition of lobby groups and lobbying is helpful at this early stage. Yet, the literature demonstrates that the classification of such groups, and explaining what exactly lobbying is, have proved immensely difficult. Developing cogent definitions of both 'lobby group' and 'lobbying' is not as easy as it might first appear.

To define an 'interest group' or 'lobby group', different classification schemes have been used in the literature. For example, in a study on the EU, Watson and Shackelton (2003: 89) provided a useful typology to classify different types of lobby actors, distinguishing between bodies that promote private interests (i.e. that pursue specific economic goals) and those that promote public interests (i.e. that pursue non-economic aims). Chari and Kritzinger (2006) extended this by considering three types of groups: economic groups (including individual corporations and business organisations), professional groups (such as trade unions and farmers) and public groups (including groups that are concerned about issues such as human rights, the environment, animal rights and health and safety). Chari and Kritzinger (2006: 30) define an interest/lobby organisation, whether motivated by economic, professional or public concerns, 'as any group, or set of actors, that has common interests and seeks to influence the policy-making process in such a way that their interests are reflected in public policy outcomes'. Some everyday examples include: corporations trying to ensure that the finance ministry has a policy of minimising corporation tax; a farming organisation that lobbies the agriculture ministry in order to ensure maximum subsidies for the goods farmers produce; and an environmental group that wants to make sure the ministry of the environment has strong legislation in place to control carbon emissions.

With regard to the activity of lobbying itself, two eminent scholars in the field have pointed out that 'the word lobbying has seldom been used the same way twice by those studying the topic' (Baumgartner and Leech, 1998: 33). These authors define lobbying parsimoniously and clearly as 'an effort to influence the policy process' (Baumgartner and Leech, 1998: 34). In the US, the National Conference of State Legislatures (2008) specifies that 'all states share a basic definition of lobbying as an attempt to influence government action'. For Nownes (2006: 5), 'lobbying is an effort designed to affect what the government does'. Hunter *et al.* (1991: 490) argue that 'a common definition of a lobbyist is "someone who attempts to affect legislative action"'.

In essence, lobbying can take two forms: in-house and the hiring of professional lobbyists. In-house lobbying refers to the practice whereby the lobbyist is an employee of the organisation engaged in the lobbying. Paid lobbying takes the form of professional lobbyists who perform that function for a fee.

Taking ideas from the above contributions to the literature, in either case we can regard lobbying as the act of individuals or groups, each with varying and specific interests, attempting to influence decisions taken at the political level. Such lobby groups may include, but are not necessarily limited to, those with economic interests (such as corporations), professional interests (such as trade unions or professional societies) and civil society interests (such as environmental groups). Such groups may directly, or indirectly through consultants they have hired (professional lobbyists), seek to have public policy outputs reflect their preferences. The attempts to influence political decisions may take place by many means, including direct communications with government officials, presentations to state officials, draft reports to public officials wherein specific details of policy itself are suggested, and even simple telephone conversations with government personnel, to name but some mechanisms.

When turning to the concept of regulation, a leading scholar in the field points out that 'regulation is a notoriously inexact word, but its core meaning is mechanical and immediately invokes the act of steering' (Moran, 2007: 13). For the purposes of our book, the concept of 'regulation of lobbyists' refers to the idea that political systems have established 'rules' which lobby groups must follow when trying to influence government officials and public policy outputs. The idea of 'must follow' is a significant one for the purposes of the study: it is not simply a matter of voluntarily complying with suggestions made by the political system, as presently seen in the case of the European Commission (see Chapter 2, p. 55). Rather, the regulations represent a set of codified, formal rules which are passed by parliament and written in law (which is enforced), and so must be respected. The latter point suggests that the risk lobbyists run in not complying with the rules is penalisation, whether that is a fine or, potentially, a jail sentence. Examples of rules that lobbyists may have to follow include: registering with the state before contact can be made with any public official; clearly indicating which ministry/public actors the lobbyist intends to influence; providing the state with individual or employer spending disclosures; having a publicly available list with lobbyists' details for citizens to scrutinise; and ensuring that former legislators cannot immediately jump into the world of lobbying once they have left public office (referred to as a 'cooling off' period). The theoretical justification for such rules is based on ensuring transparency and accountability in the political system. Or, taking from Francis (1993: 12), such regulations, or state constraints on the activity of interest organisations, 'help promote the public interest', a discussion to which we now turn.

Theoretical reasons for regulating lobbying, or not

In this section we consider the two sides of the debate regarding the theoretical reasons to regulate, or not. On the one hand, proponents of lobbying regulation discuss the importance of deliberative democracy, transparency and accountability. On the other hand, opponents stress that regulations pose dangers, such as serving as a barrier to entry. We consider both arguments in turn.

Theoretical justifications for regulating lobbyists: the importance of deliberative democracy, transparency and accountability

Deliberative democratic theory, as a subgroup of participatory democracy, argues that representative democracy can be bettered through discussion and reflection (Chambers, 2003: 308; Pateman, 1976). This results in a more legitimate polity for all citizens. As Stasavage (2004: 668) contends, 'advocates of deliberative democracy emphasize that the deliberations that occur in public increase the quality and the legitimacy of decisions taken'. The main ideas behind deliberative democracy are that the reasons for, and details behind, policy decisions should be publicly available, while decision makers ought to be publicly accountable (Gutmann and Thompson, 2004: 135; O'Flynn, 2006: 101). Young (2002: 17–32) suggests that deliberative democracy promotes inclusion, equality in the policy process and publicity. Naurin (2007: 209) argues that 'transparency is believed to strengthen public confidence in political institutions and increase the possibilities of citizens holding decision makers accountable'.

What is the relation between ideas raised in deliberative democratic theory and the need for lobbying regulation? As Stasavage (2004: 668) succinctly argues, 'the more that citizens know about the actions of government officials, the easier they will find it to judge whether officials are acting in the public interest'. In this regard, it is important to confront the absence of transparency in decision making by establishing rules that allow the public to gauge 'who is influencing what' when policy is formulated. Although deliberative democratic theory argues against the concept of 'more regulation', lobbying regulation constitutes an exception, perhaps a necessary evil, until other solutions can be found. Stasavage (2003: 389) argues that 'the most direct way to eliminate problems of moral hazard is to make an agent's behaviour more observable'. This is something which McCubbins *et al.* (1987) note can be achieved through 'sunshine laws' which allow public access to information. Through increasing transparency and accountability, lobbying regulation is seen to shed light on an aspect of the black box of policy making referred to above, and improve the overall nature of the political decisions reached by a polity (Dryzek, 2000; Elster, 1998; Keohane and Nye, 2003).

With this in mind, it is necessary at this point to define two key terms which underpin deliberative democratic theory: transparency and accountability. Taking from Broz (2002: 861), 'transparency' refers to the ease with which the public can monitor not only the government with respect to its activity, but also which private interests are attempting to influence the state when public policy is formulated. This encapsulates the motives of all policy-making actors and the clarity of policy objectives (Geraats, 2002: 540). As Héritier (1999) and Scharpf (2006) show, transparency not only increases policy actors' responses to public demands, but also helps prevent misconduct. Or, as Finkelstein (2000: 1) contends, 'transparent policies are better than those that are opaque'. Although there may be no direct material benefits *per se*, Geraats (2002: 562) shows that there are benefits associated with transparency, such as bettering the democratic quality of life, something which makes citizens become less apathetic towards the world of politics. Naurin (2007: 209) highlights another benefit: the increased legitimacy of public institutions in the eyes of the public.

By 'accountability', we mean answering to and taking responsibility for actions (Moncrieffe, 1998: 389; Scott, 2000: 40). At the political level, actors who are accountable for their actions include politicians, who must seek re-election on a regular basis. Increasingly, other actors, such as civil servants and regulators, are also under the spotlight. Gutmann and Thompson (1996: 95) argue that exposing the details of decision making helps 'purify' politics, a concept which was espoused in the 1800s by theorists such as Bentham (James *et al.*, 1999). Risse (2000: 32) suggests that not only political but also economic elites are increasingly having to justify their actions to citizens. Much of the world was witness to this idea when many banks and financial regulators came under the microscope during the economic and banking crisis of 2008 and 2009.

Lobbying regulations are thus justified in order to render government officials more accountable and to promote the transparency of lobbyists' actions (Thomas and Hrebenar, 1996: 12–16). Lobbying regulation invariably takes the form of the establishment of a register of lobbyists, run by a registrar's office or similar institution in the jurisdiction within which the lobbying itself takes place. Largerlof and Frisell (2004: 16) contend that lobbyist registration in and of itself helps promote transparency. Moreover, 'by imposing an obligation on lobbyists to disclose the identity of those on whose behalf action is being taken, a government is making laws that take account of the public interest' (Garziano, 2001: 99). In the words of Thomas (2004: 287), such rules 'constrain the actions of lobbyists and public officials alike, even if they do not ultimately affect which groups are powerful and which ones are not'.

This is not to say that the goal of regulating lobbying is to outlaw bribery – most liberal democracies have well defined mechanisms for this already, including laws that deal with corruption. Rather, the role of regulation is to make the public aware of the interests behind proposals and the links between lobbyists and policy makers. This helps bring policy making under closer scrutiny (Gray and Lowery, 1998: 90) and increases knowledge of how the political system and the actors within it work. Without such scrutiny, 'it may be difficult for electors to judge whether a representative has taken their interest in consideration when bargaining over policy, or alternatively, whether unseen actions by lobby groups are dominating outcomes' (Stasavage, 2004: 672).

Theoretical justifications for not regulating lobbyists: barriers to entry, need for confidentiality and costs

From a theoretical perspective, why do some political systems choose not to regulate lobbying? We consider three factors: barriers to entry, the 'dangers' of shedding light on the policy process and costs.

With regard to the first point, the literature suggests that political systems choose to not pursue lobbying rules because such regulations may be viewed as barriers to entry to participation in the policy process, particularly as far as citizens are concerned. This idea is seen in arguments by rational-choice scholars such as Ainsworth (1993) and Brinig *et al.* (1993). This was also a conclusion shared by the Committee on Standards in Public Life in the UK in the mid-1990s (Nolan Committee, 1995) when it stated that 'regulation could create the perception that the only legitimate route through which outside interests might engage with parliament would be via the offices of registered commercial lobbyists' (see Dinan, 2006: 56). The Nolan Committee subsequently called for the maintenance of the status quo, where relations between politicians and lobbyists were to be based upon informal rules and a type of self-regulated 'good conduct'. Jordan (1998: 524) observes that 'successive parliamentary inquiries [in the UK] have examined this issue, but their recommendations (if any) have had limited impact'. Gray and Lowery (1998: 78) also conclude that reluctance to institutionalise lobbying regulation relates to the concern that such 'regulation may have a direct bearing on levels of lobbying activity if the stringency of regulations and their enforcement influence the numbers of registrations'.

Secondly, Naurin (2007) suggests that resistance to formal lobbying rules is actually based on the potential dangers that may be associated with increased transparency, an argument which directly challenges the deliberative democratic theory scholars (see above). The idea here is that, in order to formulate 'good policy', confidential negotiations are sometimes necessary (Fisher *et al.*, 1999: 36). Transparency in this regard is really more part of the disease than of any cure: it impedes effective problem solving and 'sunshine laws' can in fact harm the efficiency of the negotiations (Groseclose and McCarty, 2001: 100). One example of a country with an opaque policy process is Japan, where, as Hrebenar *et al.* (1998: 554) state, 'almost all important lobbying aimed at influencing takes place behind closed doors', and they cite Johnson (1982: 91–92), who states that 'the invisible political process is much more important for actual decision-making'.

A third reason for not regulating lobbyists relates to costs to the state: regulating lobbying by its very nature necessitates the setting up of a register, hiring staff to monitor it and later enforcing the rules if there are breaches, which all cost significant amounts of money. Formulating and implementing the rules essentially means a loss of state funds that might otherwise be used for other purposes, which becomes especially important during economic recession. We revisit and re-evaluate this argument in more detail in Chapter 5 (p. 129).

Democracies that regulate lobbying: international trends and contextualising the phenomenon

We started this chapter with a discussion of why lobbying is important in the political system and what is meant by the terms 'lobbying', 'lobby groups' and 'regulation of lobbyists'. We then considered the theoretical underpinnings for justifying lobbying regulation and contemplated theoretical concerns against such legislation.

The question we turn to in this section is rather simple: which political systems in the democratic world regulate lobbyists? To this end, Table 1.1 (pp. 10–11) summarises the situation in major states, as well as the EU, and considers the rules in place governing lobbyists as of 2008. A first observation from Table 1.1 is that advanced industrial democracies which have lobbying regulations are relatively rare: there are no lobbying rules in most jurisdictions.

Notwithstanding the rarity of regulating lobbyists, there are nine political systems throughout the democratic world with lobbying rules in place: Australia, Canada, the EU, Germany, Hungary, Lithuania, Poland, Taiwan and the US. Of these, the systems that established such regulations in the 1900s, thus constituting systems with rules for a longer time than the others, are the US (since 1946), Germany (since 1951), Canada (since 1989) and the European Parliament (since 1996; neither the European Commission nor the Council has formal lobbying rules in place, although the Commission has had a voluntary scheme in place since June 2008 – see Chapter 2, p. 55). The US also sees regulations in all of its 50 states, while Canada has regulation in six of its 10 provinces. The other jurisdictions, namely Hungary, Lithuania, Poland and Taiwan, have all enacted lobbying laws relatively recently, in the 2000s. The case of Australia witnesses a state that flirted with lobbying regulation in the 1980s, abandoned it in 1996, only to revisit the issue in 2008.

When considering developments in the 27 member states of the EU (the EU-27), one sees that only four have national laws: Germany, Lithuania, Poland and Hungary. Interestingly, three of these four are countries associated with the former USSR and also represent 'new entrants' that joined the EU in 2004. In other words, more established EU states (other than Germany) have not enacted lobbying regulations, although it is noteworthy that some parts of Italy have done so at the regional level. Nor have other member states which are negotiating entry into the EU (such as Croatia, Turkey, Bosnia and Herzegovina and Serbia) and nor have those which operate within the European Economic Area (such as Norway and Switzerland).

Table 1.1 also tells us that economic heavy-weights with sizeable populations, such as Japan and India, do not have lobbying laws. In fact, apart from Taiwan, there are no other democracies in Asia with lobbying rules; nor has any African or South American state implemented formal regulations to date.[1]

The main questions that guide the book

Despite the works noted above that have offered some analysis of the development of lobbying legislation, there is a fourfold void in the literature. First, from a more descriptive perspective, no study has attempted a broad overview of the historical development and the exact details of the regulations in each of the systems throughout the world that have established lobbying legislation: the US, Germany, Canada, the EU, Lithuania, Poland, Hungary, Taiwan and Australia. Secondly, from a more analytical perspective, no study has offered a comparative analysis that classifies the types of laws in the political systems where lobbying rules are in place. This will allow for better theoretical understanding of the different regulatory environments one finds in this area. Thirdly, few studies have analysed the views of key agents involved in the process, including politicians, lobbyists and regulators, and how these compare and contrast across the different regulatory environments of the four political systems with the longest established record of lobbying legislation: the US, Germany, Canada and the European Parliament (EP). And finally, little analysis has been performed on institutions (such as the European Commission) and other jurisdictions within Canada and the US that have not enacted lobbying legislation. Examination of political and bureaucratic actors' views, as well as those of interest groups, will allow political scientists better to gauge why lobbying legislation was not pursued in these jurisdictions even though their neighbours have adopted it, and whether or not it is worth implementing.

As such, six central questions guide the analysis of the book:

1 What is the brief history of the regulations in each system which established lobbying rules during the 1900s – the US, Canada, the European Union and Germany (Chapter 2)?
2 What is the nature of the regulations in political systems that more recently established them, in the 2000s – Lithuania, Poland, Hungary, Taiwan and Australia (Chapter 3)?
3 From a comparative perspective, how can the different types of systems established throughout the world be theoretically classified (Chapter 4)?
4 By focusing on those systems which have had regulations longest, namely the US, Canada, the EP and Germany, what insights can be gained with

Table 1.1 Contextualising lobbying regulations: regulations in place in democratic states and the European Union

Country	Rules governing lobbyists as of 2008
Australia	As of 1 July 2008 there have been national rules in place and a register. Originally formulated and implemented in the 1980s, lobbying rules were then abandoned in 1996. See Chapter 3 (p. 91) for more details on Australian regulations
Austria	No statutory rules
Belgium	No statutory rules
Bosnia and Herzegovina	No statutory rules
Bulgaria	No statutory rules
Canada	*Federal level*. Rules and register since the Lobbyists Registration Act of 1989. This legislation was amended in 1995, 2003 and 2008 *Provincial level*. Since the 1990s, lobbying regulations in Ontario, Quebec, British Columbia, Nova Scotia and Newfoundland. Alberta was scheduled to introduce legislation in 2009. See Chapter 2 (p. 36) for more details on Canadian regulations
Chile	No statutory rules, although a bill on regulating lobbying was being debated at the time of writing
Croatia	No statutory rules
Cyprus	No statutory rules
Czech Republic	No statutory rules, although a voluntary code of ethics, including guidance on how elected officials should maintain relations and communications with interest groups, was introduced in 2005
Denmark	No statutory rules
Estonia	No statutory rules
Finland	No statutory rules
France	No statutory rules, although, at the time of writing, a motion for a resolution on lobbying was being debated. Article 26(1) of the general directives of the Bureau of the National Assembly also states that those with special cards issued personally by the president or by the quaestors may have access to the Salon de la Paix (a chamber which regularly hosts debates with Members and invited guests on topical issues)
Germany	Regulation and registration were introduced through rules of procedure of the Bundestag in 1951; later amended in 1975 and 1980. See Chapter 2 (p. 61) for more details
Greece	No statutory rules
Hungary	Regulation of lobbying activity since 2006. See Chapter 3 (p. 82) for more details
Iceland	No statutory rules

India	No statutory rules
Ireland	No statutory rules
Israel	No statutory rules
Italy	No statutory rules at national level. Nevertheless, regional schemes were introduced in the Consiglio regionale della Toscana in 2002 and Regione Molise in 2004
Japan	No statutory rules
Latvia	No statutory rules
Lithuania	Regulation since 2001. See Chapter 3 (p. 74) for more details
Luxembourg	No statutory rules
Malta	No statutory rules
Mexico	No statutory rules
Netherlands	No statutory rules
New Zealand	No statutory rules
Norway	No statutory rules
Poland	Regulations since 2005. See Chapter 3 (p. 79) for more details
Portugal	No statutory rules
Romania	No statutory rules
Serbia	No statutory rules
Slovakia	No statutory rules
Slovenia	No statutory rules
South Korea	No statutory rules
Spain	No statutory rules
Sweden	No statutory rules
Switzerland	No statutory rules
Taiwan	Lobbying Act passed in August 2007, came into force in August 2008. See Chapter 3 (p. 87) for more details
Turkey	No statutory rules
UK	No statutory rules in either the House of Commons or the House of Lords
US	*Federal level.* Lobbying Act 1946, amended in 1995 and 2007 *State level.* All states have lobbying regulations. See Chapter 2 (p. 20) for more details

European Union (EU)

European Parliament	Regulated by rule 9 of the Rules of Procedure, 1996. See Chapter 2 (p. 50) for more details
European Commission	Before 2008, 'self-regulation' was the model adopted by the Commission. However, in June 2008 the Commission opened a register of interest representations, although interest groups are not formally required to register. See Chapter 2 (p. 55) for more details
Council of Ministers	No statutory rules

Sources: Chari *et al.* (2007); Malone (2004); McGrath (2008, 2009).

regard to how effective these regulations have been? Here we seek better
to understand:

* how regulations may or may not foster transparency and accountability in the democratic process;
* the potential loopholes in the system;
* the potential financial costs and how the rules have affected lobbying
  (Chapter 5).

5 Why is there no lobbying legislation in the European Commission or
  some jurisdictions in Canada and what are the different actors' views
  regarding pursuing lobbying regulations (Chapter 6)?
6 What are the various pros and cons of regulating lobbyists and, based
  on the experience of jurisdictions with regulations, what lessons can be
  learned by other states without regulations, including democracies in
  Asia, South America and Africa (Chapter 7)?

Method of analysis and approach

We believe that all good work in social science is based on firm evidence.
That is not to say that we are hard-core positivists who rely only on
'data-sets'. In fact, we have seen the limitations on the use of data-sets:
a researcher's interpretation of such (limited) data may result in a complete misrepresentation of what is being studied. Nevertheless, if a social
scientific study is not based on cogent evidence, it may result only in a
debilitating interpretivist exercise based entirely on the opinions of the
authors. Presenting good evidence to back up claims allows other social
science researchers to verify or falsify scientific findings, as discussed by
authors such as Popper (1963). In a nutshell, any study should be replicable
in order to allow our scientific knowledge to be built on.

With these ideas in mind, the main research questions presented above
will be answered by using three broad methods of analysis, combining
both quantitative and qualitative techniques. The first is a textual analysis
that generates numerical scores. The second is a compilation of responses
to surveys, to allow for analysis of trends. And the third is a more qualitative analysis, of findings from a series of elite interviews. We consider
each in turn.

First, this study examines the exact regulations on lobbying activity in
the nine political systems by way of detailed textual analysis of legislation.
In order to gain a complete view of the existing regulations, two strategies
were taken. First, an exhaustive search was performed in order to find
the specific relevant legislation for each political system. When turning to
the three (federal) systems with the longest history of regulation – the US,
Canada and Germany – we used various sources, including contacts with
other researchers as well as government officials, to collect *all* relevant
pieces of legislation. This, in itself, was a mammoth task not previously

done in any study: while there is only one piece of legislation in Germany and the EU, the US sees 51 pieces of legislation at the federal and state levels, while Canada has federal legislation plus that of six provinces. Textual analysis of the specific legislation was also performed for those states which have more recently established regulations, namely Lithuania, Hungary, Poland, Taiwan and Australia.

Once we had a firm idea of the exact regulations in each of the political systems, we determined how regulations in all the political systems compared. This allows us to see similarities and differences between the jurisdictions. This was accomplished by applying the quantitative method of analysis developed by the Center for Public Integrity (CPI, discussed in detail in Chapter 4). In essence, the CPI methodology consists of assigning values to 48 questions measuring certain aspects of lobbying legislation, resulting in a score between 1 and 100: the closer the score of the legislation is to 100, the more 'developed' the regulation is considered to be (or 'tighter' in terms of regulating lobbyist behaviour). By carefully studying each piece of lobbying legislation, points were assigned by the authors on each of the 48 questions. Questions covered rules on individual registration, rules on individual spending disclosure, methods for registration, availability of information to the public and state enforcement capabilities. This method of analysis allows for a more cogent understanding of the nature of the regulation, allowing us to theoretically classify different regulatory environments.

With regard to the second main method of analysis, we determined the effectiveness of such regulations in the four jurisdictions with the longest-standing lobby regulation in place by developing a questionnaire targeted at interest groups (those who lobby) and political and administrative actors (those who are lobbied). It was decided to concentrate on these four jurisdictions – the US, Canada, the EP and Germany – precisely because they have had lobbying laws for the longest time and it was felt that more reliable data on the effectiveness of such regulations could be attained from these jurisdictions, given that lobbying regulation was not a 'new' phenomenon *per se*. The actors who were approached were representative of a large sample of the main types of lobby groups (economic, professional, single-interest, etc.), regulators and political officials in all four jurisdictions. Three main types of question were asked and later answered by over 140 respondents across Canada, the US, the EU and Germany in a survey which we administered in 2005. The first type of question gauged the knowledge of the actors on the regulation, the second sought their views on the effectiveness and transparency of the legislation, and the third questioned how they believed that the regulation could be improved in relation to cost, transparency and accountability. A separate questionnaire was also given to actors in institutions and jurisdictions in those systems where there was no lobbying law in place in 2005, but whose 'neighbouring jurisdictions' had lobbying legislation. In the case of the EP, these were the

European Commission and the Council of Ministers; in Canada, provinces such as Prince Edward Island, New Brunswick, Manitoba, Saskatchewan and Alberta;[2] and in the case of the US, the state of Pennsylvania.[3] This questionnaire was given in order to illuminate why these jurisdictions did not pursue lobbying legislation and whether or not there may be advantages to adopting a regulatory system.

Thirdly, once the questionnaire responses had been coded and analysed, we followed up with open-ended elite interviews in 2006 with some of the respondents in each of the four political systems, with a view to probe some of their answers more deeply, in an informal setting, to better understand other issues such as loopholes in the system, the burden the system imposed on lobbyists and politicians and its enforceability. Over 25 on-site semi-structured elite interviews were conducted with various lobby groups, regulators and politicians from these political systems; we received frank and clarifying views. In our interviews, we were concerned with two key issues: the pros and cons of the regulatory system, and an assessment of which aspects of the rules in place might be of value to countries without lobbying legislation. Interviews were also carried out with politicians, lobbyists and state officials working in unregulated jurisdictions.

Structure of the book

Answering the first of our six main questions, Chapter 2 offers the reader an overview of the history and context of each of the four political systems with the longest history of lobbying regulations – the US, Canada, the EU and Germany – and then examines the lobbying legislation in place. In the case of the US and Canada, attention is also paid to developments with regard to state/provincial regulations. After briefly considering the nature of government and the nature of lobbying in each system, we focus on the names of the acts and when they came into existence, what the legislation covers and note any changes over time. Thereafter, Chapter 3 examines developments in those states which have more recently established such rules – Lithuania, Poland, Hungary, Taiwan and Australia.

The goals of Chapter 4 are twofold, helping us answer the third of our six questions. First, we use a quantitative index, based on the model offered by the CPI, to measure how strong or weak the regulations are in each system. The second objective is to develop a theoretical classification of the different types of lobbying regulatory environment. We argue that there are three regulatory environments: low, medium and high regulation. The evidence demonstrates that Germany, Poland and the EU all represent low-regulation systems; all the Canadian jurisdictions plus several US ones, as well as Lithuania, Hungary, Taiwan and Australia, represent medium-regulation systems; and 50 per cent of the American states, plus the most recent federal initiative, are representative of high-regulation systems. We close the chapter by considering what factors may help explain why different countries have implemented different regulatory environments.

Chapter 5 is devoted to measuring the opinion of political actors, interest groups and regulators in the US, Canada, the EP and Germany as measured through questionnaires and elite interviews conducted throughout the study, in order to see how effective the regulations have been as per our fourth main question. We also see whether there are any trends that can be found between the different types of system and the opinions of the actors we surveyed. Some main arguments we make are that actors in highly regulated systems claim to know more about legislation, are more likely to argue that accountability is ensured and feel that there are fewer loopholes in the system than are respondents from low-regulation systems. Nevertheless, we argue that even in relatively highly regulated systems, the rules can be undermined under the 'if there is a will there is always a way' principle. We close the chapter by examining the impact of different regulatory environments on the practice of lobbying.

Chapter 6 turns to our fifth main question and we offer an analysis of why some provinces/states in Canada and the US as well as the European Commission have not (or had not at the time of the survey, in 2005) pursued lobbying legislation. The aim here is to show what attitudes prevail towards the idea of regulating lobbying in unregulated jurisdictions. While most jurisdictions across the world have no lobbying regulations in place, and have no experience of such regulation, in the jurisdictions sampled here there was widespread knowledge of what lobbying legislation is about, precisely because these jurisdictions/institutions are encompassed within larger polities where lobbying is mostly regulated. Our objective is thus to discover what the attitudes are towards lobbying regulations, given the understanding of the topic in these locations. Are such regulations regarded as beneficial to democracy? Or are they seen merely as bureaucratic red tape?

The final chapter summarises the findings of the research, and assesses the lessons that can be taken from this study of relevance to democratic states that do not have lobbying legislation in place.

In sum, this book seeks to give an understanding of where the regulation of lobbying stands in comparative terms, and what can be learned from political systems throughout the globe currently active in this field. This book, in doing both, breaks new ground in this area, and seeks to provide significant insights into the regulation of lobbyists. As this is an area that will become of greater concern to governments in the coming decades, the answers to these questions will provide a foundation for better understanding lobbying regulations across the world and, potentially, will serve as a guide for policy makers in those political systems contemplating implementing such regulations.

Notes

1 In 1998, Georgia passed its Law on Lobbying Activities. However, Georgia has been ranked by the Freedom House as being only a 'partly free', not a fully democratic state, and will therefore not be considered in detail for this study. Even though lobbying legislation does exist in the country, most interest groups have not registered and many officials are unfamiliar with the process of registration. See SME Support Project (2006).
2 Lobbying legislation was introduced in Alberta in 2008. This was due to become fully operational in early 2009.
3 Lobbying legislation was introduced in Pennsylvania in 2007.

2

Political systems with regulations in place in the 1900s: the US, Canada, the European Union and Germany

Introduction

This chapter is concerned with providing a detailed understanding of the regulations in place in those systems that implemented them throughout the 1900s, thereby representing jurisdictions that have the longest history of formal lobbying legislation. This includes the US, Canada, the EU and Germany, all of which established lobbying rules in the last century.[1] This chapter is thus structured into four parts, one for each political system, and the analysis of each is further divided into three categories. In the first, we offer a brief examination of the history of the country and its nature of governance. The second considers the nature of lobbying in the jurisdiction. And finally, we turn to an analysis of the actual lobbying legislation, first focusing on the names of the acts and when they came into existence. We then offer a more detailed examination of the regulations in place, consider what the legislation covers and note any changes over time. For readers who wish to see the texts of the actual lobbying laws for each of the political systems presented in this chapter, we have set up a webpage that accompanies this book, www.regulatelobbying.com, where links to each of the legal texts and regulations can be found.

The US

Brief history

The US was born in a revolutionary war against colonial Britain between 1775 and 1783. It declared its independence from Britain in 1776 and enacted a republican system of government in its constitution, which was ratified in 1789 and further amended in 1791 with the inclusion of the first 10 amendments, the famous Bill of Rights. At the heart of the American political tradition ever since has been the tension between the federal government and the states making up the union. Originally 13 in number, there are now 50 states, each with its own constitution, government and laws. From its inception, some individual states viewed membership of the new United States of America as somehow revocable and it was not until the end of the American Civil War in 1865 that this idea would be refuted after the victory for the northern states over their southern counterparts which had attempted to secede from the union in 1861.

The US government operates at a federal level, with a national government and individual state governments; the latter have significant powers and send representatives to the legislative branch of government, the Congress, made up of the House of Representatives and the Senate. There is also an executive branch, headed by the President of the United States, and an independent judiciary. At its simplest, lobbying in the US revolves around the First Amendment to the constitution, which states: 'Congress shall make no law respecting an establishment of religion, or prohibiting the free exercise thereof; or abridging the freedom of speech, or of the press; or the right of the people peaceably to assemble, and to petition the Government for a redress of grievances'.[2]

Since the ending of the Civil War, lobbying has been an issue never far from the political surface in the US and the regulation of lobbying and lobbyists remains extremely contentious to this day. Beginning with the populist movement in the 1870s, much of the pressure for reform has come from the public or certain sections of it (Thomas, 1998: 502). Extremely questionable practices by a number of railroad lobbyists in the years following the Civil War led to significant demands to regulate those who sought to influence railway prices in the vast amount of railroad building that took place across the country at this time (Kolko, 1965).[3] The House of Representatives in 1876 attempted to require lobbyists to register but was unsuccessful. Since 1911, lobby regulation has been considered in almost every session of Congress (Thomas, 1998: 504). Such demands for lobbying reform were, however, never acceded to and it was not until the New Deal presidency of Franklin Delano Roosevelt that advocates of reform found a potential ally in the White House.

The nature of lobbying in the US
Lobbying is big business in the US. The Center for Responsive Politics estimates that total lobbying spending increased from $1.44 billion in 1998 to $3.28 billion in 2008 (see Table 2.1). This lobbying is carried out by myriad organisations, including private companies, labour unions and a host of other cause-centred organisations which lobby Congress and other federal agencies in the hope of getting legislation passed which is to their benefit and advantage. While campaign contributions to candidates for public office are one way to attempt to influence policy, some special interests retain lobbying firms, many of them located along the legendary K Street in Washington, DC. Other special interests have specific lobbyist arms within their own organisations.

The number of registered lobbying firms which receive these vast sums is actually relatively small, with the same organisation estimating that these stood at 15,038 in 2008, up from 10,676 a decade earlier (Table 2.2). Table 2.3 shows how much the top firms spent over the decade and Table 2.4 the main industries involved.[4]

We investigate in the next section where all this lobbying has emerged from and how it works.

Table 2.1 Total lobbying expenditure in the US, 1998–2008

Year	Expenditure
1998	$1.44 billion
1999	$1.44 billion
2000	$1.56 billion
2001	$1.63 billion
2002	$1.81 billion
2003	$2.04 billion
2004	$2.18 billion
2005	$2.42 billion
2006	$2.61 billion
2007	$2.85 billion
2008	$3.28 billion

Source: Center for Responsive Politics, www.opensecrets.org/lobby/index.php.

Table 2.2 Number of registered lobbying firms in Washington, DC, 1998–2008

Year	Number of firms
1998	10,676
1999	13,280
2000	12,719
2001	12,056
2002	12,334
2003	13,143
2004	13,380
2005	14,393
2006	14,771
2007	15,311
2008	15,038

Source: Center for Responsive Politics, www.opensecrets.org/lobby/index.php.

Table 2.3 The top US lobbying firms by total spend between 1998 and 2008

Lobbying firm	Total spend
Patton Boggs LLP	$302,917,000
Cassidy & Associates	$276,895,000
Akin, Gump *et al.*	$246,665,000
Van Scoyoc Associates	$198,348,000
Williams & Jensen	$145,474,000
Hogan & Hartson	$133,153,907
Ernst & Young	$129,857,556
Quinn, Gillespie & Associates	$115,363,500
Barbour, Griffith & Rogers	$114,430,000
PMA Group	$110,925,132
Greenberg Traurig LLP	$107,088,249
Holland & Knight	$94,069,544
PriceWaterhouseCoopers	$92,114,084
Verner, Liipfert *et al.*	$88,595,000
Alcalde & Fay	$83,720,660
Carmen Group	$81,900,000
Dutko Worldwide	$78,268,411
Clark & Weinstock	$77,785,000
Timmons & Co.	$74,388,000
Washington Group	$74,257,000

Source: Center for Responsive Politics, www.opensecrets.org/lobby/top.php?indexType=l.

Lobbying legislation at the federal and state levels
The US has the longest history of lobbying regulation of all modern democracies. The individual states led the way with lobbying regulations, implementing legislation long before the federal government did so (Thomas, 1998: 500). In this regard, the state legislatures have a longer history of dealing with the issues surrounding the regulation of lobbying than does Washington, DC, or any other democratic jurisdictions in the world, for that matter. The result has been that the lobbying regulations introduced at state level have often been more coherent in their structure, more thorough in their scope and more transparent in their operation than similar legislation found at the federal level. By the early 1950s, 38 states, and the then territory of Alaska, had put in place lobbying regulations (Thomas, 1998: 505). Lobbying regulations at the federal level date back to 1935 and the first presidency of Franklin Delano Roosevelt. Amid worries about electricity provision, the Public Utilities Holding Company Act of 1935 included within its various provisions a requirement for anyone employed or retained by a registered holding company to file reports with the

Table 2.4 The US main industries involved in recruiting lobbying agencies and using in-house lobbying supports between 1998 and 2008, by total sums spent

Industry	Total spend
Pharmaceuticals/health products	$1,499,696,090
Insurance	$1,136,697,438
Electric utilities	$1,037,772,258
Computers/internet	$839,486,564
Business associations	$779,555,724
Education	$738,121,498
Oil and gas	$705,615,303
Real estate	$703,817,220
Hospitals/nursing homes	$659,899,092
Miscellaneous manufacturing and distributing	$625,668,155
Health professionals	$616,642,035
Civil servants/public officials	$582,620,478
Securities and investment	$576,000,802
Television, movies, music	$563,780,283
Air transport	$538,142,342
Automotive	$533,385,321
Miscellaneous	$520,320,864
Telecommunications services and equipment	$508,838,581
Telephone utilities	$428,718,593
Defence, aerospace	$423,093,103

Source: Center for Responsive Politics, www.opensecrets.org/lobby/top.php?indexType=i.

Securities and Exchange Commission (SEC) before attempting to influence Congress, the SEC or the Federal Power Commission. This was the first piece of legislation ever enacted by Congress to be directly applicable to the lobbying of government agencies (Hrebenar, 1997: 271). The following year, reacting to scandals in the shipping industry over the granting of maritime mail hauling contracts and the lobbying practices of the industry in attempting to influence a maritime subsidy bill, Congress included a lobby registration provision in the Merchant Marine Act of 1936. Section 807 of that act required lobbyists of shipping corporations and shipyards receiving government subsidies to report their income, expenses and interests on a monthly basis. These initial efforts at lobbying regulation were, however, deeply flawed by their limited coverage of only the power and maritime industries and by the enforcement agencies' lack of interest in using their provisions (Hrebenar, 1997: 272).

Two other major pieces of legislation were also passed in this era: the Foreign Agents Registration Act of 1938, whose aim was to attempt to register anyone representing a foreign government or organisation, and the Federal Regulation of Lobbying Act of 1946, which comprised the first general federal lobby registration laws. The latter piece of legislation was really a supplement to the Legislative Reorganization Act of the same year, was only four pages long and had a very modest set of objectives. It merely provided for the registration of any person hired by someone else for the principal purpose of lobbying Congress and required that quarterly financial reports of lobbying expenditures be submitted as well (Thomas, 1998: 507). As a piece of legislation, it has widely been seen as a failure. It covered only Congress, so in essence the executive branch, regulatory agencies and other government organisations were exempt. Financial reporting was left to the lobbyists and there was little (if any) investigation and enforcement of the Act. Nevertheless, the Act remained in place for nearly 50 years, to be replaced only in November 1995, by the Lobbying Disclosure Act.

The Lobbying Disclosure Act, 1995. The Lobbying Disclosure Act refers to the federal level exclusively. It was the culmination of much effort by advocates of lobbying reform, advanced a definition of lobbyists to include all those 'who seek to influence Congress, congressional staff, and policy-making officials of the executive branch including the president, top White House officials, Cabinet secretaries and their deputies, and independent agency administrators and their assistants' (Hrebenar, 1997: 280). Lobbying is said to occur when a lobbyist communicates either orally or in writing with certain public officials on behalf of a client or employer, 'concerning legislation, rules and regulations, programs, grants, loans and nominations subject to Senate confirmation' (McGrath, 2005: 168–169). The public officials range from the President to congressional staff. Moreover, all commercial lobbyists who anticipate being paid more than $5,000 over six months must register with Congress, as must all in-house lobbyists who expect to spend more than $20,000 over the same period. The registration form asks for details about the lobbyist and the client or employer, and also about the policy issues which will be the subject of the lobbying activity. Another report must be filed retrospectively at the end of each six-month period, specifying precisely which policy issues and legislation the lobbyist worked on, as well as setting out which congressional chamber and/or executive agencies were lobbied. A lobbyist who knowingly or wilfully fails to make a full disclosure can be imprisoned for up to five years, under a separate piece of legislation enacted in 1996 (McGrath, 2005: 169). The Lobbying Disclosure Act also significantly tightened registration and reporting rules. Nevertheless, it exempts grass-roots lobbying and lobbying by religious groups from the reporting requirements (Thomas, 1998: 509).

The successful enactment of the Act in 1995 had three major strategic objectives: to leave out the controversial provisions of previous bills, to make a bipartisan coalition, and to allow no amendments to bills that have successfully passed through the first chamber in which they were debated. Yet among the key amendments defeated in the House were provisions to establish an enforcement agency. In the new law, non-compliance is first determined by the officers of the House and Senate and then referred to the US Attorney for Washington, DC, who can prosecute and request civil fines of up to $50,000 for further non-compliance (Hrebenar, 1997: 280). Nevertheless, the fact that a bipartisan law, in an era of extreme partisanship between the Clinton Democratic White House and the Republican Congress, was finally passed in the House on a vote of 421 to 0 showed that there was a common view within the US political system that some regulatory system for lobbying had to be put in place.

The current context. Former Republican lobbyist Jack Abramoff was sentenced to 5 years and 10 months in prison on 29 March 2006 after pleading guilty to fraud, tax evasion and conspiracy to bribe public officials in a deal that required him to cooperate with an investigation into his dealings with members of Congress.[5] The scandal prompted Republican House leader Tom DeLay of Texas and Robert Ney of Ohio, Chairman of the House Administration Committee, to resign their leadership posts. A former Abramoff associate, David H. Safavian, most recently the top contracting official in the White House Office of Management and Budget, was first indicted for lying about his dealings with Abramoff then sentenced to 18 months in prison in October 2006, after he was found guilty of covering up his dealings with Abramoff. In June 2008, however, the US Court of Appeals for the District of Columbia Circuit unanimously reversed Safavian's convictions. Abramoff was sentenced to a further four years in federal prison on 4 September 2008 by US District Judge Ellen Segal Huvelle.[6] In the context of the Abramoff scandal, lobbying has returned to centre stage in American politics.

Lobbying, as we pointed out above, is protected by the First Amendment. When individuals or groups lobby, they are exercising their basic right 'to petition the Government for a redress of grievances'. According to the Public Affairs Council, based in Washington, DC, the leading association for public affairs professionals or lobbyists, as 'the government has grown in size and complexity, more lobbyists have been needed to explain how business operates, how technology works, how legislation would affect various interests, and how consensus can be achieved in public policy-making'.[7] At the federal level, the 1995 Lobbying Disclosure Act remains in place. Within this act, a lobbyist is defined as someone who is employed or retained for financial or other compensation for services that include more than one lobbying contact, other than an individual whose lobbying activities constitute less than 20 per cent of the time engaged in the services provided by the individual to the client or employer over a six-month period. 'Lobbying contacts' do not include: requests for meetings or status reports that do not attempt to influence a legislative or executive official; testimony before a congressional panel; the provision of information at the request of a government official; or communications made in response to government notices requesting comment from the public. A lobbyist must register with the Secretary of the Senate and the Clerk of the House and must file semi-annual disclosure reports. These reports cover lobbying expenditures, payments to contract lobbyists and the income a contract lobbyist receives for lobbying.

Significant changes were made by the 110th US Congress in 2007 to the Lobbying Disclosure Act and to internal House and Senate rules on ethics and procedures, by the passage of the Honest Leadership and Open Government Act.[8] This resulted from concerns over a variety of lobbying and gift scandals, as mentioned above, and questions of undue influence through the preferential access of certain special interests to public officials.

The statutory and internal congressional rule changes which were adopted address five general areas of reform:

1 broader and more detailed disclosures of lobbying activities by paid lobbyists, and more disclosures concerning the intersection of the activities of professional lobbyists with government policy makers;
2 more extensive restrictions on the offering and receipt of gifts and favours for members of Congress and their staff, including gifts of transportation and travel expenses;
3 new restrictions addressing the so-called 'revolving door', that is, lobbying activities by former high-level government officials on behalf of private interests;
4 reform of the government pension provisions with regard to members of Congress found guilty of abusing public trust;
5 greater transparency in the internal legislative process in the House and Senate, including 'earmark' disclosures[9] and accountability.[10]

These changes have their genesis in the US Senate debate on a lobbying reform bill, the Legislative Transparency and Accountability Act of 2006 (S. 2349), early that year. If passed, the act would have curbed trips and meals paid for by lobbyists, and required increased disclosure for special funding provisions added late in the legislative process. It would also have increased disclosure of: lobbyists' campaign contributions; grass-roots lobbying; travel paid for by lobbyists; and gifts to members of Congress. During floor consideration of the bill, the Senate rejected an amendment to create an office of public integrity to investigate ethics rules, but adopted an amendment to require Senators to publicly disclose holds they have on bills.[11] The Senate passed its lobbying reform bill on 29 March 2006 by a vote of 90 to 8.[12]

Parallel to this the House of Representatives was debating its own bill, the Lobbying Accountability and Transparency Act of 2006. The House passed this bill on 3 May by a narrow margin, 217 to 213. This bill provided for amending, strengthening and enhancing the Lobbying Disclosure Act of 1995 and would have required quarterly filing by lobbyists, up from twice a year. Registered lobbyists would have had to disclose: contributions to federal candidates, political action committees (PACs) and political party committees; the amount and date of any gift stipulated as counting towards the cumulative limit; and the date, recipient and amount of funds contributed to (or on behalf of) an entity named for a member or established, financed, maintained or controlled by a member.

As the bills that originally passed the House and Senate were different, a conference committee met to iron out the differences, which resulted in a compromise bill passed in the House and Senate on 30 July and 2 August 2007, respectively. The vote in the House was 411 to 8 and in the Senate 83 to 14. President Bush signed the bill into law in September 2007 under the name Honest Leadership and Open Government Act. He declared:

> This bill represents some progress towards ethics, lobbying, and earmark reform, all of which I strongly support. Strengthening the ethical standards that govern lobbying activities and beginning to address meaningful earmark reform are necessary steps to provide the public with a more transparent lawmaking process. The essence of successful ethics reform is not laws and restrictions, but full disclosure. The legislation includes minimal improvements in the area of disclosure, both for lobbying and earmarks. But there is still more to be done – and I will work with the Congress to improve upon this legislation.[13]

One of the key questions relating to lobbying in the US continues to be why lobbyists get involved in fundraising. The simple answer is that campaign costs are huge for politicians. In that context, the Federal Election Campaign Act (FECA) of 1971 (as modified by the Bipartisan Campaign Reform Act of 2002) sets very specific limits for campaign contributions by individuals and PACs. In their modern form, PACs are a creation of the FECA of 1971 amended in 1974. The number of PACs grew dramatically in the first decade after FECA was enacted, but levelled out at about 4,000 in the mid-1980s and has now declined to just under 4,000. However, the amount of money generated by PACs has grown dramatically. In the bitter partisanship that marked US politics since the extremely close and divisive presidential election of 2000, there was a significant surge in PAC money-raising activity (Kernell and Jacobson, 2003: 494–495). PACs exist legally as a means for corporations, trade unions and other organisations to make donations to candidates for federal office, something that they cannot do directly. Corporations and labour unions are not permitted to make contributions, including in-kind contributions, to federal candidates or committees. Individuals may contribute up to $2,000 per election to candidates, up to $5,000 per year to PACs, up to $10,000 per year to federal accounts of state party committees and up to $25,000 per year to national party committees. In aggregate, an individual may contribute up to $95,000 per two-year election cycle. A qualified corporate or trade association federal PAC may contribute up to $5,000 per election to a candidate for federal office. Many contract lobbyists, in particular, play a major role in congressional fundraising. Some lobbyists help to organise fundraising events for candidates whom they and their clients support. Others attend such events and make contributions to like-minded candidates.[14]

State-level regulation

As Thomas (1998: 509) points out: 'with fifty governments, a variety of political sub-cultures, histories and levels of political development, experience with lobby regulation in the states is quite diverse'. State oversight of lobbying generally takes four forms: states establish registration requirements by defining what lobbying is and who is a lobbyist; they require lobbyists or the interests that hire them to periodically disclose their expenditures and earnings; they regulate the 'revolving door' between government and the private sector by establishing a cooling-off period during which ex-government officials are prohibited from lobbying the government they once served; and they define the range of permissible lobbying activities, such as providing free gifts or meals (Gordon, 2005).

Massachusetts, in 1890, was the first state to introduce a lobbying regulation law (Opheim, 1991: 405). With the adoption of Pennsylvania's new Lobbying Disclosure Act on 1 January 2007, all of America's 50 states now have legislation regulating lobbyists. While Pennsylvania initially introduced lobbying regulations in 1998, with the Lobbying Disclosure Act, this legislation was struck down in May 2000 by the Pennsylvanian Supreme Court as unconstitutional as it pertained to attorneys: the Court stated that the efforts of the General Assembly of Pennsylvania to monitor the activities of lobbyists amounted to illegal regulations on the practice of law. This then invalidated the whole law. In 2002, the Supreme Court re-affirmed its decision. In December 2003, the Supreme Court issued a new rule requiring lawyers acting as lobbyists to comply with requirements that they disclose information related to their clients. The Pennsylvania State Senate in January 2003 and again in January 2005 adopted rules requiring all those who lobby the Senate to register and file quarterly reports with the Secretary of the Senate.[15] In March 2006, Governor Edward G. Rendell took steps to enact legislation at the executive level when he signed an executive order amendment to the Governor's Code of Conduct, establishing new registration and disclosure standards for those who want to lobby the executive branch of state government. Under the Governor's amendment, anyone who lobbied a member of the executive branch – basically, decision makers – had to register and file quarterly expense reports relating to their activities. The Governor's Code of Conduct set the ethical standards for some 78,000 state employees under the Governor's jurisdiction.[16] Finally, after much deliberation and discussion with interested parties, in November 2006 a revised Lobbying Disclosure Act was signed by Rendell and became law in January 2007, thus removing Pennsylvania from the anomaly of being the only state in the union without any form of state lobbying regulation.

Pennsylvania is important in that it gives us insights into the perception that politicians and policy makers in the US have when it comes to lobbying regulation. In a number of interviews conducted in 2006 with legislators and legislative aides in Harrisburg, Pennsylvania, it was stressed to the authors that Pennsylvania felt itself to be something of 'an ugly duckling in legislative terms' by being the only state not to have lobbying legislation. One senior aide said:

> while I don't think the average citizen is too bothered by the lack of legislation, it sure as hell bothers the politicians. They think everyone else is looking down on them and that as much as anything else is what is driving lobbying reform in this state.[17]

All reporting responsibility lies with the companies or organisations that directly employ lobbyists, known as lobby principals or lobby employers. Washington State is often ranked as one of the most regulated in the US (Chari *et al.*, 2007; Opheim, 1991). For Washington:

> The public's right to know of the financing of political campaigns and lobbying and the financial affairs of elected officials and candidates far outweighs any right that these matters remain secret and private.[18]

This quotation from the policy provisions of Washington State's Open Government Act, better known as the Public Disclosure Law, aptly summarises both the impetus for and the purpose of that statute. Washington recognises lobbyists as those who lobby both the executive and legislative branch. The origin of this disclosure law can be traced to the efforts of concerned citizens who came together in 1970 believing that the public had the right to know about the financing of political activity in the state. Following an unsuccessful attempt in 1971 to generate legislative action and only minimal success in 1972, these concerned citizens – now calling themselves the Coalition for Open Government (COG) – turned to the people. COG gathered nearly 163,000 signatures in order to place Initiative 276 on the November 1972 ballot. Initiative 276 was approved by 72 per cent of the voters and became law on 1 January 1973.

In 1992, reform-minded voters in Washington State again passed an initiative resulting from a comprehensive campaign. Over 72 per cent supported reform and this time around approved contribution limits and other campaign restrictions. Yet, for all the comprehensive nature of regulation in Washington State, the CPI recently reported that the spirit of the state's exemplary disclosure law was being undermined by lobbyists who reported their clients' purposes on disclosure forms in vague, non-descriptive terms (Gordon, 2005).

Washington is the most advanced state in the US when it comes to disclosure. It has public access via the internet to registered lobbyists, and discloses to the public the names of lobbyists, and how much they earned and spent. It breaks down lobbying activity into 40 different sectors.[19] The website of Washington State's Public Disclosure Commission enables registered lobbyists to file all disclosure information online. This is voluntary rather than mandatory, although the Commission hopes to make all filing electronic in the near future.[20]

Wisconsin is another highly developed state in terms of disclosure. The state legislature is of the view that the operation of an open and responsible government requires that the fullest opportunity be afforded to the people to petition their government for the redress of grievances and to express freely to any officials of the executive or legislative branch their opinions on legislation, pending administrative rules and other policy decisions by administrative agencies, and on current issues. In a 2005 bill concerning the application of the lobbying regulation law, the state legislature declared that:

> essential to the continued functioning of an open government is the preserva-
> tion of the integrity of the governmental decision-making process. In order to
> preserve and maintain the integrity of the process, the legislature determines
> that it is necessary to regulate and publicly disclose the identity, expenditures
> and activities of persons who hire others or are hired to engage in efforts to
> influence actions of the legislative and executive branches.[21]

This bill's aim is simply to give meaningful public access to information about the financing of political campaigns, lobbyist expenditures and the financial affairs of public officials and candidates, and to ensure compliance with disclosure provisions, contribution limits, campaign practices and other campaign finance laws. All lobbyists in Wisconsin must register, no matter how much money they make or spend.

Wisconsin has had lobbying regulations dating back to 1858 and lobbying is regulated by the Wisconsin Ethics Board. For Wisconsin, the purpose of regulating lobbying activity is:

> [to] make sure that no inappropriate lines are crossed when it comes to
> peddling influence. The laws attempt to ensure a level playing field for indi-
> viduals who do not have many resources to lobby local or state officials. After
> all, lobbying is based on the idea that everyone has the right to address his or
> her government.[22]

Yet, while Wisconsin has significant lobbying regulation processes, there is no 'cooling off' period before legislators can become lobbyists and

Wisconsin does not recognise as lobbyists those who lobby the executive branch of state government.

While all the states and the federal government now have regulatory frameworks in place, there are significant differences between individual jurisdictions. While Montana, for instance, does not by statute require individual lobbyists to file spending activity reports, all lobbyists must register, no matter how much money they make or spend. Lobbyists are recognised as those who lobby both the state and executive branches of government. Montana has a Commissioner of Political Practices, who monitors the regulation of lobbyists in that state. However, the Commissioner's office has only four people in it, and there is no online access to lobbying disclosures of expenditure. In January 2005, Montana Governor Brian Schweitzer called for a two-year cooling-off period covering executive and legislative branch officials. The 2005 legislative session closed with the proposed legislation at a virtual standstill in both legislative chambers.[23]

Florida has laws on lobbying both the state legislature and executive. Florida's Commission on Ethics asserts that it has been a leader among the states in establishing ethics standards for public officials.[24] In April and May 2005, the Florida Senate approved, revised and re-approved ethics measures that would, among other changes, require lobbyists to report their earnings and expenditures. Registration is required before any state agency can be lobbied and is renewable annually. In addition, lobbying firms must file quarterly 'compensation reports'. Lobbyists must register, no matter how much money they make or spend. There is a two-year cooling-off period, one of the longest in the US, before legislators can register as lobbyists, but this refers only to former office holders who lobby the particular government body or agency that employed them. There is no online system of filing in Florida. Lobbyists can print out forms from the website of the Commission on Ethics but they must fill them in and return them manually. The Center for Public Integrity reported that expenditure on lobbying in Florida declined by 59 per cent in 2004, and was at its lowest in a decade (Gordon, 2005). Florida, along with Illinois and Ohio, does not require lobbyists to disclose campaign contributions, so presumably one of the main reasons for the large decline was the 2004 election, when lobbyists and their employers probably channelled a significant proportion of their resources towards campaign activities. In Florida, lobbyists outnumber legislators by a ratio of almost 13 to 1.

Wyoming recognises only legislative branch lobbyists, but all these lobbyists must register, no matter how much money they make or spend.[25] Up until 1998, when it enacted a lobbyist reporting bill, Wyoming was the only state that did not require lobbyists to report any of their spending. The 1998 law did not require lobbyists to report all the expenditures they (and their employers) made in their efforts to influence Wyoming legislators. The Wyoming law requires reporting of only: the lobbyist's 'sources of funding; loans, gifts, gratuities, special discounts or hospitality' exceeding $50 in value; the cost of special events held for legislators; and the cost of advertising to influence legislation (without any definition of what that might be). This places Wyoming at the bottom of the comparative ranking in terms of what states require lobbyists to disclose. For example, in other western states bordering Wyoming there are more rigorous regulations. Nebraska, Colorado and Montana require complete reporting of all expenditures related to lobbying activity, including lobbyist compensation. Idaho requires reporting of all expenses for entertainment (including food and beverages), advertising, travel and lodging for public officials' office expenses. South Dakota simply requires reporting of all costs incurred for lobbying except the lobbyist's personal expenses and compensation.

As we can see, there are substantial differences across the states when it comes to regulating lobbyists and lobbying behaviour. While all states now have some form of regulation, what is clear is that lobbying regulation continues to be a highly contentious political issue. While the Abramoff scandal turned the focus in the US back on federal-level legislation, the Honest Leadership and Open Government Act of 2007 has gone some way to allaying concerns of improper access and influence by lobbyists. Nevertheless, it is important to note that, because of the importance of state governments in the US, lobbying regulations at the state level are in many ways as important as the federal lobbying regulations, if not more so.

Canada

Brief history
Founded in 1867, Canada is a federal country consisting of 10 provinces and three territories. The federal government has two law-making bodies: the House of Commons (the lower house, consisting of 301 directly elected members) and the Senate (the upper house, consisting of 105 members, who are appointed by the Prime Minister). Of the two houses, the most significant in terms of law-making power is the House of Commons: the party with a plurality of seats in the House forms the government, whose head is the Prime Minister, who plays a major role in appointing the core executive (i.e. the cabinet) as well as imposing party discipline on Members of Parliament (MPs) from the governmental party.

The leader of a provincial government is called the premier, who heads the party with the most seats in the provincial legislative assembly (the only house at the provincial level; members of provincial legislative assemblies are referred to as MLAs). In Canada's history, the two main parties in government at the federal level have been the Liberals and the Conservatives, although Canada itself sees many other parties at the federal and provincial levels, such as the National Democratic Party (similar to the UK's Labour Party) and the Bloc Quebecois (from Quebec, and which seeks independence from, or at least some form of sovereign association with, Canada).

The power of the cabinet at both levels of governance becomes apparent when one considers how a bill becomes law. In terms of the cabinet and legislative process at the federal level, a cabinet member usually submits a proposal, which is studied and approved by the cabinet committee. The draft of the bill is then confirmed by cabinet as a whole, signed off by the Prime Minister and introduced in the House of Commons. First and second readings take place in the House (at which time no amendments can be made); a parliamentary committee examines the bill thereafter (at which time amendments can be made); it is approved by the House on the third reading (when limited amendments can be made); the bill is then sent to the Senate, which usually 'rubber stamps' it, given that this institution is of mostly symbolic value to Canadian government; and then final assent is made by the Governor General, who is Canada's official head of state, representing the British monarchy, even though the Prime Minister has effectively the most political power. Almost absent in the legislative process are the actions of individual MPs. This is due to the strong imposition of party discipline in the Canadian political system: MPs are usually 'whipped' to follow the party line and very few 'free' votes have taken place in Canada's history. The compliance of individual MPs is usually attained by promises that they will be promoted in the future.

With these dynamics in mind, one can see that law making is a strongly centralised process around a few key actors, whom lobbyists attempt to influence. In its history, Canada has seen situations in which political actors might have been perceived to be acting in a manner that was less than transparent, in the interests of some private groups. One example was in the late 1800s, when the Canadian Pacific Railway was built: Canada's first Prime Minister, John A. MacDonald, built the Canadian Pacific Railway as a means to unite Canada from east to west. However, the process itself was deemed by many to cater to some private interests that would financially gain from the building of the railway. Another example is seen in the case of the province of Quebec under Maurice Duplessis in the 1950s and 1960s, when government contracts for initiatives such as building highways were seen as a means to attract votes. Even as recently as the 1980s, with the federal governments under Brian Mulroney (Conservative), and the 1990s and 2000s, under Jean Chrétien and Paul Martin (Liberals), there were reports of different ministers favouring some private interests over others with the view of gaining payoffs. As Dyck (2004: 369) explains with regard to the Mulroney years:

> In the Mulroney era, ministers were allowed to set up large offices full of personal or partisan assistants headed by a chief of staff with which to provide strong direction to the bureaucracy. As a result, lobbyist efforts were often focussed on ministers' offices and even though most firms took on lobbyists with Liberal connections too, Tory partisan links were particularly important.

In this context, lobbyist legislation was pursued and later amended by both the Conservatives and Liberals at the federal level throughout the 1980s, 1990s and 2000s in order to increase the transparency of public policy making. Before considering the nature of lobbying legislation at both the federal and provincial levels in Canada, we turn to a discussion of the nature of lobbying in Canada.

The nature of lobbying in Canada

As with all countries where lobbying takes place, Canada is home to several professional organisations that lobby on behalf of their clients, whether that includes corporations, industry, professional interests or even non-governmental organisations (NGOs). Table 2.5 lists the top 10 lobbyists that represented companies and organisations in Canada, ranked by total spending over 1998–2004.

Table 2.5 Top 10 professional lobby organisations in Canada, 1998–2004

	2003 spending (US$)	2004 spending (US$)	1998–2004 total spending (US$)
DLA Piper Rudnick Gray Cary LLP	$1,480,000	$880,000	$5,440,000
WPP Group plc	$620,000	$240,000	$3,783,000
Chambers, Conlon & Hartwell	$360,000	$360,000	$2,510,000
Interpublic Group of Companies, Inc.	$400,000	$460,000	$2,260,000
Akin Gump	$80,000	$40,000	$1,900,000
Palmetto Group	–	–	$1,080,000
MGN Inc.	$160,000	$200,000	$1,040,000
Mayer Brown & Platt	$360,000	$200,000	$1,000,000
Williams Mullen	$148,000	–	$964,000
Van Ness Feldman	$240,000	$120,000	$940,000

Source: Center for Public Integrity, http://projects.publicintegrity.org/lobby/profile.aspx?act=countries&year=2003&co=ca&sub=2.

Who has used the services of these lobbyists? We take the example of the highest-ranked lobbyist in the time period, DLA Piper Rudnik Gray Cary LLP, and see main corporations such as: Starwood Hotels & Resorts Inc., Lockheed Martin, Merrill Lynch & Co. Inc., Visa Inc., Citigroup, Lloyds of London/Lloyds of America Inc., Diageo North America, GenCorp Inc., R. J. Reynolds Tobacco Holdings, Inc., Time Warner, Staples Inc., and General Motors Corporation.

Equally important, in-house lobbyists from various corporations have also been active, spending hundreds of thousands of dollars in lobbying the state. Table 2.6 outlines the top 10 companies and organisations that have used in-house lobbyists in Canada, ranked by total spending.

Table 2.6 Top 10 companies and organisations in terms of in-house lobbying in Canada, 1998–2004

	2003 spending (US$)	2004 spending (US$)	1998–2004 spending (US$)
Canadian National Railway Co.	$1,760,000	$1,380,000	$8,370,000
Bombardier Inc.	$542,500	$500,000	$4,628,981
British Columbia Lumber Trade Council	$860,000	$800,000	$4,340,000
Methanex Corporation	$480,000	$220,000	$4,239,000
Barrick Gold Corporation	$360,000	$260,000	$3,042,000
Interactive Gaming Council	$148,000	$120,000	$1,404,000
The Thomson Corporation	$215,000	$110,000	$1,318,000
Free Trade Lumber Council	$115,300	$121,000	$1,116,300
CGI Group Inc. (including former American Mgmt Systems Inc.)	$380,000	$60,000	$1,098,000
Placer Dome Us, Inc.	$160,000	$210,000	$1,090,000

Source: Center for Public Integrity, http://projects.publicintegrity.org/lobby/profile.aspx?act=countries&year=2003&co=ca&sub=1.

What policy areas are both professional and in-house lobbyists involved in? Although the federal and provincial levels have different jurisdictional powers, as outlined in articles 91 and 92 of the Canadian constitution, one can see that there is much overlap in terms of what subject matters are lobbied at the two levels of government when comparing Figures 2.1 and 2.2. Comparison of the figures shows some striking similarities: one can see that many of the 'top 10' subject areas for which lobbyists are registered remain the same between the provincial and federal levels of governance. More concretely, the top 10 areas found in both levels include: industry, environment, taxation and finance, energy, science and technology, transportation and health. Economic development and trade was ranked the highest in Ontario, while international trade was ranked fourth at the federal level precisely because of its constitutional responsibilities

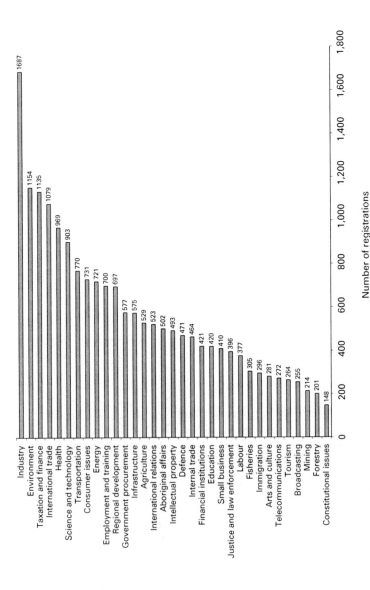

Figure 2.1 Subject matters lobbied at the federal level in Canada, as of 9 August 2008

Source: Office of the Commissioner of Lobbying of Canada

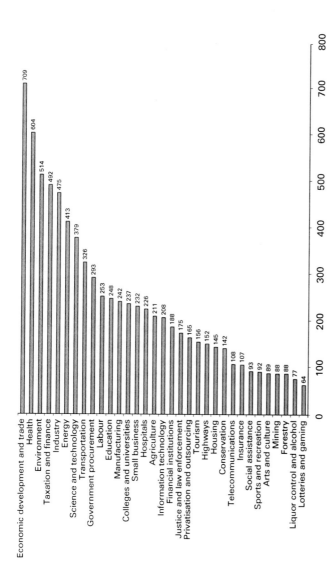

Figure 2.2 Subject matters lobbied in Ontario
Source: Ontario Lobbyists Registration Office

in this jurisdiction under article 91 of the constitution. While government procurement was ranked twelfth at the federal level, it is ranked slightly higher, at ninth, at the provincial level. Taken together, this suggests that much overlap exists in terms of subject matters that lobbyists try to influence at both the provincial and the federal levels, thereby suggesting that having expertise in a certain subject matter will allow lobbyists to work easily between levels.

Lobbying legislation in Canada and the provinces
Turning to the federal level, in 1989 the Canadian government initiated lobbying legislation, by way of what was referred to as the Lobbyist Registration Act (Canada), with the goal of promoting transparency and openness in policy making. As discussed in more detail below, this act has as its main objective the compulsory registration of groups lobbying national governmental actors on a national registry. The 1989 act was amended in 1995 by the Amendment to Lobbyist Registration Act, which attempted to beef up the information that was required to be forwarded by lobbyists when registering.

The next major amendment to the federal Lobbyist Registration Act came with Bill C-15 in 2003 (which came into force in 2005), which helped clean up loopholes in the previous system with regard to what could be considered 'lobbying'. The final major amendment was in July 2008, when the Lobbyist Registration Act was renamed the Lobbying Act, which saw new obligations and heavier fines for lobbyists, as discussed in more detail below.

Nova Scotia, Quebec, Ontario, British Columbia (BC) and most recently Newfoundland are provinces in Canada that have followed the federal government's suit and similarly enacted lobbying legislation. In December 2007, Alberta passed a lobbyists act which provides for the establishment and maintenance of a registry of lobbyists. While an ethics commissioner has been appointed, the legislation provided for in the act had not been enforced at the time of writing. Thus, not all of the Canadian provinces have legislation with regard to regulation of lobbying activity, as will be discussed in detail in Chapter 6. In the case of Nova Scotia, the Lobbyist Registration Act (Bill 7) was passed in 2001; Quebec passed its Lobbying Transparency and Ethics Act (Bill 80) in 2002; Ontario, which was the first province to pursue lobbying legislation after the federal government, established the Lobbyist Legislation Act in 1998; BC pursued its Lobbying Registration Act in 2001; and the most recent example is that of Newfoundland, which implemented its lobbying legislation in 2005. Thus, in the past decade five provinces have moved towards regulating lobbyists, and a sixth is in the process of doing so.

It is important to point out that these different acts were introduced by different parties, across the ideological spectrum, which suggests that the legislation was not ideologically based *per se*. For example, the first federal legislation was approved by the Conservative Party under Brian Mulroney, later amendments were made by the Liberals under Jean Chrétien, and further reforms were made by the recent Conservative government led by Stephen Harper.

The nature of the regulations: a comparative analysis of Canada. Rather than offer a descriptive narrative of the contents of each of the pieces of legislation in Canada referred to above, this section offers a comparative analysis of their contents by focusing on key elements within them. We therefore consider each of the following sub-themes and questions in turn, which helps us better understand what the legislation covers, how much it covers, and some of the changes over time:

- What is the principal focus of Canadian legislation?
- How does Canadian legislation define 'lobbying', 'lobbyist' and 'public office holder', and which actors' actions are *not* scrutinised in the acts?
- What information do lobbyists have to give when registering in Canada?
- Are there 'codes of conduct' in Canadian lobbying legislation?
- What rules surround lobbying by former public office holders?
- By which means do lobbyists register?
- What are the penalties for non-compliance with the legislation?

The following sub-sections consider each of these questions in turn.

The principal focus of the Canadian legislation – registration. A key idea behind the lobbyist registration legislation in Canada, also reflected in the provincial legislation in Alberta, Ontario, Quebec, Nova Scotia, Newfoundland and BC, is the act of making lobbyists register with the state. Registration of lobby groups in itself *is* the objective. The objective is *not* to monitor what is going on when lobbying activity itself takes place; *nor* does the legislation require disclosure of all financial information (i.e. spending reports) of the lobby group or the client represented (although political campaign contributions in Canada must be reported under the Canada Elections Act, as discussed below); *nor* does the legislation place any responsibilities for politicians to ensure that those who lobby them are registered. In the words of Guy Giorno, a leading expert on Canadian lobbying legislation who in 2008 took the position of Chief of Staff of the Prime Minister's Office under Harper, Canadian legislation on lobbying is 'principally concerned with the requirement of the process of registration [of lobbyists].... [and therefore] shares the same basic structure' (Giorno, 2006a: 3).

Based on the belief that lobbying is a legitimate political activity, the principal reason for having a registry, as reflected in the legislation and mentioned in several elite interviews in this study, is that it helps to ensure transparency and openness in the democratic process, from which citizens, lobby groups and politicians can benefit. If citizens, lobby groups and public office holders know who is lobbying whom, then this will allow for a better idea of who is trying to influence policy. Citizens will benefit because they can see which private interests are seeking to affect policy and influence state institutions; other lobbyists will benefit because they can see what their competitors might be doing; and politicians benefit because they can be seen as being open and helping to increase legitimacy in the political process because there is increased transparency in policy making as far as citizens are concerned. In short, it is a positive-sum game where everyone wins.

Defining lobbying, lobbyists and public office holders. As set out in section 5 of the Lobbyist Registration Act of 1989, which is similar to the provincial legislation, *a lobbyist* can be defined as an individual who 'for payment, on behalf of any person or organisation' seeks:

1 to communicate with a public office holder in an attempt to influence
   * the development of any legislative proposal by the government of Canada or by a member of the Senate or House of Commons
   * the introduction, passage, defeat or amendment of any bill
   * the making or amendment of any regulation
   * the development or amendment of any policy programme
   * the awarding of any grant, contribution, or other financial benefit
   * the awarding of any contract
2 to arrange a meeting between a public office holder and any other person.

It is noteworthy that while the 1989 Act stated that lobbying occurs 'when a person or organization communicates with a public office holder in an attempt to influence the latter', this concept would be slightly changed over time in order to allow the federal law to have more force. More concretely, Bill C-15 of 2003 replaced the idea of communication 'in an attempt to influence' to communication 'in respect of' government decisions (p. 11). This has the effect of broadly covering all forms of communication, whether or not they actually have the goal of influencing or not: 'lobbying will consist of "any oral or written communication made to a public office holder"'.[26] It is also worth mentioning that while the 1989 Act stated that someone invited by government to speak to political officials was exempt from registering, Bill C-15 closed this loophole by stating that such lobbyists also had to register, whether or not there was an actual 'attempt to influence'.[27] To date, all provincial governments have maintained the 'attempt to influence' clause, save Quebec, which 'applies both an objective and subjective test to the communication' (Giorno, 2006a: 11).[28]

Regardless of whether or not the term 'attempt to influence' or 'in respect of' government decisions is used in the legislation, analysis of all legislation in Canada reflects this similar principle of lobbying: any communication by a lobbyist/interest group to sway any governmental decision is considered lobbying and anyone so doing must register. Indeed, one may argue that the definition of 'governmental decision', which is covered by all the acts, is rather all encompassing: it includes any legislative proposal – the introduction of any bill or resolution, as well as its passage, defeat or amendment; the amendment of any government programme or regulation; and the awarding of grants and contracts.

In the words of Dyck (2004: 368), the acts

> acknowledged that lobbying public office holders was a legitimate activity, but required lobbyists to register because it was desirable that officials and the public knew who was attempting to influence government and because paid lobbyists should not impede free and open access to government.

It is interesting to note that all of the acts in Canada do define what is meant by the term *public office holder*. As Giorno (2006a: 4) explains:

> There are slight differences among (Canadian) jurisdictions, but as a general rule public office holders include: elected members of the jurisdiction's legislature or parliament; members of their staffs; employees of the jurisdiction's government and government agencies; and individuals whom the jurisdiction's government has appointed to government. In Quebec only, public office holders also include elected members of municipal councils and employees of municipal governments.

The 2008 federal Lobbying Act explicitly refers to the idea of 'designated public office holder' (DPOH), that is, a key policy maker: DPOHs are defined as 'Ministers, Ministers of State and their exempt staff; Deputy Heads; Associate Deputy Ministers; Assistant Deputy Ministers; any positions that have been designated by regulation, such as certain senior members of Canadian forces, and others' (Government of Canada, 2008: 4).

As well as Canadian legislation defining a 'public office holder' (one who is lobbied), it also defines what is meant by 'lobbyists' (those who lobby), who have to register on two fronts, in terms of function and in terms of structure. First, as above, in terms of function, a lobbyist is anyone who seeks to influence, or sway, any public office holder with the aim of affecting final government outputs. Secondly, taking all Canadian legislation together, the laws differentiate between the types of organisational structures of lobbyists at play in the political system. In the words of Giorno (2006a: 3, 17–20), the laws 'distinguish between those who lobby on behalf of clients (also referred to as *consultant* lobbyists) and those who lobby on behalf of their employers (which may be either corporations or organisations; these are also referred to as *in-house corporate or in-house organisational lobbyists*)'.[29] While consultant lobbyists have always had to register since 1989, the changes introduced in 1995 stipulated that in-house lobbyists also had to disclose details similar to consultant lobbyists (Nelson, 2007: 6). Table 2.7 shows the numbers of active consultant, in-house corporate and in-house organisation lobbyists at the end of 2008.

Table 2.7 Numbers of active lobbyists at the Canadian federal level,
19 December 2008

Type of lobbyist	Number
Consultant lobbyists	889
In-house corporate lobbyists	1,617
In-house organisation lobbyists	2,329
Total	4,835

Source: Office of the Commissioner of Lobbying of Canada.

The top 20 federal-level institutions as of December 2008 that lobbyists seek to influence are listed in Table 2.8.

While all lobbyists are required to register when lobbying government institutions, certain other officials are not. These include: MPs, senators, MLAs, governmental employees, elected municipal officials and their employees (except in Quebec), Aboriginal (or, First Nations Canadians) leaders, diplomats, and members of international organisations (such as the United Nations) working in Canada (Giorno, 2006a: 14–15).

What information is required by lobbyists when they register in Canada and what is the frequency of reporting?   Although there is some variation across the federal and provincial levels according to whether or not a lobby group is acting as a consultant or in-house lobbyist, the following information – as taken from the federal-level rules for a consultant lobbyist who is working on behalf of a client – offers a good indication of the information that must be disclosed by a lobbyist when registering:[30]

- name, position, title and business address of the lobbyist;
- name and business address of the lobbying firm/corporation;
- client's name and business address (if consultant lobbyist);
- name of the principal representative of the client;
- name and business address of any person or organisation that controls or directs the client's activities;
- if the client is a corporation, the name and business address of the parent corporation and those subsidiaries which directly benefit from the lobbying;
- if the client is a coalition, the names and business addresses of the corporate and organisational members;
- if the individual is a former public office holder, a description of the offices held and at what time;

Table 2.8 Canadian government institutions identified in active registrations by lobbyists

Institutions	Number
1. Industry Canada (IC)	2,024
2. Finance Canada (FIN)	1,532
3. Privy Council Office (PCO)	1,300
4. Environment Canada (EC)	1,185
5. Foreign Affairs and International Trade (DFAIT)	1,164
6. Members of the House of Commons	1,160
7. Prime Minister's Office (PMO)	1,104
8. Health Canada (HC)	1,054
9. Transport Canada (TC)	902
10. Natural Resources Canada (NRCan)	815
11. Treasury Board of Canada (TBS)	752
12. Agriculture and Agri-Food Canada	703
13. Public Works and Government Services Canada (PWGSC)	639
14. Revenue Canada	633
15. Senate of Canada	629
16. Indian and Northern Affairs Canada (INAC)	605
17. National Defence (DND)	559
18. Human Resources Development Canada (HRDC)	547
19. Canadian Heritage (PCH)	518
20. Justice Canada (JC)	457

The numbers refer to active registrations by lobbyists, as of 19 December 2008.
Source: Office of the Commissioner of Lobbying of Canada.

- subject matters, including the specific legislative proposal, bill or resolution, regulation, policy, programme, grant, contribution, other financial benefit or contract sought;
- name of each department or other governmental institution lobbied;
- source and amount of any government funding provided to the client;
- whether payment is contingent on the success of the lobbying (at the federal level, however, the 2008 legislation states that contingency fees are now banned);
- the communication techniques used, including grass-roots lobbying.

It is significant to consider what is meant by 'grass-roots lobbying', something which is mentioned in the federal, Ontario and Nova Scotia legislation, but not in that of either Quebec or BC. Grass-roots communication can be defined as:

> appeals to members of the public through mass media or by direct communication to persuade them to communicate directly with a public office holder

to place pressure on him or her to endorse a particular opinion ... [although] these Acts do not state explicitly that grass-roots communication constitutes lobbying or communication with a public office holder.... The conclusion is implicit in their language. (Giorno, 2006a: 9)

Once registered, lobbyists have to re-register for as long as they are pursuing political activity. Depending on the jurisdiction (and potentially the type of lobbyist), the frequency with which re-registration takes place varies. For example, at the federal level, all lobbyists have to re-register every six months. If, however, contact is made with a federal-level DPOH, the 2008 legislation states that re-registration must take place monthly. When re-registering on this basis, the lobbyist is required to give a report to the federal Commissioner of Lobbying which states with which DPOH they met, when and on what matter. Although not every return will neces-sarily be verified, the Commissioner may subsequently 'require any present or former DPOH to verify information derived from one or more monthly returns' (Government of Canada, 2008: 5). In Ontario, consultant lobbyists have to re-register annually, while in-house lobbyists have to re-register every six months (Giorno, 2006a: 25–26).

In terms of other dimensions that lobbyists have to report, as men-tioned earlier, under the Canada Elections Act, lobbyists must report all financial contributions to political parties. However, the Lobbying Acts themselves do not stipulate that lobbyists cannot contribute to political parties. In fact, many of them do, within the limit of $1,000 allowed by the Canada Elections Act for corporations, trade unions and associations.[31] Interestingly, a loophole within the system allows lobby groups to provide 'consultancy services' to political parties for free during election times, and many do so.[32]

Codes of conduct for lobbyists? In most Canadian lobbying legislation there is no explicit code of conduct imposed on lobbyists. The exceptions to this are the cases of Quebec and the federal legislation (where it is not a statutory instrument). But even in these cases, one may argue that the main shortcoming relates to vague (if not normative) generalisations in the code. That is, even though such codes, as in the case of Quebec, do suggest how lobby groups ought to operate in terms of general guidelines, with 'duties and obligations', 'respect for institutions', 'honesty and integrity' and 'professionalism', these broad definitions are open to interpretation. For example, with regard to the last, both federal and Quebec legislation prevents lobby groups from exerting 'improper influence' on government officials. However, this is something that is difficult to measure: what may be 'improper influence' to some may not be deemed so by others. As Giorno (2006b) questions, 'does political fundraising or assistance on a political campaign constitute an improper influence?' With this in mind, there is little surprise there has not been any case of a lobbyist being investigated for having breached any code.

Cooling-off periods. Whether as part of the lobbying rules, or as part of a separate piece of related legislation, all jurisdictions in Canada have a mandatory 'cooling off' period, which refers to a minimum amount of time in which former ministers or high-level civil servants cannot engage in lobbying activity, given potential conflicts of interest.[33] The 2008 federal legislation states that DPOHs have a mandatory cooling-off period of five years; Quebec and BC's legislation stipulates that politicians cannot act as lobbyists for two years after leaving office; in Ontario and Newfoundland, this time limit is lowered to one year; and in Nova Scotia this limit reaches a low of all jurisdictions, at six months. High-level provincial civil servants, in Ontario, Newfoundland and Quebec, have a cooling-off period of one year; BC has a cooling off period in this regard of two years; and in Nova Scotia the time limit is again six months.

How do lobbyists register? The primary means through which lobbyists register, and which is recommended by the registrars of all jurisdictions, is via the internet. At the federal government level, and in Ontario and Quebec, there is no charge for any consultant to register, renew registration or change registration details if this is done via the internet. In fact, in the case of the Registrar's Office in Ontario, state-of-the-art sophisticated software developed at a cost of over $50,000 was introduced to ensure a smooth, trouble-free method of registering by way of computer. The great advantage of having such software is that it decreases resources and the workforce necessary to keep all the files in order: in the case of Ontario, only one person needs to be in charge of all technical aspects of the office. When the authors were allowed access to the managing system in Ontario, we saw how the person in charge sees which registrants have made recent requests (either for initial registration or for renewals). The software allows the person in charge of the system to go to the main menu and have easy access to the various registrants on the file, including consultant and in-house lobbyists (corporations and organisations). The Ontario software also reflects its sophistication in its ability to monitor when a lobbyist has missed the renewal period, by flagging to the operator on a daily basis those whose registration has lapsed.

The only three jurisdictions where there is a charge for internet registration are Nova Scotia, Newfoundland and BC.[34] Paper registration in all districts, however, requires a fee of between $27 and $150. Charging higher prices for paper registration is a result of the extra work that is required for the registrars to get the lobbyists' file into the system. The effect is that virtually all lobbying registration in Canada is done online, and citizens are allowed free access to the registries of all lobbyists in all jurisdictions.[35]

The penalties a lobbyist may incur.   Given the overall objective that lobbyists register when pursuing political activity, the main penalty under the acts is for not registering with the level of government where political activity (lobbying) is taking place. A related failure includes giving false or misleading information when registering. This failure to register, or to renew, or to correct any misleading/incorrect information, or to notify the state when lobbying has ceased can result in one of two penalties.[36] The first is a fine, where the amount that can be imposed varies according to jurisdiction. Quebec has a minimum fine of $500 and a maximum of $25,000; in Nova Scotia, Ontario and Newfoundland the fine is $25,000 for the first offence, with a maximum one of $100,000 for infringements thereafter; and at the federal level, the 2008 legislation saw fines double from those under the previous legislation, and they now range from $50,000 (if prosecuted summarily) to $200,000 (if prosecuted on indictment). The second penalty that may be paid by lobbyists who infringe the rules, and which is seen only at the federal level, is imprisonment (theoretically ranging from six months to two years). The 2008 federal legislation extends the investigation and prosecution period of potential breaches by lobbyists from 2 to 10 years. Further, the 2008 legislation gave the Commissioner the right to 'name and shame' the convicted lobbyist by publishing the names of violators in reports, as well as the power to prevent any convicted person from lobbying at the federal level for two years.

There has so far been only one case that resulted in penalties being imposed: in March 2006, an immigration lawyer in Quebec was fined $3,105 for not having registered as a lobbyist before lobbying immigration officials.[37] The low number of penalties imposed allows some more positive observers to conclude that lobbyists are generally complying with the legislation. Yet, other, more critical observers suggest that more needs to be done to empower the state to investigate potential infringements. For example, even though state agencies can conduct mandatory reviews, lobbyist registrars infrequently prosecute violations of regulations, as they lack both resources and information.[38] With the exception of the revamped federal Office of the Commissioner of Lobbying in 2006–7, which now has 20 staff, most registrars in Canada have only a handful of staff. In fact, one of the smallest operations exists in Nova Scotia, which has one person working virtually half-time.

The European Union

Brief history and nature of EU institutions
There are presently 27 member states of the EU, covering a population of over 460 million people and an area of over 4,300,000 km^2. The original six member states were Belgium, the Netherlands, Luxembourg,

France, Italy and (West) Germany, which signed the 1951 Treaty of Paris establishing the European Coal and Steel Community (ECSC). Six years later the Treaty of Rome establishing the European Economic Community (EEC) was signed by the same countries. In 1973 the UK, Ireland and Denmark joined, while the next decade saw 'southern' expansion bring in Greece (1981), Spain (1986) and Portugal (1986). In 1995 Austria, Sweden and Finland became members and less than 10 years later further expansion saw Cyprus, the Czech Republic, Estonia, Hungary, Latvia, Lithuania, Malta, Poland, Slovenia and Slovakia become part of the EU in 2004. The latest entrants were Romania and Bulgaria in 2007.

From its inception after the Second World War, the rationale behind deeper economic integration was that tying together European countries would greatly lessen the chances they would go to war again. In that context, European integration was seen as guaranteeing European peace. Although the European project started with much optimism, it was clear that with the economic decline in Europe throughout the 1970s as well as continued protectionism on the part of some member states, the 1980s needed to see a deeper push towards further economic integration. This push was achieved with the Single European Act (SEA) in 1986, which created a true, free-trade single market. The 1992 Maastricht Treaty took economic union further by adding monetary union. While 2005 saw the failure to introduce a European constitution, which would represent a step towards closer political union, three years later the Lisbon Treaty attempted to rekindle such ideas. At the time of writing, its future still remained somewhat uncertain (Chari, 2008).[39] However, regardless of the fate of Lisbon, all previous milestones – the SEA (1986), the Maastricht Treaty (1992), the Amsterdam Treaty (1999) and later the Nice Treaty (2003) – reflect the increasing importance of the supranational level: throughout the last 30 years there has been a transfer of power in several policy areas from the member-state level to the supranational level of governance, including trade, competition, economic and monetary union, agriculture as well as elements of justice and security policies and external relations. A consequence of this transfer has been the increasing drive of different lobby groups to attempt to influence EU policy making (Chari and Cavatorta, 2002; Coen, 1997).

In order to better understand the significance of the lobbying regulations in place at the EU level, and to better understand which institutional structures lobbyists seek to influence, it is important to note the triumvirate of the major institutions of the EU wherein supranational policy is made: the European Commission, the Council of Ministers and the European Parliament.[40] The first two of these – the Commission and the Council – have been likened by some to a 'dual executive' for the EU (Hix, 2005): executive power is not held by one institution *per se* as seen in domestic politics but is held in tandem by two main ones. On the one hand, the Commission has a leading role in initiating regulations in key policy areas as well as in ensuring that policies are implemented. On the other, the Council can amend or reject Commission proposals, while defining the long-term EU goals. The main strength of this dual character is that it 'facilitates extensive deliberation and compromise in the adoption and implementation of policies', while its main weaknesses is that it 'lacks overall leadership' (Hix, 2005: 70–71). This last point emphasises that even if one agrees with the idea that there is some sort of 'executive' power, policy making in the EU is not necessarily centred exclusively in one of these main institutions.

The European Commission has 27 members: each member state has one Commissioner. Commissioners theoretically represent the interests of the EU, not the member state from which they come. They lead what are known as Directorates General (DGs), which can be considered a Brussels-level equivalent to a ministry found in domestic politics. Examples of Directorates General include Internal Market, Competition, Economic and Financial Affairs, Agriculture, Employment, Environment, Justice, Freedom and Security, and External Relations. In terms of policy-making power, the Commission has the sole right among all EU institutions to initiate legislation in most policy areas. However, as discussed below, this does not mean that the Commission can act unilaterally: in fact, the Council often rejects Commission proposals. A second power, which relates to its role in the implementation phase and closely mirrors a bureaucratic function, is ensuring that member states comply with EU legislation. Yet, this is an increasingly difficult task for a staff of approximately 30,000 civil servants. There have been several instances of member states not complying with Commission decisions over the last 15 years, especially in areas such as competition policy and state aid (Chari, 1998).

The Council of Ministers, or the Council of the European Union, represents the interests of each of the member states. Before May 2004, there were 15 member states, but the 2004–7 enlargement, which saw 12 central and eastern European states join, increased this number to 27. There is no one Council *per se*, but, rather, several, each of which consists of the national ministers in a particular policy area. Some of the most significant are General Affairs (with representation from foreign ministers) and ECOFIN (finance ministers), as well as the 'European Council' (comprising the 27 heads of state), which attracts the most media attention. The Council presidency rotates every six months and the European Council is held every six months. The most important meetings are those taking place at various times throughout the whole year, where details of policy are discussed. The Council's first main power is to reject or amend Commission proposals. While this may seem insignificant vis-à-vis the power of the Commission, some authors argue that this means that the Council exercises power over the Commission (Moravscik, 1993). Moreover, there is nothing to stop the Council from informally leaning on the Commission to initiate a piece of legislation in a specific policy area that is in the former's interest (Christiansen and Piattoni, 2004). In this regard, the Council is empowered to define the long-term goals of the EU, effectively 'delegating' its power to the Commission as the Council sees fit.

The European Parliament (EP) is the third main institution in EU policy making. The EP is the only one of the three main institutions that is directly elected; the 736 Members of the European Parliament (MEPs) are chosen by EU citizens every five years. Once elected, MEPs sit not along national lines, but as members of party groups. Although the literature generally agrees that the axis of executive power lies between the Council and the Commission, the exact role of the EP in the policy-making process has been debated. More pessimistic observers argue that the EP is a symbolic institution (or 'talking shop') that has virtually no substantive power other than offering the façade of a representative assembly. Optimists demonstrate that formal EP power is increasing, particularly since the early 1990s and with the 1997 Treaty of Amsterdam (Hix, 2002), in four dimensions. First, policy in the major EU areas must attain the EP's approval, including: the admission of new member states; major international agreements between the EU and outside countries (but not including foreign policy initiatives); the method of election to be used in EP elections; and the role of the European Central Bank (ECB). Second, since 1993 the EP has gained an active role in the appointment of Commissioners (Hix, 2005). Third, although the Commission and Council clearly have strength in determining the details of the budget, the EP can amend and even reject the budget on the final reading (although this has not occurred since the 1990s). Fourth, the EP has gained substantial power via the use of the 'co-decision' procedure, by which it can reject and/or amend legislation in specific policy areas, including internal market, public health, consumer protection, and culture and education.

The nature of EU lobbying

Of the 15,000 lobbyists working in the EU, it is estimated that 70 per cent work directly or indirectly for corporate/industrial interests, 20 per cent represent the interests of the regions, cities and international organisations, and 10 per cent represent trade unions and NGOs (Corporate European Observatory, 2005: 8).

Turning to the first category, Brussels is home to numerous professional lobbyists who work directly for corporate and industrial interests. Many of the professional lobbyists who specialise in public affairs (PA) and public relations (PR) have their offices close to the headquarters of either the Commission (in the Berlaymont building) or the EU Council of Ministers (the Justus Lipsius building), on Rue de la Loi. According to a 2005 report by the Corporate European Observatory (2005: 8), the five largest public affairs and public relations organisations in Brussels which offer consultancy services are: APCO, Burson-Marsteller, Fleishman-Hillard, Hill and Knowlton, and Weber Shandwick. These specialists are hired in order to attempt to influence officials in the EU's institutions on behalf of industrial and corporate interests, or to give strategic advice to such economic actors when they choose instead to engage in direct lobbying. With the latter point in mind, Coen's (1998) work demonstrates that corporations are increasingly choosing to do so, by having in-house lobbyists who attempt to influence European political actors. Firms, whether European or internationally based – such as Airbus, Boeing, Telefónica, DuPont and Dow Chemical – all have lobbying offices in Brussels. Beyond hiring professional lobbyists and using in-house lobbyists, corporations may also lobby through European-level umbrella organisations such as the Union of Industrial and Employers' Confederations of Europe (UNICE) or the European Round Table of Industrialists (ERT) that champion the cause on behalf of the corporation or industrial partner. This is seen in Cowles' (1996) work, which highlights the role played by the ERT in the lead-up to the 1992 Maastricht treaty on European Union, as well as that of Chari and Kritzinger (2006: chs 4, 5 and 6), who highlighted the importance of the ERT in shaping single-market, merger, as well as economic and monetary policies at the supranational level.

Beyond corporate and industrial interests that seek to influence the EU policy process, there are professional interests such as trade unions and farmers. For example, the European Trade Union Confederation (ETUC) is an umbrella organisation that represents 82 national trade union confederations from 36 different European countries (extending beyond the EU), plus 12 industry-based federations. In its own words, its main objective since it was founded in 1973 has been to 'promote the European Social Model and to work for the development of a united Europe of peace and stability where working people and their families can enjoy full human and civil rights and high living standards'.[41] It hails as some of its main achievements: having taken part in the annual Tripartite Social Summit, which assesses progress on the 2000–10 Lisbon Agenda; having been consulted on EU decisions affecting employment, social affairs and macroeconomic policy; and participating in EU advisory bodies, including the European Economic and Social Committee (EESC) and the EU agencies for vocational training, working conditions, and health and safety.[42]

Founded in 1958, the Committee of Professional Agricultural Organisations (COPA) is an umbrella group representing the interests of 60 farming organisations in the EU. In 1962, it merged with the General Committee for Agricultural Cooperation (COGECA), which presently represents agricultural cooperatives in the EU. Today, COPA–COGECA represents some 15 million people who work full or part time on EU agricultural holdings, as well as 30,000 agricultural cooperatives. In terms of influencing EU institutions, the organisation: meets frequently with the Agriculture Commissioner

as well as officials from DG Agriculture on the development of the Common
Agriculture Policy (CAP); meets regularly with the EP's Committee on Agriculture and Rural Development, as well as the EP's various political groups;
and occasionally meets with the President of the Council.[43]

Various NGOs representing the concerns of members interested in
developments in a particular policy area – such as human rights, the
environment, animal rights, and health and safety – also have a lobbying
presence in Brussels. Examples of international organisations operating
in the EU include the International Lesbian and Gay Association (ILGA),
Greenpeace and Amnesty International. European-based groups include
the European Council of Refugees and Exiles (ECRE) and the European
Environment Bureau. Some studies have found that such NGOs do exercise
influence in environmental policy making as well as, somewhat interestingly, areas related to freedom, justice and security policies.[44]

It is noteworthy that many civil society groups in the EU – such as trade
associations, youth groups, professional institutions and religious organisations – receive Commission funding in order to operate. Table 2.9 shows
what types of organisation these are.

Table 2.9 Interest groups that receive EU Commission funding

Type of organisation	Number	Percentage of total
Citizen organisation	28	44
Youth/education	11	17
Trade association	5	8
EU integration group	5	8
Professional association	3	5
Association of institutions	3	5
Religious organisation	2	3
Political association	2	3
Federation of associations	2	3
Labour union	1	2
Business association	1	2
Research group/foundation	1	2
Total	64	*100*

Source: Mahoney (2004: 447).

Regardless of where they receive their funding, how successful are the
different types of EU lobbies? In order to better gauge the effectiveness
of industry lobbyists and NGOs, Burson-Marsteller (2005: 10) surveyed
150 senior representatives of the three key EU policy-making institutions.

Industry was considered by EU policy makers to have more effective lobbying strategies in the following policy areas: energy; financial services; electrical and electronics; defence and aerospace; healthcare and pharmaceuticals; and information technology and telecommunications. NGOs and other civil society groups gained some slight comparative advantage over industry only in the areas of consumer goods and the food and drinks sector.

In terms of how successful lobbyists in the EU see themselves, Mahoney's comparative data with the US suggests that EU lobbyists overall fare better than their American counterparts, not so much in terms of attaining all of their goals, but in terms of attaining compromises. She argues:

> more US lobbyists, at 23%, attained all of their lobbying goals compared to the EU figure of 17%, and more US lobbyists at 46% attained none of their lobbying goals compared to those in Europe where only 39% attained nothing. While only 31% of US lobbyists attained a compromised success, in the EU that figure was 43%. On average, therefore, EU lobbyists are more likely to attain lobbying success, but a compromised success – a type of success that comes from policy resolutions where everyone wins, at least a little. (Mahoney, 2007: 44–45)

That said, how important are lobbyists to EU policy makers when they are looking for information? Interestingly, the Burson-Marsteller (2005) report also sheds light on which sources of information decision makers rely on when having to make informed decisions, which can help us gauge how effective EU lobbying is when decisions are taken. One of the lessons from that study is that all senior decision makers in the Commission, Council and EP value the information gleaned from staff members, colleagues and personal research more than that from lobbyists, whether from industry or NGOs.[45] That is not to say that EU lobbying is ineffective; rather, it is to say that lobbyists have to lobby the right people, namely those who work closely with senior EU decision makers. Secondly, beyond staff members, colleagues and personal research, Commission senior officials rank information coming from industry lobbyists as the next highest source. While Council officials feel that industry lobbying is of slightly lower importance ·as a source of information than the media, it actually ranks the lowest of all sources for MEPs, who instead rely more heavily on local constituency information, the media and NGOs. All senior officials from all three institutions did nevertheless agree that three best ways to receive information from lobbyists were through face-to-face meetings, written briefing material, and conferences, seminars and workshops (Burson-Marsteller, 2005: 15).

The nature of the regulations in the EU
The above overview of the main institutions of the EU as well as of the main types of interest representation in the EU helps us better understand the significance of the lobbying legislation initiatives that have been pursued

at the EU level: to date, the only EU institution to have pursued a lobbying registry which all lobbyists must sign up to has been the EP, by way of Rules of Procedure 9, in 1996. There is no lobbying legislation with regard to the Council or the Commission, although a *voluntary* registry was adopted in the Commission in June 2008 (see below, p. 55). Thus, the two main policy-making powers in the EU have not pursued lobbying regulations. Moreover, it is also important to note, and as will be shown in Chapter 4 when we offer a comparative analysis of the political systems studied in this book, that when compared with the Canadian and US systems, the legislation in place for the EP is relatively weak.

In order to better understand this, this subsection examines the stages of development of the EP lobbying initiative and then analyses what is covered (and what is not covered) in the legislation. Thereafter, we close with a brief discussion of recent developments at the Commission level.

History of EP legislation

The rationale for a registry of lobbyists was based on perceptions of less than transparent practices having occurred in the EP throughout the 1980s and 1990s. As the EP itself stated, there were 'charges that some MEPs' assistants could have been paid by interest groups and that some MEPs even could have acted as interest representatives themselves' (European Parliament, 2003: 36). As a consequence, in the early 1990s calls were made to establish 'minimalist standards' in order to clean up the situation, something which was spearheaded by Marc Galle, chairman of the Committee for Rules and Procedure (European Parliament, 2003: 36). However, little progress was made at the time, given the upcoming EP election in 1994 and given the EP's inability to clearly agree to key terms, such as what was meant by 'lobbying' and 'lobbyist'.

Nevertheless, there was a renewed impetus following the elections: led by Glyn Ford, the Labour member for South West England, there was a proposal that 'the College of Quaestors should issue permanent passes to persons who wished to enter Parliament frequently with a view to supplying information to members within the framework of their parliamentary mandate' (European Parliament, 2003: 37). As Bouwen (2003: 8) explains, the EP elects the five Quaestors of the College, who 'have an important internal function within the Parliament as they are responsible for administrative and financial matters directly concerning the members'. And with the final acceptance of Ford's recommendations in 1996, the College was doubly

> politically responsible for the implementation of the rules of 'lobbying in parliament' and 'transparency and Member's Financial Interests' (Rules of Procedure Annex I and IX).... These rules are the cornerstone of the Parliament's policy to regulate the interaction of members of Parliament and private interests. (Bouwen, 2003: 8)

We thus turn to a more detailed discussion of what this policy does (and does not) entail.

EP legislation in place: what it covers (and what it does not cover)

How are lobbyists defined? The EP offers the following definition of lobbyists:

> Lobbyists can be private, public or non-governmental bodies. They can provide parliament with knowledge and specific expertise in numerous economic, social, environmental and scientific areas.[46]

When comparing the last part of the definition with the Canadian definitions quoted above (p. 38), for example, one may argue that the EP definition portrays lobbying activity as an utterly altruistic, good-hearted act: the importance of lobbyists lies in what they can give to the institution, in terms of knowledge and expertise. In other words, there is no explicit mention in this EP definition of interest groups 'attempting to influence' institutions in order to attain outcomes that are in their favour. Considering that, at present, there are over 5,000 institutions accredited to lobby in the EP, one would have thought that an 'attempt to influence' was clearly part of their mandate.[47]

Nor is there an exhaustive attempt to define 'public office holder' as seen in the Canadian legislation, for example. The above definition seems broad, if not vague, as it does not clearly define *who* can be the object of a lobbying strategy (i.e. it may involve not only MEPs, but also their staff as well as civil servants).

What are the responsibilities of the Quaestors and the lobbyists? The 'door pass' system. It is worth quoting at length Rule of Procedure 9(4), in order to better understand the responsibilities of the Quaestors and lobbyists in the registration process:

> The Quaestors shall be responsible for issuing nominative [i.e. individual named] passes valid for a maximum of one year to persons who wish to enter Parliament's premises frequently [defined as five or more days per annum] with a view to supplying information to Members [i.e. MEPs] within the framework of their parliamentary mandate in their own interests or those of third parties.
>
> In return, these persons shall be required to:
>
> • respect the code of conduct published as an annex to the Rules of Procedure;
> • sign a register kept by the Quaestors.
>
> This register shall be made available to the public on request in all of Parliament's places of work and, in the form laid down by the Quaestors, in its information offices in the Member States.[48]

There are three main points brought out in Rule of Procedure 9. First, passes for a maximum of one year are granted to those who lobby the EP, where lobbying is defined as 'supplying information to Members' (not, as above, an explicit attempt to influence) at a frequency of more than five days per year. These passes allow for access to the Parliament, and state the lobbyist's name and the organisation for which the lobbyist works. In other words, anyone wishing physically to enter the Parliament building has to have a pass, and this pass requires registration: email, telephone conversations and meetings off-site are all allowed without registering. The merits of this, as some lobbyists and even some politicians feel, is that the minimalist regulation in place allows room for an element of informal lobbying outside the EP institutional structure. A downside, however, is that because only physically entering the building is regulated, several lobbyists active in the EP are not registered, as stated in interviews with two Commission officials responsible for monitoring the Commission's new voluntary registry (discussed below).[49]

Secondly, a register of all who lobby will be available to the public on the EP website. It is significant to note, however, that while names of lobbyists are available to the public, other information stated on the registration form, such as the nature of the lobbyist's work, the interests for which the lobbyist is acting, and which MEPs may have served as references for the lobbyists, is not publicly available (European Commission, 2006: 7).

Thirdly, in order to get a pass, a lobbyist must respect the code of conduct and sign the register. The code of conduct, however, is a set of mostly either minimal standards (such as stating the interests they represent, under article 3.1.b), or broad definitional concepts through which it would be difficult to penalise anyone (such as refraining from action designed to obtain information 'dishonestly', under article 3.1.c), or actions that would be virtually impossible to trace (such as not to circulate for a profit to third parties copies of documents obtained from Parliament, under article 3.1.e).[50]

What information does a lobbyist have to give when registering with the EP? According to the rules, lobbyists must provide, in writing, general information about their activities, including the name of the lobbying organisation, the general interests (in terms of policies) of their organisation, their own name and their position, their home address (plus a copy of their passport) and for how long they seek to lobby the EP. Comparing the information needed to lobby the EP with that required to lobby the different jurisdictions in Canada and the US, one can see that *less* information is required. For example, the lobbyist does not have to state: the name of each committee, department or other institution lobbied; the subject matters, such as the specific legislative proposal, bill or resolution, regulation, or programme; whether or not there are contingency fees involved; and the communication techniques used when lobbying. Nor do lobbyists have to state whether or not they are former public office holders. In fact, there are not even specific regulations surrounding 'cooling off' periods for former EP officials who may seek to undertake lobbying. Nor are there rules on complete individual spending disclosure (i.e. a lobbyist is not required to file a spending report) or on employer spending disclosure (i.e. an employer of a lobbyist is not required to file a spending report). Taken together, one may argue that though there are rules requiring an individual to register, fewer details have to be given than is the case in the US or Canada.

The potential penalties that EP lobbyists face – the lack of an effective gatekeeper.   Rule of Procedure 9(1), annex 1, article 2, is directed at MEPs rather than lobbyists directly:

> If after the appropriate request a Member does not fulfil his obligation to submit a declaration pursuant to (a) and (b), the President shall remind him once again to submit the declaration within two months. If the declaration has not been submitted within the time limit, the name of the Member together with an indication of the infringement shall be published in the minutes of the first day of each part-session after expiry of the time limit. If the Member continues to refuse to submit the declaration after the infringement has been published the President shall take action in accordance with Rule 124 to suspend the Member concerned.[51]

Despite this, authors such as Bouwen have concluded that 'it would be wrong, however, to conclude on the basis of the Rules of Procedure that the quaestors act as effective gatekeepers of the EP' (Bouwen, 2003: 8). Highlighting the importance of 'informal governance' in the lobbying registration process in the EP, and reflecting comments which were made by different officials we interviewed, Bouwen (2003: 8–9) explains how enforcement of lobbying legislation is limited and how sanctions are insignificant:

> In practice, hardly any requests for passes based on the Rule of Procedure (2) are refused. The responsible quaestor explained to me that he grants access to the different interests on the basis of two informal rules: 1. A maximum of 6 passes can be granted to the same organization, 2. Interests that constitute a security risk are not granted a pass. It is important to emphasize that neither the public or private character of interests nor their organizational form matters when the nominative passes are issued. The only sanction for interests that breach the code of conduct is the withdrawal of the pass issued to the persons concerned.... According to an administrator of the secretariat of the college of quaestors, the application of the rules over the last years has shown that passes are almost never withdrawn. In addition, the implementation of Rule of Procedure 9(1) does not really shape the interaction between the private interests and the MEPs. The same administrator added that members do not take the declarations for the register very seriously and often do not update the required information. *Due to the quaestors' lenient implementation of the Rules of Procedure, it is impossible to conceive of the college of quaestors as the gatekeeper of the European Parliament.* (Emphasis added)

The European Commission: towards mandatory lobbying registration? Well,
not just yet... Some 2,500 lobbyists have offices in the European capital,
spending annually around €60–95 million in their efforts to influence the
Commission (Cronenberg, 2006): the Commission is *the* hot-bed of EU
lobbying activity, particularly given its prominent role in the policy process.
Yet, the European Commission does not run a compulsory register of
organisations that deal with it. This contrasts with the EP's position, which,
as above, has an accreditation system whereby passes are needed in order
to lobby within the Parliament building. This does not mean, however, that
little debate has taken place with regard to whether or not a registry should
be adopted at the Commission level. In fact, much debate has ensued since
the 1990s and, as shown below, the Commission set up a voluntary – not
mandatory – registry in June 2008.

As early as 1992, the Commission stressed the need for an 'open and
structured dialogue with special interest groups' and nearly 10 years later
under the Prodi Commission, its 2001 White Paper stressed the need for
openness and transparency in government (European Commission, 1992,
2001). As Michalowitz (2006: 14) argues:

> With the White Paper, the European Commission has taken steps towards
> rendering its decision-making structures more open and predictable than
> before. As regards measures for increasing civil society involvement in
> decision making, the Commission envisaged in this document to grant a
> larger role to actors whom it accepted as representatives of important civil
> society actors – churches, unions, employers' organisations.... The idea was
> to define more clearly who should be consulted and who should not, and to
> make consulted actors accountable themselves.

In response to the White Paper, CONECCS (Consultation, the European
Commission and Civil Society) was developed. CONECCS was a 'voluntary
database' to which civil society organisations (including, for example, trade
unions, business associations and NGOs) could sign up in order to provide
better information about the Commission's consultative process. Nevertheless, and even in the Commission's own words, CONECCS remained
somewhat toothless:

> CONECCS is used as an information source for Commission departments
> and the general public. However, there is no requirement or incentive for a
> civil society organisation to register. Equally, there is no disincentive against
> failing to register. (European Commission, 2006: 7)

Less than 7 per cent of all lobbyists (i.e. less than 1,000 lobbyists of the
over 15,000 estimated) signed up to the voluntary registration system
(Smyth, 2006). The CONECCS database was eventually closed as the
Commission moved to create a formal voluntary register of interests.

The debate over what type of register to have was opened up again
under the leadership of Anti-Fraud Commissioner Siim Kallas, who started

a consultation process on the theme by pursuing two related initiatives. First, in November 2005 the Commission approved the so-called 'Transparency Initiative', which has a broad goal to foster the idea that 'European leaders, businesses, civil society and citizens … are making policies in an open and inclusive way'.[52] Secondly:

> a Green Paper was published in May 2006 to launch a debate with all the stakeholders on how to improve transparency on the Community Funds, consultation with civil society and the role of the lobbies and NGOs in the European institutions' decision-making process.[53]

In the Green Paper, the Commission considered that a credible system for greater transparency in the EU would consist of a voluntary registration system and tighter self-regulation by lobbyists themselves in terms of their conduct. Voluntary registration was considered better than a mandatory system because it was felt that the latter 'would take a long time to come into force and … could include many loopholes' (Smyth, 2006) (Kallas did not fully specify exactly what the loopholes were). More critical observers of the Commission's Green Paper, such as Erik Wesselius of the Corporate Europe Observatory, nevertheless stated that 'you need some good incentives to encourage lobbyists to sign up for a voluntary system, but the Commission's proposals are very weak and unconvincing on this' (as quoted in Smyth, 2006). Other critics noted that not only has Kallas ignored the advantages of mandatory registration, as seen in cases such as Canada and the US, but also that he has seemingly back-tracked on his own proposals of summer 2005, when it was reported that 'Kallas said he would "certainly" go ahead with plans for a central register of Brussels lobbyists'.[54]

On 21 March 2007 the Commission went on to approve the idea of a *voluntary* public register for all interest representatives working to influence decisions taken in EU institutions.[55] This voluntary public register took effect from June 2008. Although there are rules on what information registrants have to supply, this register is *completely voluntary*, in contrast to developments in the EP, as well as those in other countries studied in this chapter, where registration is mandatory. In other words, lobby groups can attempt to influence the Commission at any time and any place, whether or not they are on the registry. Those on the voluntary public register are also expected to comply with the voluntary codes of conduct.[56]

Why is the Commission's 2008 registry voluntary and not mandatory? In its press release on the new registry, the Commission somewhat naively stated:

> The Commission is ready to trust the profession. The register offers lobbyists legitimacy and recognition as a profession. With self-declaration, the registrant takes responsibility for supplying correct information, and the Commission believes this trust should first be tested, before considering the possibility of more binding regulation.[57]

The Commission also suggested that a mandatory register would need legislation, which would seemingly result in a much narrower definition of interest representation. It also repeated the idea of loopholes as originally raised in the Green Paper of 2006, again without fully defining what the loopholes specifically are. It stated:

> The Commission wants the register to cover a broad assortment of stake-holders. A mandatory register would require legislation, and with legislation a much narrower definition of 'interest representative' would apply. This would create loopholes, and make the playing field uneven. Given the length of legislative procedures, it would also mean no tangible results during this Commission's term of office. In any event, after one year of operation, the Commission will evaluate the register, in particular regarding participation. If it proves to be unsatisfactory, compulsory registration and reporting will be considered.[58]

With the last point in mind, after a one-year trial period with the voluntary register, the Commission intended to revisit the issue regarding whether or not there will be a mandatory one. In October 2008, Commission officials in charge of the register indicated to the authors that if many of the major lobbyists had signed up to the voluntary register within that trial period, the Commission would probably decide that there will be no need to make registration mandatory.[59]

Even though this register is voluntary and was launched only on 23 June 2008, it is worth considering what is required when registering. Three main categories of lobbyists can register: professional consultancies and law firms; corporate 'in-house' lobbyists and trade associations; and NGOs and think-tanks. All registrants must disclose: name of the company, who is the head of the organisation, contact details in Brussels, goals and remit of the organisation, fields of interest of the organisation, and information on the organisation's membership. Signatories must also disclose: total revenues relating to lobbying EU institutions (for professional consultancies and law firms), an estimate of costs associated with direct EU lobbying (in-house lobbyists), or the organisation's overall budget and its main sources of funding (NGOs and think-tanks). Although there is no direct pay-off in signing up for the voluntary register, the Commission states that, in return for registering, 'lobbyists will receive alerts from the EU executive giving details of upcoming public consultations on policy areas of interest to them'.[60]

How effective has the voluntary registry been to date? As it is only months after its launch at the time of writing, it is difficult to tell. Nevertheless, several observers have criticised the Commission's efforts, or, perhaps better said, lack thereof. Earlier in 2008, the EP was already openly stating that it wished to have a mandatory register for all lobbyists who attempt to influence all institutions in the EU,[61] similar to a type of one-stop shop for lobbying registration outlined by organisations such as the European Centre for Public Affairs.[62] MEP Monica Frassoci, the co-President of the Greens/EFA Group, went further:

> The Commission's voluntary lobbyists register falls well short of Parliament's position on 8 May [2008], which called for mandatory participation. The European Transparency Initiative is increasingly being exposed as a very pale imitation of the US' far-reaching Lobbying Disclosure Act.... [The register is] a Commission PR exercise that offers semblance but not substance of greater democratic scrutiny.... It is an insult to the European Parliament and damaging to European citizens' trust in EU institutions and processes.[63]

By 12 December 2008, there were 657 registered lobbyists, which seems a small fraction of the thousands that lobby the Commission on a daily basis.[64] It is also a number that pales in comparison to the 4,500 individuals and organisations that are found in the EP registry. Of those registered with the Commission, 38 were professional consultancies or law firms, among which Burson-Marsteller is the only one of the five major professional lobbyists mentioned earlier listed; 389 were in-house lobbyists; 180 were NGOs or think-tanks; and 50 were 'others', including academic institutions and religious organisations. In the words of a 2009 report by Alter–EU which analyses the development of the Commission's voluntary registry, 'the compliance rate is alarmingly low and the overall quality of information disclosed is very poor'.[65]

Chapter 6 offers a more in-depth discussion on the views of those working in the Commission with regard to mandatory registration and considers whether or not they are really of the opinion that 'self-regulation' is sufficient, a view which has been historically held by the Commission.

Germany

Brief history
There is a long tradition of interest group involvement in the policy process in Germany. This involvement tends to be based around representation on a collective basis, whereby lobbying has largely been pursued by interest associations whose contacts developed primarily with government.

Interest group organisation has developed systematically in Germany since the mid-nineteenth century. Prior to 1871, a fragmented pattern of organised interests appeared. In the aftermath of the Franco-Prussian War and the unification of Germany, this pattern was reshaped over the following decades through the emergence of new social interests in society and the creation of new state institutions. The early development of interest group representation in Germany points to the fact that a sincere effort to organise interests voluntarily along the lines of collective action was made (Ronit and Schneider, 1998: 559–560). Nevertheless, at the same time, the autocratic governments from 1871 to the outbreak of war in 1914 strongly influenced the development of collective action by defining and indeed limiting the channels open to interest groups in the decision-making process. Yet, these governments did introduce generous social reform and welfare legislation after input from various associations.

The period in German history from 1914 to 1945 is a dark one. The optimism of the Weimar Republic, after the bitterness left by Germany's defeat in the First World War and the country's humiliation at Versailles, was displaced by the rise of Nazism and the horrors of the Second World War. Nevertheless, post-war Germany and its place at the heart of Europe, both in terms of the European project and as an independent nation state, is one of the great success stories of the modern world. From the formation of the Federal Republic of Germany in 1949, German democracy has proved remarkably durable and successful.

A new constitution, the Basic Law, was adopted in 1949.[66] There are very few references to the role of associations in the Basic Law: the most explicit references relate to freedom of association, information, assembly and speech. Nevertheless, a regulatory system for relations between private actors and associations and political institutions was formulated over some decades. At times, this has proved contentious. In the mid-1970s, there was a debate about whether a special law on associations should be adopted to regulate interest group behaviour. This arose when the Christian Democrats and the Free Democrats expressed concern that associations had gained too much power in society, partly through their access to parliament and government. Their explicit party political goal was to curb associational power in the policy process and reduce the influence of the unions over the economy. Indeed, their main political opponents, the Social Democrats, saw the proposal as concerned less with associations in general than with trade unions. Instead of a regulation of associations, they proposed an economic and social council, to integrate key economic interest organisations into a corporatist body. This idea was rejected by the Christian Democrats and Free Democrats, as well as by a federal commission that was then considering constitutional reform (Ronit and Schneider, 1998: 561). The issue of what role organised interests should play in politics was addressed without any new legislation being adopted and the federal-level register of associations, administered by the President of the Bundestag, was thus established.

The nature of lobbying in Germany

Germany operates a bicameral parliamentary structure that is federal in nature. The Bundestag (lower house) consists of 662 members (328 directly elected from individual constituencies; 334 elected through party lists in each state so as to obtain proportional representation). Parties must win at least 5 per cent of the national vote, or three constituency seats, to gain representation. The Bundesrat (upper house) consists of members nominated by the governments of the 16 federal states (*Länder*, individually known as *Bundesland*).[67] All states have elected legislatures, which have considerable responsibilities, including education and policing. The Bundesrat exemplifies Germany's federalist system of government. As noted, members of the Bundesrat are not popularly elected, and tend to be *Bundsesland* government ministers. The Bundesrat has 69 members. The *Länder* with more than 7 million inhabitants have six seats (Baden-Württemberg, Bavaria, Lower Saxony and North Rhine-Westphalia). The *Länder* with populations of between 2 million and 7 million have four seats (Berlin, Brandenburg, Hesse, Mecklenburg-Western Pomerania, Rhineland-Palatinate, Saxony, Saxony-Anhalt, Schleswig-Holstein and Thuringia). The least populous *Länder*, with fewer than 2 million inhabitants, receive three seats each (Bremen, Hamburg and the Saarland). This system of representation, although designed to reflect *Bundesland* populations accurately, in fact affords greater representation per inhabitant to the smaller *Länder*. The presidency of the Bundesrat rotates annually among the *Länder*. By law, each *Bundesland* delegation is required to vote as a bloc in accordance with the instructions of the *Bundesland* government.

It is necessary to emphasise that lobbying in Germany has been seen mainly as association lobbying throughout the decades, and German parties have, until recently, not been very shy to support candidates who have some relation to associations, so there are still many 'built-in lobbyists' at both national and state parliaments.[68] In essence, the interplay between interest groups and parliamentarians in Germany is legislated by the provision of a wide corpus of legislation to regulate the behaviour of members of parliament and the civil service. The German philosophy in terms of regulation is based around setting codes of conduct for members of the cabinet, members of parliament and civil servants. The rules for civil servants and elected representatives are relatively strict in terms of corruption avoidance. For members of the Bundestag, this includes a number of rules making publication of membership of external bodies (corporate boards for example) mandatory, and informing the President of the chamber of additional income (a very limited and non-publication rule). Both the Bundestag and the 16 *Landtage* (state legislatures) have such codes, which require reporting of various gifts, travel expenses, and campaign and party fundraising.[69] On the other side of the equation, two associations that organise lobbyists and public affairs professionals have implemented national-level voluntary codes of conduct for lobbyists. Both the Deutsche Gesellschaft für Politikberatung (German Association of Political Consultants) and the Deutsche Public Relations Gesellschaft (German Public Relations Society) assert that lobbying is an important part of the interaction between citizens and their government, and in that context they maintain that lobbying needs to be open and transparent. Thus, they advocate that all their members sign up to such codes of conduct.[70]

Regulation in Germany

Bundestag legislation. Within the EU, the German Bundestag is currently the only parliament that has adopted specific formal rules on registration of lobbyists. Yet as Ronit and Schneider (1998: 559) point out, in German politics, 'lobbying has always been and still is considered a foreign word with strong connotations of secretive policy processes where illegitimate influence is sought'. Relations between government and different kinds of private actors (business, churches, trade unions) are never really referred to as lobbying. Each year a public list is drawn up of all groups wishing to express or defend their views to parliament. Interest groups are required to provide some basic information when registering but there is no requirement to provide any financial information. The register is drawn up every year and is published in the *Federal Gazette (Bundesgesetzblatt).*[71] Those wishing to lobby at either the Bundestag or the federal government (or both) must register on this public list. The procedure is overseen by the President of the Bundestag. The register is published annually and a registered association has access to buildings and may participate in the preparation of federal legislation.

In addition, various types of less formal procedure exist to involve interest groups in the preparation of federal or regional legislation. This point was made by EU Commissioner Siim Kallas in an address to the Zukunftskolloquium Politikberatung ('Political Consultancy Future Colloquium') in Berlin in October 2007, when he stated:

> For decades, it seemed lobbying in Germany was shaped by your corporatist traditions and that lobbying in Bonn was an affair involving a limited number of the major industry associations. The move of the Federal government to Berlin seems to have heralded a change in that culture. I understand that companies wishing to defend their interests now lobby directly or use professional consultancies. (Kallas, 2007)

In principle, lobbyists cannot be heard by parliamentary committees or be issued with a pass admitting them to parliamentary buildings unless they are on the register. However, the Bundestag can invite organisations that are not on the register to present information on an ad hoc basis. This in essence means that not being on the register is no real barrier to being in contact with parliamentary committees or members of the Bundestag. The Bundestag makes quite clear that consulting with interest groups and professional associations is very important when it comes to drafting legislation. Paragraph 1, article 77, of the Basic Law provides for legislative bills to be adopted by the Bundestag. The Bundestag is of the view that many people should participate in the substantive elaboration of bills, but responsibility for enacting the bills must be assumed by those elected for this purpose. Once a bill is drafted by the civil service, the head of the division of the civil service to which the bill relates to will invite organisations and groups which will be affected by the draft law to attend discussions for an exchange of views and information. In essence this means that representatives of interest groups will often learn that a bill is being prepared sooner than will members of the Bundestag themselves. This also means that interest groups can influence the bill at a very early stage. Indeed, such groups are involved before they meet members of the Bundestag, for instance at committee hearings, where they express their views and place their expertise at the Bundestag's disposal.[72] Ministers can receive delegations according to article 10 of the General Rules of Procedure of the federal government. According to Ronit and Schneider (1998: 562), it is at this stage, 'when agendas are set, investigations are undertaken and laws drafted, that intense lobbying exists'.

Article 23 of the Basic Law emphasises that the ministries should cooperate only with national federations, that is, organisations which represent interests across the *Länder* and are thus compatible with the federal ministries. Reference is also made to the hierarchical level of organisations: consultation should be with peak associations primarily. The trade unions and business organisations are the prime examples. The German Federation of Trade Unions (Deutscher Gewerkschaftsbund, DGB) is the umbrella organisation for trade unions in Germany and consists of eight member unions. There are also some smaller unions. In 1990, trade union membership stood at 13.7 million, but this had decreased to 8.5 million in 2005. The combined membership of the Federation has also been decreasing substantially since the early 1990s and in 2005 stood at 6.77 million, or about 80 per cent of all unionised employees.[73]

Within the business community there are three different peak organisations in Germany, but crucially these do not compete against each other. The Federation of German Industries (Bundesverband der Deutschen Industrie, BDI) concentrates on the political representation of business; the Confederation of German Employers' Associations (Bundesvereinigung der Deutschen Arbeitgeberverbände, BDA) deals with social policy and collective bargaining; and the Association of German Chambers of Industry and Commerce (Deutschen Industrie- und Handelskammertages, DIHK) deals with trade and commerce (Gallagher *et al.*, 2006: 447–448). The key point, though, is that all three organisations coordinate their activities and often function as a single entity. Such association patterns may be one of the reasons why a large part of the interest group landscape in Germany has been organised around peak associations. Such peak organisation influence in the policy process dates back to 1967, when in response to the recession of 1966–67, the Economy Minister, Karl Schiller, moved towards a type of macroeconomic consensual planning by bringing together employers, trade unions, the *Länder* and the municipalities to manage the economy with the government in a form of concerted action (Pulzer, 1995: 132). While this particular form of planning lasted only into the early 1970s, the principle of trade unions and employers being central players in the economic policy process remains.

For the Bundestag, involving interest groups in decision making is important, as it brings specific expertise to the process, balances interests and wins the support of those affected by a legislative proposal without parliament simply endorsing the opinion of one group or another. Yet the Rules of Procedure of the German Bundestag and Rules of Procedure of the Mediation Committee, in annex 2, state quite clearly that entry on the list shall not entitle an association to obtain a hearing or a pass. These rules require that representatives of trade and industry are issued with a pass only if the following information is furnished:

> name and seat of the association; composition of the board of management and the board of directors; sphere of interest of the association; names of the associations' representatives; and address of its office at the seat of the Bundestag and of the Federal Government.[74]

In light of this process whereby groups that represent certain sections of society more often than not get to examine potential legislation before members of the Bundestag, the registration of lobbyists is seen as making sure that the system is open and transparent. However, the rules are somewhat contradictory. On the one hand, groups that register have no entitlement to be heard, while, on the other, groups that have not registered simply have to be invited by the Bundestag in order to get a hearing. Moreover, the register lists only trade and professional organisations, so, for instance, various individual corporations that are actively engaged in lobbying government and the Bundestag do not have to register if they are invited in. In that context, it is difficult to estimate the number of active professional lobbyists engaged in lobbying in Germany. Kallas (2007) reckons there are some 5,000 but it is difficult to be accurate about the precise figure because of the way the system operates.

Länder legislation. There is no legislation regulating lobbying in Germany either at *Länder* level or Bundesrat level (the Bundesrat comprising members from the various *Länder*). *Länder* have their own constitutions, their own government and their own parliament but there is no legislation regulating lobbying at the *Länder* level. Each Bundesland has articulated its own rules of procedure governing members but that is the extent of any regulation.[75] However, similar to the federal level, the right to give access to parliamentary buildings is a parliamentary privilege and can be seen as a form of lobbyist regulation. This so-called 'pass policy' is administered in much the same way at *Länder* level as at federal level. We examine a number of *Länder* to give us an idea of the way the system works.

In Hamburg, for instance, one of the *Länder* with the smallest populations, the Geschäftsordnung der Hamburgischen Bürgerschaft (Rules of

Procedure of Hamburg Parliament), paragraph 58(2), regulates the presence of lobbyist groups or their representatives in public committee sittings and in essence states that the committees may give experts, lobbyist representatives and other persons entitled to public comment the opportunity for oral or written statement before the committee.[76] Mecklenburg-Western Pomerania, a middle-sized *Land* in terms of population, operates on the same principle. Article 6 of the state's constitution basically asserts that the parliament is to listen to federations formed from municipalities in the consultation of bills that affect the interests of the municipalities directly.[77]

In Brandenburg, another middle-sized *Land*, article 97 of its constitution, regarding municipal self-government, states that municipalities and associations of municipalities (in the form of their local authority associations) shall be heard in good time, before general questions are regulated by law or a statutory instrument that affects them directly. According to Ingo Borkowski of the Brandenburg parliamentary office, most of the lobbying organisations are working countrywide and the competences of the state parliaments are not wide enough to influence the interest of the lobbyists, in that state parliaments are mainly concerned with the transfer into state law of legislation set by the European Parliament or the German Bundestag.[78]

In North Rhine-Westphalia, one of the *Länder* with a large population, there is no formal mechanism within the constitution for discussion between legislators and lobbyists. The committees of its parliament thus compile different lists of organisations and invite experts from these organisations to hearings to get their views on different political issues and bills which are likely to affect their interests.[79]

Because of the peak associational framework of organised interests, *Länder* are not subject to the same lobbying interests as the Bundestag. This seems to be a common interpretation of lobbying in the *Länder* and is the most likely explanation for the lack of legislation in the separate German *Länder*.

Conclusion

This chapter has considered the history and nature of lobbying and the regulations in place in the four political systems which have had lobbying rules for a long time, throughout various stages in the 1900s. We started the analysis with the United States, a country with the longest history of lobbying laws, and then paid attention to its northern neighbour, Canada, which established such rules later, in the 1980s. We then turned to an examination of developments in Europe, first focusing on the political system of the EU and then Germany. One of the main objectives of this book is to compare and contrast the nature of the regulations in each of these states in order to gain insights into their similarities and differences, something which will be done in Chapter 4. Beforehand, however, the next chapter considers those states that have recently implemented lobbying laws, that is, in this millennium – Lithuania, Poland, Hungary, Taiwan and Australia. One of the interesting findings that the reader will note is that while only four political systems developed lobbying laws in the twentieth century, as seen in this chapter, five countries have already enacted such regulations within the first decade of the twenty-first century.

Notes

1 Australia is not included here because its lobbying rules, originally pursued in 1984, lapsed in 1996. Nor, moreover, were such rules representatives of a formal law passed by parliament, as they were simply based on an executive decision. See Chapter 3 (p. 91) for more details.
2 The constitution of the United States is available at www.usconstitution.net.
3 For two differing accounts of railroad regulation in this period, see Kolko (1965), who argues that there was too little enforcement of inadequate regulation, and Martin (1971), who argues that there was too much regulation and too much enforcement.
4 Note that the figures reported in Tables 2.1–2.4 run to the last full year available, and that they are subject to ongoing revision by the Center for Responsive Politics.
5 *Washington Post*, 30 March 2006.
6 *Washington Post*, 5 September 2008.
7 Interview with senior official, Public Affairs Council, 3 April 2006, Washington, DC.
8 See http://assets.opencrs.com/rpts/RL34166_20070918.pdf.
9 'Earmarks' have proved extremely controversial in US politics. The Office of Management and Budget (http://earmarks.omb.gov) defines an earmark as 'funds provided by the Congress for projects, programs, or grants where the purported congressional direction (whether in statutory text, report language, or other communication) circumvents otherwise applicable merit-based or competitive allocation processes, or specifies the location or recipient, or otherwise curtails the ability of the executive branch to manage its statutory and constitutional responsibilities pertaining to the funds allocation process.' In effect, earmarks allow US members of Congress to secure significant funds for projects without subjecting them to open scrutiny by their congressional colleagues.
10 See http://opencrs.com/document/rl34166.
11 A hold is basically a procedure that allows a Senator to prevent a bill from reaching a vote on the Senate floor.
12 See www.independentsector.org/programs/gr/S2349.html.
13 Whitehouse press release, 14 September 2007, available at www.coherentbabble.com/Statements/SSs1-110th.pdf. The full bill can be accessed at www.fec.gov/law/feca/s1legislation.pdf.
14 Information from the website of the Public Affairs Council, www.pac.org.
15 Senator Robert D. Robbins, Pennsylvania, to the authors, 28 November 2005.
16 See www.state.pa.us/papower/cwp/view.asp?A=11&Q=450761 for the Governor's press release (March 2006) announcing this decision.

17 Interview with senior public official in the Pennsylvanian Senate, 30 March 2006, Harrisburg, Pennsylvania.

18 Information from www.pdc.wa.gov, the website of the Public Disclosure Commission in Washington. See particularly:
www.pdc.wa.gov/archive/compliance/pdf/BriefHearingBrochure.pdf.
Similar points were brought out in an interview with a senior official of the Public Disclosure Commission, 28 March 2006, Olympia, Washington.

19 See www.pdc.wa.gov/public/Lobbyist/lobexp.aspx.

20 Interview with senior official, Public Disclosure Commission, Washington State, 28 March 2006.

21 The amendment act pertains in particular to attempts to influence state procurement decisions. It is available at:
www.wispolitics.com/1006/large/contract_sunshine_act_lrb_1_.pdf.

22 See www.legis.state.wi.us/lrb/gw/gw_8.pdf for background to lobbying regulation in Wisconsin.

23 Information on lobbyist disclosure practices in Montana can be accessed at the website of the Montana Commissioner of Political Practices:
http://politicalpractices.mt.gov/4lobbying.

24 See the website of the Florida Commission on Ethics at www.ethics.state.fl.us.

25 Information on lobbyist disclosure in Wyoming can be accessed at the website of the Wyoming Secretary of State, Elections Administration:
http://soswy.state.wy.us/Elections/LobbyistInfo.aspx.

26 See the Government of Canada's Office of the Registrar of Lobbyists at:
www.ocl-cal.gc.ca/eic/site/lobbyist-lobbyiste1.nsf/eng/nx00104.html.

27 Many lobbyists at the federal level were stating that they did not need to register, given that the 1989 and 1995 Acts stated that only lobbyists who 'sought to influence' needed to do so. An obvious loophole in this regard is to say, as a lobbyist, that you were 'asked' by government to give information when a decision was being made; hence, lobbyists could claim that they did not seek to influence *per se*. Bill C-15 closed this loophole by stating that all forms of communication, whether solicited or not by government, require registration by all lobbyists.

28 Giorno (2006a: 11) further argues in the case of Quebec that 'it covers both communication "in an attempt to influence" and communication "that may reasonably be considered by the initiator of the communication as capable of influencing the decision...." The former standard is subjective, and depends on the state of mind of the individual making the communication; the latter is objective, and involves an assessment of how a reasonable person would view the communication' (Giorno, 2006a: 11–12). It is also significant to note in interviews with high-level public servants that Ontario may be considering changing the 'attempt to influence' clause to that found at the federal level.

29 Consistent with ideas raised in this paragraph from Giorno, it is useful to note that the website of the Government of Canada's Office of the Registrar (www.ocl-cal.gc.ca/eic/site/lobbyist-lobbyiste1.nsf/eng/nx00009.html) gives the following definitions:
Consultant lobbyists. 'These are individuals who, for pay, lobby for clients. They must complete and file the Consultant Lobbyists Registration form when they begin lobbying for a client, when information previously submitted changes, and when the lobbying activity terminates or is completed.'

In-house corporate lobbyists. 'These are employees who, as a significant part of their duties, lobby for an employer that carries out commercial activities for financial gain. These employees must complete and file the In-House Lobbyists (Corporate) Registration form when they begin to lobby for their employer and thereafter annually. They must also report any changes to information previously submitted, or report if they have ceased their lobbying activities or have ceased to be employed by the employer.'

In-house organisation lobbyists. 'These are not-for-profit organizations in which one or more employees lobby, and the collective time devoted to lobbying amounts to the equivalent of a significant part of one employee's duties. The senior officer of the organization must complete and file the In-House Lobbyists (Organizations) Registration form when the organization begins to lobby and semi-annually thereafter.'

30 Taken from a guide to registration (Ottawa) found at www.ocl-cal.gc.ca/eic/site/lobbyist-lobbyiste1.nsf/eng/home.

31 See www.elections.ca/content.asp?section=loi&document=fs02&dir=gui&lang=e&textonly=false.

32 This assertion is based on ideas raised by interviewees in Halifax and Toronto in March 2006.

33 In the case of Quebec, regulations surrounding cooling-off periods are found in the Lobbying Registration Act; at the federal level, such regulations are found in the Conflict of Interest and Post-Employment Code for Public Office Holders; in BC and Nova Scotia, the Members' Conflict of Interest Acts; and in Ontario, the Conflict of Interest and Post-Service Directive.

34 In the case of Nova Scotia, only consultant lobbyists and in-house (corporate) lobbyists must pay a fee if registering by the internet; in-house (organisational) lobbyists do not. In the case of Newfoundland, only consultant lobbyists must pay a few if registering via the internet.

35 In the authors' opinion, and after having confirmed this idea in several elite interviews in Canada, by far the best internet system in Canada is that set up in Ontario. See http://lobbyist.oico.on.ca/ and click on 'lobbyist login', 'getting started' to see how to register as a lobbyist.

36 The only jurisdictions wherein a penalty cannot be given to a lobbyist who has not ceased to register are Nova Scotia and Ontario.

37 See http://communiques.gouv.qc.ca/gouvqc/communiques/GPQF/Mars2006/16/c3033.html.

38 This assertion is based on ideas raised in elite interviews.

39 For an analysis of the Irish rejection of the Lisbon Treaty, see Chari (2008).

40 The fourth main EU institution is the European Court of Justice (ECJ). There is no doubt that some of the ECJ's decisions have shaped policy subsequently developed in the EU. A prime example was when the ECJ served as a catalyst in the drive towards the completion of the single market with its ruling in the infamous *Cassis de Dijon* case (for an account of this, see Chari and Kritzinger, 2006, ch. 4). However, while ECJ decisions may influence policy, the institution is not 'lobbied' *per se* by different interest groups in the policy process as are the other three institutions. As such, this analysis will not pay attention to institutional developments in the judiciary branch of the EU.

41 See www.etuc.org/r/2.

42 *Ibid.*
43 See www.copa-cogeca.be.
44 See, for example, Chari and Kritzinger (2006: ch. 6) for the role of the European Council on Refugees and Exiles (ECRE), which called for less rigid rules to be applied to asylum seekers wishing for family reunification when the Family Reunification Directive of 2003 was negotiated.
45 On a scale of 1–10, Commission officials ranked the following as being the most reliable sources of information: their own staff members (7.9), their colleagues (7.5), their own personal research (7.4), industry representation (5.7), media (5.5), NGO representation (5.2) and constituency/local information (4.2). Rankings done by the permanent representatives of the member states (in the Council) were as follows: their colleagues (8.0), their own staff members (7.7), their own personal research (7.5), media (5.4), industry representation (5.2), constituency/local information (5.2) and NGO representation (4.8). EP rankings were: their own staff members (8.5), their own personal research (8.0), their colleagues (7.4), media (6.1), constituency/local information (6.6), NGO representation (5.9) and industry (5.7). See Burson-Marsteller (2005: 13).
46 Taken from www.europarl.europa.eu/parliament/expert/staticDisplay.do?id=65 &language=en&redirection.
47 Data taken from:
    www.europarl.europa.eu/news/public/focus_page/008-25231-168-06-25-901-20080331FCS25217-16-06-2008-2008/default_p001c001_en.htm.
48 Taken from:
    www.europarl.europa.eu/sides/getLastRules.do?language=EN&reference= RULE-009.
49 Interviews with Commission officials held in Brussels, October 2008.
50 For the full code of conduct, see www.europarl.europa.eu/omk/sipade3?L=EN &OBJID=3091&HNAV=Y&MODE=SIP&NAV=X&LSTDOC=N.
51 Taken from:
    www.europarl.europa.eu/omk/sipade3?PUBREF=-//EP//TEXT+RULES-EP+20040501+ANN-01+DOC+XML+V0//EN&HNAV=Y.
52 Taken from the website of Siim Kallas, Vice President of the Commission, http://ec.europa.eu/commission_barroso/kallas/transparency_en.htm#3.
53 *Ibid.* We are grateful to Eoin Corrigan of the Irish Department of the Environment for providing us with a copy of the Green Paper shortly after it was released.
54 See the Euroactive article that quotes Kallas from on 19 July 2005, at: www.euractiv.com/en/pa/kallas-press-registry-brussels-lobbyists/article-142799. To be fair to the Commissioner, the article does go on to state that 'Kallas remained careful about his intentions, saying he would prefer to see self-regulation by the profession rather than forcing a compulsory system of registration defended by NGOs' and that he was also 'keeping all the possibilities open'.
55 See http://europa.eu/rapid/pressReleasesAction.do?reference=IP/07/367&format =HTML&aged=0&language=EN&guiLanguage=en.
56 With regard to the voluntary code on those lobbying that the Commission adopted for those who registered, many of these points suffer from the same ambiguities seen, for example, in the code of conduct in the province of Quebec, as discussed earlier (especially points b–g below). According to the

Commission, those lobbying shall always: (a) identify themselves by name and by the entity(ies) they work for or represent; (b) not misrepresent themselves such that registration may mislead third parties or EU staff; (c) declare their interests or, where applicable, those of the clients or the members which they represent; (d) ensure that, to the best of their knowledge, information which they provide is unbiased, complete, up to date and not misleading; (e) not obtain or try to obtain information, or any decision, dishonestly; (f) not induce EU staff to contravene rules and standards of behaviour applicable to them; (g) if employing former EU staff, respect their obligation to abide by the rules and confidentiality requirements which apply to them. See: https://webgate.ec.europa.eu/transparency/regrin/infos/codeofconduct.do;REG RINSID=1OYLLCdTvgTZqh9wWB2mLVvSCNqhhPNScbfkCvBBGhTGt1Td0 nbV!1914171189.
The 'penalty', if found guilty of breaking these rules after a Commission investigation, is that the lobbyist may face temporary suspension or exclusion from the register. Yet, not being on the Commission register does not mean one cannot lobby the Commission. As such, it is hard to see how this can be a meaningful penalty. See http://ec.europa.eu/transparency/docs/323_en.pdf (section 3).

57 From http://europa.eu/rapid/pressReleasesAction.do?reference=MEMO/08/428 &format=HTML&aged=0&language=EN&guiLanguage=en.

58 See http://europa.eu/rapid/pressReleasesAction.do?reference=MEMO/08/428& format=HTML&aged=0&language=EN&guiLanguage=en.

59 Interviews with two officials, October 2008.

60 See www.euractiv.com/en/pa/commission-launches-lobbyists-register/article-173591.

61 See www.europarl.europa.eu/news/public/focus_page/008-26498-168-06-25-901-20080414FCS26495-16-06-2008-2008/default_p001c004_en.htm.

62 See www.publicaffairs.ac/inindex.php?in=main.htm.

63 See www.euractiv.com/en/pa/commission-launches-lobbyists-register/article-173591.

64 See https://webgate.ec.europa.eu/transparency/regrin/consultation/statistics.do.

65 See www.alter-eu.org/en/system/files/files/alter-eu/publications/Commission+ Register+Fails+Transparency+Test.pdf

66 The Basic Law of the Federal Republic of Germany is in essence the constitution governing the country. It was amended by the Unification Treaty of 31 August 1990 and Federal Statute of 23 September 1990. It can be accessed in its English versions at www.constitution.org/cons/germany.txt and at www. iuscomp.org/gla/statutes/GG.htm.

67 The *Länder* are as follows: Baden-Württemberg, Bavaria, Berlin, Brandenburg, Bremen, Hamburg, Hesse, Mecklenburg-Western Pomerania, Lower Saxony, North Rhine-Westphalia, Rhineland-Palatinate, Saarland, Saxony, Saxony-Anhalt, Schleswig-Holstein and Thuringia.

68 Dr Marco Althaus, Director of the German Institute for Public Affairs, Berlin, to the authors, 26 July 2005.

69 *Ibid.*

70 See www.degepol.de/eng for information on the German Association of Political Consultants and www.dprg.de/statische/itemshowone.php4?id=140 for information on the German Public Relations Society.

71 The *Federal Gazette* is available at http://frei.bundesgesetzblatt.de.
72 See the website of the German Bundestag at www.bundestag.de/htdocs_e/legislat/04intgroup.html for information on the input of interest groups in the framing of legislation.
73 See www.eurofound.europa.eu/eiro/2006/04/articles/de0604039i.htm.
74 Rules of Procedure of the German Bundestag and Rules of Procedure of the Mediation Committee, annex 2, p. 88, available at www.bundestag.de/interakt/infomat/fremdsprachiges_material/downloads/goEN_download.pdf.
75 Christian D. de Fouloy, President of the Association of Accredited Lobbyists to the European Parliament, to the authors, 25 July 2005.
76 Tanja Blätter, Hamburg, to the authors, 15 July 2005.
77 Correspondence from the parliament of Mecklenburg-Western Pomerania, 15 August 2005.
78 Ingo Borkowski, Landtag Brandenberg, to the authors, 17 August 2005.
79 Hans Zinnkann, Nordrhein-Westfalen, to the authors, 12 July 2005.

3

Political systems with regulations in place in the 2000s: Lithuania, Poland, Hungary, Taiwan and Australia

Introduction

In the 2000s, within seven years of each other, a series of democratic states across the world implemented lobbying legislation – Lithuania (2001), Poland (2005), Hungary (2006), Taiwan (2008) and Australia (2008) – pointing to the increasing zeal with which states throughout the world are regulating lobbying. In this chapter, we turn to discussion of developments in each of these states, following a similar structure as seen in the previous chapter: the countries' history and structure of government; the nature of lobbying; and the main aspects of the legislation in place. We present the states in the order in which they established regulations. As mentioned in the previous chapter, readers seeking the full text of the regulations in each of these countries can go to our website www.regulatelobbying.com.

Lithuania

The nature of government

Lithuania is located on the south-eastern shores of the Baltic Sea, bordered to the north by Latvia, the south-east by Belarus and to the south and south-west by Poland and Russia's Kaliningrad Oblast. During the late middle ages, the country grew to become the largest in Europe; however, by the eighteenth century it was in terminal decline. Thereafter, Lithuania, like its close ally Poland, disappeared from the maps of Europe, its territories confiscated by its avaricious neighbours, only to reappear briefly between 1919 and 1939.[1] During the Second World War, Lithuania was occupied first by the Soviet Union, then by Nazi Germany, before being taken back by the Soviets in 1944. There it was to remain for the next 45 years, forming one of the republics of the USSR.

In early March 1990, Lithuania became the first of the Soviet republics to declare its independence (Serrill, 1990). Since independence, Lithuania has sought closer ties with the west, and joined the North Atlantic Treaty Organization (NATO) and the EU in 2004 (and became a member of the

Schengen Agreement in 2007).[2] Although income levels still lag behind those found in the western member states of the EU, Lithuania's economy has performed consistently well since 2000, with growth rates, in terms of gross domestic product, being between 8 and 10 per cent over the past half decade.[3]

The overarching governmental framework within Lithuania is that of a parliamentary representative democracy. The constitution (article 91) stipulates that the executive branch of the state consists of the Prime Minister and ministers, while the President is the official head of state.[4] As such, according to some definitions, Lithuania is classified as a semi-presidential regime (Roper, 2002). The parliament of Lithuania, the Seimas, is a unicameral institution with 141 members, elected for a four-year term. The Prime Minister is selected from the membership of the Seimas and then formally appointed by the President (article 92 of the constitution). Just over half of the Seimas's deputies, 71 in all, are elected from single-member constituencies. The remaining 70 are selected by a nationwide vote according to the principles of proportional representation.[5] In order to be represented within the Seimas, a party must acquire at least 5 per cent of the national vote,[6] and coalition governments have tended to be the norm.

The main duties of the executive include protecting the national territory, guaranteeing security, protecting public order, preparing budgets and maintaining relations with foreign states (article 94 of the constitution). Similar to the situation in many other parliamentary systems, the Council of Ministers consists of 13 ministers chosen by the Prime Minister and then appointed by the President. Government ministers are accountable for the directing of the activities of the branch of the administration entrusted to them, and specifically are responsible to the Seimas and the President (article 96). If a Prime Minister happens to die, or resign, then the government is required by the constitution to resign (article 101). Government policies are adopted by means of a vote of all ministers (article 95). The President's duties include the formal appointment, upon the Seimas's approval, of the Prime Minister; the President also appoints, and dismisses, ministers upon the submission of the Prime Minister (article 84). In relation to national defence, the President is considered to be the commander-in-chief of the armed forces (article 140), and he/she will declare a state of emergency if so needed (article 84). On the government's recommendation, the President also appoints and recalls ambassadors, while he/she receives letters of credence and recall from the ambassadors of foreign countries (article 84).

In terms of levels of governance, since 2000 the country has been divided up according to a three-tiered administrative structure in order to meet with EU requirements.[7] The national territory is divided into 10 counties, which are in turn subdivided into 60 municipalities, which are made up of over 500 'elderates', which manage small-scale local matters.[8]

While the counties are ruled by governors, who are appointed by central government, the municipalities are governed by locally elected officials, who serve for a term of four years.[9] However, the Lithuanian Ministry of the Interior admits that this current system of administrative division is often criticised for ineffectiveness and bureaucracy.[10] In response to this, there are proposals under consideration for a revision of these boundaries.

Interest groups

By what seem conservative estimates, there are some 200–300 lobbyists/ interest groups active in Lithuania and the Seimas is the main political institution lobbyists seek to influence (Kalninš, 2005: 55). This parliament is an open democratic institution and, to that end, parliamentary material is posted online and in various languages.[11] According to one account, public policy and interest groups 'may take part in the political process through policy advocacy, advising, and lobbying' (Piasecka, 2006: 420). However, the executive branch is noted both for adopting new laws without prior notice and for being less transparent than the legislature (Piasecka, 2008: 369).

Independent advocacy has been strengthened in Lithuania through the activities of several centre-right public policy groups. These have taken proactive stances on a variety of topical issues. However, broad-based support for civil society groups is still limited (Piasecka, 2006: 417). In fact, the Lithuanian Civil Society Institute argues that Lithuanian society, as a whole, is labouring under the prevailing belief that even by acting collectively citizens cannot make a difference, and cannot achieve significant outcomes (Žiliukaite *et al.*, 2006). There has also been a marked decline in the participation of citizens in elections (Žiliukaite *et al.*, 2006). In fact, less than 20 per cent of Lithuanians are members of NGOs, or other civil movements, and less than a quarter of working people use tax deductions to support non-profit organisations (Piasecka, 2006: 427). However, progress in civic developments is affected by both low awareness of and low support for NGOs (Piasecka, 2008: 365).

During the first half decade of the twenty-first century, the number of NGOs in Lithuanian society almost doubled, to 16,250 (Žiliukaite *et al.*, 2006: 22). Despite this, the proportion of people involved in NGO activities remained almost unchanged (Piasecka, 2007: 426). Of the three trade union peak organisations in Lithuania, the Lithuanian Trade Union Confederation (Lietuvos Profesiniu Sajungu Konfederacija, LPSK) is the largest, accounting for 60 per cent of all trade union membership in the country.[12] Formed in 2002, it currently has 26 trade unions as members.[13] Despite this, overall membership of trade unions in Lithuania is relatively low, with only 14 per cent of all workers being members.[14] All citizens are free to participate in trade unions. Despite the fact that overall union membership is low, unions are still relatively influential in society.

Lobbying legislation

Lobbying activity is regulated in Lithuania through the Law on Lobbying Activity (LLA), passed in late June 2000, which came into force in 2001 and was slightly amended in 2003.[15] Thus, when compared with its eastern European neighbours, Lithuania has had more experience in the regulation of lobbying. Yet, as McGrath (2008: 25) explains, 'the Act focuses exclusively on legislative lobbying, and entirely ignores lobbying directed at the executive branches of government'. Moreover, despite the fact that lobbying has been regulated for the best part of a decade, very few Lithuanian lobbyists have actually seen the need to comply with the legislation to the extent of formally registering themselves as lobbyists (Piasecka, 2005). The reason why representatives of interest groups do not want to register is that the word 'lobbying' has negative connotations, with suggestions of corruption and bribery (COEC, 2007: 6; Kalninš, 2005: 55). That said, and although not related to lobbying practices, the state has indeed witnessed its share of corruption scandals. For example, on 6 April 2004 the Seimas removed President Rolandas Paksas from office on three counts of violating the constitution.[16] A year later, Foreign Minister Antanas Valionis was accused of being a former officer in the KGB,[17] while two years later Finance Minister Zigmantas Balčytis resigned over speculation surrounding his son's mishandling of EU funds.[18] With this in mind, it may well be that lobbying rules can help add transparency and accountability to the political process.

Under the current legislation, lobbying refers to any activity, by individuals or other legal entities, whether paid or not, that is undertaken in order to influence the legislative process.[19] 'Thus, lobbying regulations can be applied to any publicly aired opinions on legislation or policy research' (Piasecka, 2005). This makes the law very broad in its application and, as a result, somewhat vague, as there is no differentiation between professional, paid lobbying, in-house lobbying, and the advocacy activities of interest groups.

The LLA adopts the following definitions. 'Lobbyist' means a natural or legal person recorded in the Register of Lobbyists in the manner prescribed by the law (chapter 1, article 2, section 3). 'Lobbying activities' means actions taken by a person for, or without, compensation, in an attempt to exert influence and have legal acts amended, supplemented or repealed, or to have new legal acts adopted or rejected, in the interests of the client (section 2). However, the way lobbying is defined in the legislation means that it is concerned only with the legislative branch of government (section 3) (COEC, 2007: 4).

In taking its lead from US legislation, the Lithuania legislation demands a cooling-off period after a politician leaves office. Former politicians must wait at least a year before they may become lobbyists and register with the Register of Lobbyists (chapter 1, article 3).

Once registered, lobbyists have certain rights, including the right to participate in the drafting of legislation, and to submit proposals and explanations in the drafting of legal acts (article 4). However, there is a range of conditions under which the activities of lobbyists may be considered illegal, including lobbying while not being registered as a lobbyist, and deliberately misleading politicians (article 6).

This legislation is enforced by the Chief Official of the Ethics Commission (COEC) (see Kalninš, 2005: 47). In the middle of May every year, the COEC must send an annual report on lobbying activity to the Seimas (chapter 3, article 13).

Lobbyists cannot pursue political activity unless they are registered. When registering, which can be done online, lobbyists must state:

- their name (without an accompanying picture, however);
- the name of their client;
- the bill they are lobbying on;
- the names of each employer.

Lobbyists must also:

- register annually, provided they continue to act as lobbyists;
- notify any changes of information within 6–10 days;
- provide individual spending reports and notify the registrar of salary received for providing lobbying services.

The lobbyist registrar, the Ethics Commission, is made up of five members, supported by 14 civil servants (COEC, 2007: 2). It operates under the provisions of the Lithuanian constitution and the Law on the Adjustment of Public and Private Interests in the Public Service (Klemencic, 2006: 10). The law states that 'holders of public office should make decisions solely in terms of the public interest, securing the impartiality of the decisions being taken and preventing the emergence and spread of corruption in the public service' (United Nations Development Programme, 2005). In relation to lobbying activities, the COEC registers lobbyists, inspects reports on lobbying and conducts investigations, and has the right to obtain any information deemed necessary (chapter 1, article 9, LLA), although, to date, no lobbyist has incurred any penalty. Its goals are to provide transparency in the activities of the civil service, prevent infringement of ethical standards and build trust in the institutions of the state.[20]

The COEC, nevertheless, remains critical of the different types of activities that are *not* considering lobbying under Lithuanian legislation. One such activity is the lobbying undertaken by non-profit organisations that seek to influence policies. As the COEC states, experience shows that most lobbying (in Lithuania) is done by such organisations, including the Lithuanian Builders Association, the Lithuanian Real Estate Development Association and the Association of Lithuanian Trade Enterprises (COEC, 2007: 8). Further, under the legislation, experts or specialists do not have to register when invited to participate in policy deliberation. The COEC laments that 'experience shows that lobbyists often influence decision makers to include them in workgroups as experts or specialists so they don't have to register as lobbyists' (COEC, 2007: 9). In addition to these problems, McGrath (2008: 25) notes that, as of March 2004, 'only one in seven out of an estimated 200–300 lobbyists had actually registered'.

Poland

The nature of government

Poland, more than most of its neighbours, has been both a beneficiary and a victim of its geographical location in central Europe. At various times throughout the last millennium, Poland was to find itself cast in the role of either a great power – holding sway over vast areas of central and eastern Europe – or as the victim of other great powers, being slowly dismembered until, for an interval, it ceased to exist. In the wake of the devastation of the Second World War, Poland was locked behind the Iron Curtain, located firmly within the Soviet sphere of influence (Davies, 2005). It later followed a trajectory out of the Soviet sphere, and into that of the free market, similar to its eastern European neighbours. Poland's transition was marked by the milestones of accession to NATO in 1999 and the EU in 2004, being the largest new entrant at that time, with over 40 million citizens.[21] The Polish economy is one of the healthiest among the 2004 EU entrants, with growth rates in the years after its accession exceeding 6 per cent and unemployment levels falling (Koen, 2006: 2). The effects of this economic expansion have been felt heavily in Ireland and the UK, to where a large number of Poles emigrated after May 2004, as these are now returning home to the burgeoning economy that awaits them.[22]

In terms of structure of government, 'the Constitution of 1997 establishes the rapport between the President, the Government and the parliament within the parliamentary-cabinet model' (Wyrzykowski and Cielen, 2006: 253). The government is headed by the Prime Minister and there is a multi-party system in operation.[23] It is the government that exercises executive authority, while the Sejm and the Senate exercise legislative power, under article 146 of the constitution.[24] The Sejm, the lower house of the Polish parliament, consists of 460 deputies, each of whom is elected for four years by means of proportional representation.[25] The Senate, the upper house of the parliament, comprises 100 senators, who also serve four-year mandates.[26]

The executive, or Council of Ministers, is made up of the Prime Minister and various other ministers (article 147 of the constitution), all of whom are officially appointed by the President on the advice of the Prime Minister (article 156). Thereafter, a vote of confidence in these ministers, and their programme of government, is required from the Sejm (article 156). Under the Branches of the Government Administration Act of 1999, the

Prime Minister's position was strengthened in relation to that of the other ministers.[27] His/her duties include representing the Council of Ministers, managing its work, ensuring the implementation of its policies, and co-ordinating and controlling the activities of its members (article 148). The actual title of the office, corresponding to its actual role, is President of the Council of Ministers, but Prime Minister is the term normally employed (article 147). Both chambers of parliament – the Sejm and the Senate – 'work together on new legislation and must agree upon it, with the president then signing this into law, or vetoing it' (Krajewski, 2008: 534).

The President is the country's head of state, elected popularly for a term of five years and a maximum of two terms (article 127 of the constitution). His/her duties are clearly set out in the constitution adopted in 1997: in addition to being head of state, the President is the 'supreme representative of the Republic of Poland, and the guarantor of the continuity of state authority' (article 126). The result is that he/she represents the interest of Poland in the international arena, ensures that the constitution is observed and preserves state security (articles 133 and 126). The President is empowered to appoint the Prime Minister and order the shortening of the Sejm's term of office when it fails to create a Council of Ministers or pass a budget (articles 96 and 144). Before signing a bill into law, the President can refer it to the Constitutional Tribunal to test its constitutionality (article 122). The President is also entitled to veto a bill, provided the reasons for this are given; however, the Sejm may override the veto by means of a three-fifths majority (article 122). As the supreme representative of Poland in foreign affairs, the President ratifies and renounces international agreements, appoints Poland's ambassadors and accepts other states' ambassadors (article 133).

In terms of different levels of governance, Poland is a unitary state. After administrative reforms were made in 1998, Poland was divided into 16 provinces (*województwa*) as local government was reinstituted in the wake of the collapse of communism (Yoder, 2007: 430; Regulski, 2003: 9; see also Rakowski and Rybicki, 2000). At the local level, national party politics tends to take a back seat and, as a result, independent candidates stand a good chance of success (Krajewski, 2008: 533). In fact, almost two-thirds of local councillors are independents (Krajewski, 2008: 546).

Interest groups

There is little doubt that citizens view politics, in general, negatively. In fact, a majority of Poles have expressed dissatisfaction with the way government has worked[28] and there is evidence of political apathy in the low general election turnout (Krajewski, 2008: 548). The changes that Poland experienced in the past two decades have thrown up problems in relation to corruption.[29] Such problems are partly due to the country's communist past, but are also related to its present. In 2006, Transparency

International found that 41 per cent of Poles felt their politicians were not doing enough to combat corruption, while a slightly smaller percentage felt that politicians were not doing enough to prevent bribery (Transparency International, 2006). In an effort to combat this, the government has introduced numerous measures to prohibit bribery, prevent conflicts of interest and promote transparency in the legislative process (Krajewski, 2006).

Part of this negative view of politics is directly related to lobbying and how it is portrayed in the media. As McGrath argues:

> In one case, Lew Rywin (a politically connected film producer) offered to ensure the amendment of proposed legislation affecting the communication industry, in return for a bribe of $15.5 million. Another lobbyist, Marek Dochnal, was arrested on corruption charges in 2004; he later alleged that a former Minister had accepted a $3 million bribe related to the privatization of the steel industry. (McGrath, 2008: 20)

Those cases aside, it is important to note that even as early as the 1990s the Polish lobbying industry was growing and simultaneously undergoing huge transformation. Without doubt, actors who enjoyed privileged policy-making positions under communism – including state corporations and trade unions – continued to wield significant power, particularly in the transition to democracy. In Korkut's view, democratisation in states such as Poland and Hungary (examined in the next section of this chapter) did not bring about a full and significant increase in power for all civil society organisations (Korkut, 2005). Nevertheless, it is important to note that various professional groups and organisations have formed and gained strength. For example, 2003 saw the creation of the Association of Professional Lobbyists in Poland (Stowarzyszenie Profesjonalnych Lobbystów w Polsce, SPLP).[30] The SPLP subsequently set out a voluntary ethics code for the industry and its membership,[31] even though Jasiecki (2006: 7), for instance, has stated that the 'SPLP is a passive organization, functioning outside media and public opinion perception'. Another important group is the Polish Confederation of Private Employers (*Lewiatan*, or Leviathan), which serves as an umbrella organisation for major Polish businesses. Indeed, surveys of individual companies in Poland show that, by 2004, 80 per cent saw national lobbying as important, an increase of 12 per cent from three years previously (McGrath, 2008: 18).

Yet, with scandals involving lobbyists and politicians taking place, the mid-2000s saw the need to create new strategies, including those designed to better regulate the activities of interest groups, in order to quell both the public's and politicians' concern about inappropriate lobbying. This included 'repeated incidences of voluntary assistants of MPs and high ranking officials in the public administration acting in practice as lobbyists and promoting the interests of their clients' (Galkowski, 2008: 130). We thus turn to a discussion of Polish lobbying regulation.

Lobbying legislation

On 7 July 2005, the Sejm passed the Act on Legislative and Regulatory Lobbying (ALRL), which came into force in March 2006.[32] Its passing through the legislative process since its introduction as a bill by Prime Minister Leszek Miller in 2003 shows how it evolved from a focus on 'sanction' to a focus on greater policy-making transparency (Galkowski, 2008: 131). The final bill thus sought to regulate the activity of lobbying at both the central and the sub-national levels of governance and establish rules for the maintenance of a lobbyist register. The act specifically sets out that:

- Lobbying means any legal action designed to influence the legislative or regulatory action of a public authority (article 2).
- Professional lobbying means any paid activity carried out for or on behalf of a third party with a view to ensuring that its interests are fully reflected in legislation or regulation proposed or pending (article 2).
- Professional lobbying can be carried out by a firm or by an individual – a professional lobbyist (article 2).
- The Minister of Internal Affairs and Administration is tasked with maintaining the register of lobbyists. This contains such information as lobbyists' names and addresses, and can be examined through an online database (article 10).
- Every February an annual report is to be published by the registrar outlining the level of lobbying activity conducted in the previous 12 months (article 18).
- Fines of up to €16,000 can be made against those who lobby professionally but who have not formally registered. Furthermore, this fine can be applied multiple times for repeated breaches of the rules (article 19).

In order to make the law-making process more transparent, and to allow interested parties to take part in the process, article 7 states that, every six months, the Council of Ministers must prepare a summary of information on draft legislation, the authority with responsibility for that legislation, the individual drafting the legislation, and the address of the Public Information Bulletin that will publish the proposed legislation which will be going through parliament. Such a requirement is not required for the sub-national level, however (Galkowski, 2008: 133). Articles 8 and 9 also stipulate that where a legislative proposal has been tabled before the Sejm, public hearings may be conducted.[33] Those parties which have declared an interest in the legislation before parliament are entitled to participate in these hearings.

The following information is required by the lobbyist when registering, which can be done electronically; the details are then open to free public access via the web (Galkowski, 2008: 143):

- name, company name and address of the professional lobbyist, or the first name, last name and address of a person who is not a professional lobbyist (although the lobbyist's photograph is not required);

- subject matter/bill to be addressed by the lobbyist;
- a list of employers;
- whether or not the work is compensated.

Despite the rules, the experience thus far is that the regulations seem to be largely ignored (Jasiecki, 2006: 1). According to the regulators, which are institutionally located in the Ministry of the Interior and Administration, by December 2006 only 75 lobbyists were actually registered (Galkowski, 2008: 144). The *Warsaw Business Journal* takes an even dimmer view and in February 2007 suggested that 'unofficial lobbying is flowering in the Sejm'.[34] Perhaps one reason why so few lobbyists have registered is the limited scope of the act (Galkowski, 2008: 139). An obvious criticism, as applies in Lithuania (see above), relates to the act's limitation in scope whereby private interests lobbying main institutions, such as the Office of the President, do not have to register. Moreover, the registry itself is not handled by an independent authority. Nevertheless, in the view of some observers, a positive aspect of the act is that it will 'support a professional approach to lobbying activities ... all the activities based on personal connections and "peculiar" arrangements between the world of politics and business ought to be eliminated' (Galkowski, 2008: 142).

Hungary

The nature of government

With its population of over 10 million, Hungary is located in the heart of central Europe, bordered by seven countries, currently a mixture of EU and non-EU states. Its geographical location places Hungary at the very centre of the European continent at a time when the EU is expanding eastwards. In some respects, Hungary's trajectory over the past two decades has been very similar to that of its eastern neighbours. In the late 1980s, travel restrictions were removed and there were widespread demonstrations for democracy.[35] By 1990, Hungary had become a multi-party democracy, with free elections. The following year, the last Soviet troops, present since 1944, went home.[36] Thereafter, Hungary moved willingly into the orbit of its western neighbours, joining NATO in 1999 and the EU five years later. With its free-market economy, it attracts almost one-third of all the foreign direct investment (FDI) flowing into central Europe (de Kort, 1999: 82). Strong rule of law, low corruption and the same protection for foreign and domestic capital have made the country an attractive investment option.[37] However, in late 2006, a half decade of overspending and an increasing budget deficit led to financial crisis and riots on the streets.[38] Nevertheless, the country's democratic institutions weathered the situation relatively well.[39]

Hungary is a parliamentary democracy, whose executive is headed by the Prime Minister, who is selected by way of a vote of the members of the parliament. At the same time as the Prime Minister is elected, the parliament also votes on acceptance of the government's programme for running the country. The National Assembly (Országgyülés) is a unicameral parliament and consists of 386 members, elected to serve for four years.[40] The electoral system is a mixture of single-seat constituencies (which account for 176 members) and proportional representation (using regional party lists for 152 members and the national party lists for the remaining 58 members).[41] The Prime Minister has the authority to select and dismiss cabinet ministers, which represents significant power. Nevertheless, select committees of the parliament hold hearings on the nominees for cabinet posts. Once approved by parliament, the President officially appoints them to their ministerial posts (Antal, 2005). State secretaries are the most senior administrative officials within each of the ministries.[42] They add an air of permanence at the top of the ministries by the fact that they are appointed to their posts for an unlimited period. Thus, ministers can come and go, but the state secretaries remain on, providing stability within the political system. As part of their duties, ministers may set out various decrees. However, in this regard there are limitations as to what they can do by law, as no decree may be contrary to extant legislation (Antal, 2005).

The parliament also elects the President for a term of office of five years, with a maximum of two terms, as seen in many other states.[43] Once elected, the President's functions are mostly those of a ceremonial head of state. For example, when the parliament has elected a Prime Minister, it is the President who formally appoints the person to the post. The President is also the nominal commander-in-chief of the Hungarian armed forces (Antal, 2005).

In terms of levels of governance, Hungary is divided into 19 counties and 20 urban counties. All towns and cities are legally permitted to manage their own affairs. This has resulted in a fragmented system of local government, which in turn has made it inefficient and costly. Consequently, most of the municipalities have tended to run up deficits, with the net result being that they are heavily subsidised by the central government (Kovács and Villányi, 2007: 313).

Interest groups
Much as in Poland and Lithuania, in Hungary the term 'lobbying' has certain negative connotations. Nevertheless, Hungary's laws do uphold the rights of free assembly and free association, resulting in a multiplicity of associations and NGOs. The main business organisations include the Confederation of Hungarian Employers and Industrialists (Munkaadók és Gyáriparosok Országos Szövetsége, MGYOSZ), the National Association of Entrepreneurs and Employers (Vállalkozók és Munkáltatók Országos Szövetsége, VOSZ), the Hungarian Banking Association and the Hungarian Franchise Association. In terms of influence, 92 per cent of Hungarian firms in 2004 said that national-level lobbying was important (McGrath, 2008: 118). Likewise, close to 70 per cent of senior civil servants stated that

they 'enjoyed close working relationships with major interest organizations' (McGrath, 2008: 16). With regard to civil society organisations, some observers suggest that there are over 70,000 NGOs currently registered in Hungary (Kovács and Villányi, 2006). However, data from the National Statistical Office show that only about half these NGOs are actually active.[44] As Kovács and Villányi (2007: 301) argue, although 'the most visible non-governmental organizations (NGOs) are affiliated with political parties, the majority of organizations work without any political influence, mostly providing human services to their communities', operating in areas such as community services and sports, recreational pursuits, as well as cultural programmes. The largest of the NGOs have based themselves in Budapest, including those dealing with issues such as human rights, economics and politics (Kovács and Villányi, 2007: 301). In line with Hungary's liberal laws, the trade union movement is active and open. However, unlike most western countries, which tend to have one or two peak trade union organis-ations, Hungary has six (Kovács and Villányi, 2007: 309). Despite this high number of peak organisations, the trade unions, as a whole, possess a relatively small level of membership. In fact, less than 17 per cent of all working Hungarians are members.[45] The drop in union membership has been dramatic, of the order of almost 80 per cent of overall membership in the two decades after the introduction of democracy.[46]

Lobbying legislation

In April 2006, the Hungarian parliament passed Act XLIX, Lobbying Activi-ties, which came into force in September that year.[47] The legislation, based upon the US Lobbying Disclosure Act of 1995,[48] aims to regulate the impact of interest group activities on public governance (Krishnakumar, 2006). The objective is to provide transparency as to how decisions are made in the policy-making arena, and to make public the activities of lobbyists and their interactions with Hungarian policy makers, thereby increasing people's trust in government. In this regard, the legislation is no different in its general objectives to most other acts regulating lobbying. However, it is in the examination of the particulars of the legislation that differences begin to appear. For one, the act is fairly narrow in its application, focus-ing only on the activities of contract, or professional, lobbyists, who aim to influence the executive, parliament and local government (sections 1 and 5 of the act). That is, the legislation does not deal with the activities of trade unions or non-profit advocacy groups. This has proved contentious, as some regard this type of legislation as not going far enough, as it deals only with attempts to influence legislative action for financial remuneration.

- The principal aim of the act is to publicise the activities of lobbyists and to define rules governing relations between lobbyists and decision makers (section 1).

- When lobbyists register, they must, under sections 7 and 8:
    * verify that they do not have a criminal record and, certainly dissimilar to other jurisdictions studied in this book, have a higher education degree;
    * state their name and date of birth (with a photograph);
    * state the subject matter of the bill to be addressed;
    * give the name of each employer.
- After registering, lobbyists receive a numbered licence. This contains all of their pertinent personal details, in addition to a photograph. This licence gives lobbyists open access to the bodies that are lobbied (section 14).
- The act does not affect the rights of individual citizens to contact various governmental bodies (section 1).
- The register of lobbyists is established at the Central Office of Justice, and easily accessible by the general public (section 12).
- Registered lobbyists must submit quarterly reports to the registrar. These must contain details such as the executive decision they attempted to influence, the objectives behind this, the means by which they lobbied and names of officers lobbied (section 30).
- The failure of lobbyists to comply with the law will result in their possible removal from the register (section 16). The Central Office of Justice is charged with maintaining the register and also imposing penalties for breaches of the regulations. These penalties can involve removal from the register for between one and three years, as well as financial sanctions up to the equivalent of €40,000 (section 17), where the registrar has the right to publish the names of lobbyists breaking the rules (section 20).
- Lobbyists are prohibited from using insider information, lobbying with a conflict of interest, and from engaging in unethical or illegal behaviour (section 21). They are also not permitted to give any gifts to public officials, if those gifts exceed 10 per cent of the prevailing minimum wage (section 24).

Other rules state that lobbyists are entitled to make a formal request to express their views in person to an executive decision-making body (section 25), provided a close relative is not a member of the same body (section 22). The executive decision-making body 'shall' record a brief summary of what was said in the meeting (section 26). Lobbyists are also permitted to take MPs to trade conferences and other meetings that relate to the issue upon which they are lobbying; however, they may not reimburse the MPs for the costs of such attendance (section 27). They are also entitled to send MPs various documentation relating to the issue they are lobbying on (section 28). It is noteworthy that, unlike many jurisdictions observed in the book, there is no prohibition on former MPs or ministers taking up lobbying duties immediately upon leaving office. This absence of a 'revolving door' provision, with a cooling-off period, is a significant oversight, especially if we consider that the Hungarian legislation is derived from the US legislation.

How effective has the legislation been in terms of spurring lobbyists to register? Adam Foldes, from the Hungarian Civil Liberties Union, recently pointed out that less that half of all Hungarian lobbyists have actually registered (quoted by Chatterjee, 2007). Lékó (2007: 6) suggests that one reason for this is that both lobbyists and politicians are not interested in revealing their relations, including keeping records of meetings.

Taiwan

The nature of government

The Republic of China (Taiwan) is located off the east coast of the Asian continent. It lies about 100 miles from the shores of People's Republic of China, bounded to the west by the Taiwan Strait, and to the east by the Pacific Ocean. Its geographical location places it within easy reach of the expanding markets throughout China, south-east Asia and mainland Japan to its north-east. The economies of Asia are coming to constitute an increasing share of the overall world economy, and the People's Republic of China is taking on the mantle of a superpower in the making. At the national level Taiwan is a democracy with a semi-presidential system of government, while at the sub-national level the country is divided into special municipalities, counties and provincial municipalities.[49]

After its defeat in the civil war on the mainland, the Chinese nationalist party (Kuomintang, KMT) government, led by General Chiang Kai-shek, retreated to Taiwan in 1950. It is as a direct result of the Chinese civil war that Taiwan has come to occupy the complex and sensitive position that it does today. Although the island is effectively independent, with its own government, army and foreign policy, it is not independent in name. In fact, Taiwan is regarded as a renegade province by the People's Republic of China. The result is that Taiwan lives under the threat of war from the People's Republic, should it ever decide to formally declare its independence. As serious as this is, these tensions are not confined to the Taiwan Strait, but have assumed an importance in geopolitical power politics, as the US is a strong supporter of Taiwan, and there is the danger that a conflict between China and Taiwan could assume an altogether more different nature if the US were to be drawn into such a confrontation. In 1996 there was a showdown between the People's Republic of Chain and the US in the Taiwan Strait over the international status of the island. This confrontation revealed 'how easy it can be for the United States and China to stumble into a collision' over the issue of Taiwan (Ross, 2000: 114).

Taiwan has been a fully functioning democracy only since the early 1990s.[50] The KMT government, in power since its arrival on the island, ended nearly 40 years of martial law in 1987.[51] In some respects, Taiwan's political and economic development has been akin to that of its neighbours. Democracy came gradually, but has slowly taken root. However, the difficulties of Taiwan's relationship with mainland China, and its uncertain international status, have tended to interfere in the normalisation of Taiwanese politics (Ross, 2000). This situation also ties in with Taiwan's international diplomatic relations, or formal lack thereof. In economic terms, Taiwan's economy has become powerful, dynamic and trade based. Taiwan was among the original 'tiger' economies of Asia, including the rapidly growing Singapore, South Korea and Hong Kong. A strong focus on exports has permitted the country to achieve significant trade surpluses and to earn substantial foreign reserves. In recent years China has supplanted the US as Taiwan's main trading partner and source of investment.[52] According to the Taiwanese Council for Economic Planning and Development, economic growth has averaged a consistent, and a strong, 6 per cent per annum over the past decades, while unemployment is close to its natural level.[53]

Its relationship with China is an issue that has dogged Taiwan throughout its existence. China's 'one China' policy has required that other countries must not give official recognition to Taiwan in order to maintain diplomatic relations with China – 'there is but one China and Taiwan is part of China'.[54] The constitution of the People's Republic of China, in its preamble, affirms this policy, as does the 2005 Anti-Secession Law. This law clearly set out the longstanding policy of the People's Republic of China to employ a military response in reaction to any moves by Taiwan to declare independence.[55] Partly as a result of this, only 23 countries now recognise Taiwan as a legitimate government in its own accord. The majority of countries have switched recognition from the government in Taipei to the one in Beijing. Despite this, Taiwan has maintained what are effectively embassies, but called Taipei Economic and Cultural Representative Offices, in many countries. Interestingly, each of these Representative Offices' web addresses begins with http://www.taiwanembassy.org.[56] Another result of the 'one China' policy is that the People's Republic of China will participate only in those international organisations where Taiwan is not recognised as a sovereign entity. For instance, as part of China's conditions for World Bank membership, Taiwan had to be considered to be a part of China, and not listed as a separate country.[57]

The President is the head of state[58] and represents the country in foreign relations. The President's authority includes the power to appoint the head of four of the five branches of government. These appointments include the Prime Minister.[59]

The government of Taiwan is based in the city of Taipei. It is made up of the presidency, and its five core branches, or Yuan. The most important of these branches of government are the Executive Yuan and the Legislative Yuan.[60] The Executive Yuan is headed by the Prime Minister, and is made up of eight ministers and some 31 additional commissions and agencies.[61]

The heads of these institutions are themselves appointed by the Prime Minister. It is the Prime Minister who is responsible for formulating programmes, and is charged with reporting on their progress to the Legislative Yuan. In this regard, executive power is exercised by the Executive Yuan, the highest administrative organ in the state.[62] The Executive Yuan Council consists of the President of the Republic, the Vice President, the various ministers and the Prime Minister, who acts as its chair. This body passes resolutions on all issues, and the resolutions are then sent to the Legislative Yuan for consideration.[63]

The Legislative Yuan functions in an oversight capacity in relation to the operations of the government and its various branches. It is the highest legislative body of the state,[64] consisting of 113 popularly elected representatives who serve for four years and are eligible to stand for re-election indefinitely.[65] In 2008 there was a marked change from the situation up to then, when there were 225 members in the Yuan and they held office for three years.[66] This Yuan has the power to decide upon statutory or budgetary bills, in addition to bills concerning martial law and declarations of war.[67] All acts have to be passed within the Legislative Yuan before they can become law. The Legislative Yuan also has the power to initiate impeachment proceedings against the President, as well as votes of no confidence in the Prime Minister.[68] Recently, Taiwan also revised its electoral system. It changed from a single-vote, multi-member district system to a mixed system of single-member districts and proportional representation.[69]

Following the legislative and presidential election in Taiwan in January and March 2008, the KMT came out as the strongest political party on the island. In the January legislative election, the KMT won 81 of the 113 seats in the Legislative Yuan, while its main rival, the Democratic Progressive Party (DPP), took only 27 seats.[70] Two months later, in the presidential election, the KMT candidate, Ma Ying-jeou, took 58 per cent of the vote, for a landslide victory over his rival from the DPP.[71] The KMT, which had been the ruling party in Taiwan since the 1950s, had lost power in 2000. These elections, in the first quarter of 2008, marked its triumphant return to power, and a significant mandate for its policy of better relations between Taiwan and the People's Republic of China.[72]

Interest groups
Under article 14 of its constitution, Taiwan recognizes the right of citizens to freedom of association and freedom of assembly.[73] The country respects these rights, as is evident from various peaceful demonstrations that take place in Taiwan from time to time. In this regard, while permits are necessary for public meetings conducted out of doors, these are granted as a matter of routine.[74] Civic organisations active in Taiwan must register with the government, although registration is freely approved. Organisations advocating human rights, social welfare and environmental NGOs are

also active on the island and can function openly, without any threat of prosecution.[75] However, it is noteworthy that the National Security Law has been used by the government to prevent pro-communist rallies, while rallies advocating Taiwanese independence have not been subject to the same piece of legislation and government counteraction.[76]

Taiwanese trade unions are free to operate and do so openly. The Chinese Federation of Labour is the oldest active trade union organisation in Taiwan, founded in 1948. It maintains close ties with the KMT. The other union centre active on the island is the Taiwan Confederation of Trade Unions. This organisation is much newer than its counterpart, having been recognised by the government only in 2000.[77] However, there are restrictions on the rights of association of anyone employed directly by the state, with prohibitions against their joining trade unions.[78]

Lobbying legislation

In 2007, Taiwan passed its Lobbying Act, and this came into force on 8 August 2008.[79] According to the Taiwanese Ministry of the Interior, an open and transparent lobbying process should have no negative impact upon freedom of speech, and the implementation of the act will not affect citizens' right to petition politicians.[80] The stated objective of the act (article 1) is to create open and transparent procedures for lobbying, in order to assure democratic participation. The term 'lobbying', as employed in the act, refers to the behaviour that lobbyists use to affect those they lobby in order to influence the formulation, or enactment, of legislation (article 2). The aim is to let both the general public and the media know who is lobbying the government, and specifically why they are doing so.[81] This legislation was introduced as just one of a number of 'sunshine' acts.[82]

The act covers individuals, 'legal persons' (companies, corporations, etc.), organisations and special interest groups (article 2.1). By avoiding the direct linking of lobbying to financial remuneration, the act's span of application is fairly broad – those who lobby without remuneration are still lobbying. However, unlike legislation in the US, Canada or central and eastern Europe, there is no centralised lobbyist registrar or similar institution established under the act. Instead, the Ministry of the Interior is charged with overseeing the legislation (article 3) and lobbyists are required to register with each government agency that they seek to influence (article 13).

The legislation deals with the lobbying of the President, the Vice President and the executive, along with legislators of representative bodies at various levels (article 2.1.2.3). In order for a lobbyist to engage in lobbying, in addition to registering, individual lobbyists must also pass professional and technical examinations (article 4). Relations with the mainland also find their way into this legislation, in that foreign governments are not permitted to lobby the Taiwanese government on matters concerning defence, foreign affairs and, most significantly, 'mainland affairs' (article 7). The restrictions on lobbying by those from the mainland go even further – 'people, legal persons, organisations or other institutions from mainland area shall not lobby in person or commission other lobbyists to do so' (article 8). The act also specifies that the person who was lobbied must inform the responsible agency of who lobbied them, the time when this took place and the content of the lobbyist's message (article 16). There is a responsibility on the lobbyists to prepare financial statements of the money they have expended on their lobbying efforts (article 17). All citizens are free to browse, transcribe, photocopy or photograph lobbyist registration forms as well as the financial statements that they submit (article 19).

Lobbyists who break the rules as set down in the act are subject to penalties of between TWD500,000 and TWD2,500,000 (roughly €11,000 and €55,000 at 2009 values) (article 21). In comparison with the latest lobbying legislation introduced at the federal level in both the US and Canada, these financial penalties may seem somewhat mild. However, the range of these penalties, the types of infractions monitored and the fact that punitive financial penalties can also be applied all serve to make mis-behaviour by lobbyists in Taiwan highly expensive (article 26). However, one drawback of the legislation, as noted by the *Taipei Times*, is the fact that formal registration can take up to two months, and because the registration system acts as a 'licensing system' whereby official approval is necessary for lobbying, this, in itself, constitutes a major limitation on the right to petition, and comes close to being a violation of the constitution.[83] The act also has a number of loopholes that could be exploited by lobbyists to their advantage. For example, approaching a politician's assistant with the aim of expressing an 'opinion' would not fall under the legislation; neither would claiming to be 'petitioning' or making a 'plea' rather than lobbying.[84]

Despite such drawbacks, a number of trade unions and other interest groups have expressed their support for the law. They felt that its effects would be positive, as it required open and transparent operations. However, there were also fears that the legislation would give commercial interests an advantage in influencing legislation.[85] The Speaker of the Legislative Yuan observed, just before the introduction of the legislation, that although there was room for improvement regarding the implementation of the law, people should try it first, and then discuss possible changes afterwards.[86] In subsequent chapters we examine how this legislation compares with that in other countries, and especially how it compares with that in states that have a long tradition of regulating lobbying.

Australia

The nature of government
Australia is the only country in the world that occupies an entire continent, though its population is less than one-tenth that of the US, which occupies

a similar-sized land mass. Since its creation in 1901, it has been a stable parliamentary democracy with a federal system of government; the judicial branch of government has a range of federal courts, in addition to the High Court, and the states and territories have their own parliaments.[87] Queensland is the only state to have a unicameral parliament, similar to those found in the territories.[88] The head of government in each state is known as a Premier and in each territory as a Chief Minister. Each of the states and territories is subdivided into what are called local government areas (LGAs), administered by local councils.[89] Australia's economy is prosperous, market based, with a large service sector. After 1990 the country experienced almost 17 years of unbroken economic expansion, during which economic growth averaged 3.6 per cent per annum.[90] With the slow-down in the US, the euro area, and Japan,[91] in May 2009 *The Economist* predicted slower growth for Australia.[92]

The Prime Minister, who heads the executive, is the leader of the largest party in the House of Representatives. As such, the Prime Minister and the cabinet which he/she appoints are responsible to the parliament, of which they must be elected members. The executive's main duties are 'to approve the signing of formal documents such as proclamations, regulations, ordinances and statutory appointments'.[93]

The majority of the powers of the Governor-General (the representative of the Queen and effectively the head of state) are exercised only in the context of the 'Governor-General in Council', which, according to the constitution, refers to 'the Governor-General acting with the advice of the Federal Executive Council'.[94] The federal government possesses certain centralising powers to do with matters such as international trade, taxation and defence.[95]

There are 150 deputies in the House, where each member represents an electoral area of roughly equivalent population (meaning that the states and territories with the larger populations have more deputies). The result is that the state of New South Wales, which is the most populous, has 48 deputies, while the much more sparsely populated Tasmania has only five.[96] Bills are introduced in the House and must be passed by both the House and the Senate in order to become an act of parliament.[97] The legislature also scrutinises the activities of the government, through the questioning of ministers.[98] The Senate is structured similarly to that of the US, with each of the states and territories, irrespective of its size, sending an equal number of senators to Canberra. Each state is entitled to elect 12 senators, irrespective of their population, while the mainland territories are each entitled to two.[99] This weighting of Senate representation in favour of the less populous states was designed to ensure that their views were not neglected at the federal level, and that Victoria and New South Wales did not come to dominate parliament.[100] While members of the House have to run for election every three years, senators' terms last for six. However, half the Senate's seats are up for re-election every three years, and the result is an overlap with House elections.[101] All Australian citizens over 18 years of age must enrol to vote, and are required by law to vote in both federal and state elections.[102]

The combination of elements of the UK and US systems of government has led some observes to refer to the Australian form of government as representing the 'Washminster' model (Ward, 1999). It incorporates the British parliamentary system and the concept of responsible government, but it is also a federal government with a powerful upper house. This has led some observers, such as Weller and Fleming (2003: 16), to argue that federalism, and a strong Senate, do not sit well with the principles of parliamentary government.

Interest groups
Although not codified in law, the government respects the rights of assembly and association. By the early twentieth century there was already a wide range of interest groups in operation, particularly associations to represent various industrial sectors. The increasing concentration of power in the federal government after 1901 witnessed many interest groups basing their head offices in Canberra, particularly business groups with an interest in maintaining protectionism and protectionist policies. The growing involvement of government in industrialisation over the twentieth century led to the gradual growth of other interest groups. Such groups are active in all levels of Australian society, though the fact that the country is a federal state has helped in the stratification of their activity. The numerical proliferation of interest groups, and the emergence since the 1970s of social movements, manifests at a new level the liberal-democratic promise of diversity (Marsh, 2004: 145).

In the late 1990s, over 1,000 lobbyists were active in Canberra, a number that had steadily increased over the preceding decades (Warhurst, 1998: 539). This was made up of independent professional lobbyists, employees of companies as well as employees of national associations. Warhurst (1998: 539) argues that 'in several Canberra suburbs numerous lobbyists operate cheek-to-cheek with ministers, bureaucrats, party officials, and political journalists and each other'. An example is seen in the National Farmers' Federation (NFF), made up of state-level farmers' organisations, which represents Australia's farmers in Canberra. That is not to say that such lobbyists are absent from other cities and it is important to note that the Australian lobbying community also includes those active in state capitals (Warhurst, 1998: 539). The Australian Council of Trade Unions (ACTU), which has close relations with the Labour Party, was one of the biggest interest groups that never moved its head office to Canberra, remaining in Melbourne instead. The rise in lobbies throughout Australia is due to a number of factors, among which are the increasing complexity of Australian economic and social life, better communications, and the complex nature of the Australian voting electorate. The government today recognises the right of pressure groups to represent different interests in society. At the federal level, it has encouraged groups to establish close relations with various government departments. Between July 2008, when voluntary legislation was introduced, and July 2009 (the time of writing), 276 lobbying firms registered in Canberra with the Australian Government Lobbyists Register.[103] Taking Warhurst's figures into account from a decade previously, this raises significant questions of why so few lobbyists have formally registered. This is to do with the fact that the legislation deals exclusively with third-party lobbyists. As a consequence, a majority of in-house lobbyists do not have to register and are in essence missed out by the legislation (Keane, 2008). Thus, the lack of registered lobbyists might well be to do with the regulatory process itself rather than anything to do with the probity of lobbyists themselves.

Lobbying legislation

Australia presents an interesting case in relation to lobbying regulation, as rules were first introduced at the federal level in 1983, then removed in 1996, only to be reintroduced in 2008. In 1983 the Labour government set up the Lobbyists Registration Scheme by executive decision, rather than by means of legislation (Warhurst, 1998: 544). Under this scheme, a lobbyist was defined as a person (or company) who, for advantages of one kind or another, took on the job of representing a client in dealings with the government (Sekuless, 1991). This definition proved to be highly problematic. It ignored all those lobbyists whose job involved lobbying on behalf of the corporations that they worked for. Australian lobbyists were nevertheless content with these rules, as they were fairly light and, in their view, the registration scheme conferred a level of legitimacy on lobbyists by improving their public standing without imposing the kind of rules that would normally come with a significant cost (Lloyd, 1990: 37). In fact, lobbyists were rarely requested to provide proof of registration when dealing with ministers and few enquiries were directed to the registrar (Warhurst, 1998: 545–546).

In 1996, when the Liberal–National coalition came to power it dis-banded the scheme. The reasons for this included that the rules were not being complied with and were not available for public scrutiny. Also, the government department in charge of publishing information on the register did so in a tardy fashion, providing little information initially and thereafter even less (Warhurst, 1998: 548). Echoing the concerns of the government, in 1998 Warhurst argued that the Lobbyists Registration Scheme had no teeth, served no useful purpose and appeared to be a non-event more than a failure (Warhurst, 1998: 538). The result was that the lobbying environment in Australia, although not tightly regulated prior to 1996, was even less so thereafter. Having been shelved for some 12 years, in 2008 the Australian government reintroduced the requirement for lobbyists to register, by way of the Lobbying Code of Conduct, which, this time, unlike in 1984, was passed by parliament.[104] As the office of the Australian Government Lobbyists Register wrote to the authors: 'the regulations were intended to promote trust in the integrity of government processes and ensure that contacts between lobbyists and Government representatives are conducted in accordance with public expectations of transparency, integrity and honesty'.[105] As of 1 July 2008 the register was fully operational, containing the details of lobbyists who make representations to government on behalf of their clients, and the names of the clients on whose behalf the lobbyist is acting.[106]

It is also worth mentioning that, at the state level, the governments of Western Australia (2006), New South Wales (2009) and Queensland (2009) have all introduced similar codes of conduct for lobbyists active in their state capitals. In the case of New South Wales an Independent Commission Against Corruption (ICAC) had been calling for the establishment of a register of lobbyists there since the early 1990s. In response to this, in 2006 the state government set out guidelines for ministers, their staff and public officials. This was followed up by the introduction of their lobbyist code of conduct. All three of these states operate their own registers of lobbyists akin to that operated by the federal government. Like Canada, the Australian sub-national governments' codes of conduct are similar to that found at the federal level.[107]

The other Australian states – South Australia, Tasmania and Victoria – currently have no lobbying legislation. The government of the state of South Australia was actively considering a Lobbying and Ministerial Accountability Bill, which would have been much broader in scope than the federal regulations but the bill introduced by the independent Bob Such in November 2007 fell by the wayside after debate was adjourned in November 2008. The South Australian bill would have seen the Auditor-General controlling the register and offences investigated by the Australian Crime Commission, and the definition of lobbyists would have been much broader than is set out in the federal regulations. It in effect encompassed in-house lobbyists as well as 'hired guns', thus setting a more rigorous level of regulation than found in Canberra. However, in July 2009 the state's Attorney-General, Michael Atkinson, said that while he was willing to look at the issue of a lobbying register, he believed existing laws – including the Ministerial Code of Conduct, the Pecuniary Interest Register and laws relating to the abuse of public office – prevented corrupt behaviour (Emmerson, 2009).

In the new federal regulations, 'lobbyist' means any person, company or organisation who conducts lobbying activities on behalf of a third-party client, or whose employees conduct lobbying activities on behalf of a third-party client (section 3). This does not include: charitable and religious organisations; non-profit associations; individuals making

representations on behalf of relatives or friends; members of trade delegations visiting Australia; registered tax agents, customs brokers, company
auditors and liquidators; and members of professions, such as doctors,
lawyers or accountants (section 3). Moreover, the 'code does not apply to
any person, company or organisation, or the employees of such company
or organisation, engaging in lobbying activities on their own behalf rather
than for a client' (section 3).

Lobbyists who wish to lobby a government representative must contact
the Secretary of the Department of the Prime Minister and Cabinet to have
their details recorded in the Register of Lobbyists (section 5). The Register
of Lobbyists is a searchable database located on the website of the Department of the Prime Minister and Cabinet, and easily accessible through the
internet (section 6). The code of conduct stipulates that for 18 months
after they leave office, former ministers and parliamentary secretaries shall
not be entitled to lobby on matters that they dealt with during their final
18 months in office. A similar stipulation of a 12-month cooling-off period
applies to persons who worked for ministers or parliamentary secretaries,
and senior civil service and army personnel (section 7). Lobbyists are
required to submit updated details to the Secretary of the Department of
the Prime Minister and Cabinet within 10 working days of changes to these
details occurring (section 5).

Application forms are all online and the filing process can be done
electronically, which allows for rapid updating and ease of access by the
general public. The regulations also state that a government representative
'shall not knowingly and intentionally' meet with a lobbyist who is not
registered (section 4), although no penalty is enumerated for transgression;
nor is it clear what exactly is meant by 'not knowingly and intentionally'.
Lobbyists are not required to provide any information on spending disclosures, nor has an independent body been established to oversee lobbying
registration and regulation (Griffith, 2008: 30). Apart from being struck
off the register, there is no other penalty for miscreant lobbyists.[108] As
Warhurst (2008: 5) argues, there is a potential problem due to the lack of
teeth, and lack of real sanctions, contained within the code of conduct. The
consulting company Springboard Australia responded to the governmental
initiative two months before the register came online, similarly stating that
the lack of enforcement mechanisms renders the regulations meaningless.[109]
It argues that penalties for failure to comply need to be stronger, encompassing severe fines and possible imprisonment.

When compared with the more tightly regulated jurisdictions seen in
this chapter, the regulations implemented in Australia – although much
better than nothing and certainly an improvement over what was in place
between 1983 and 1996 – could not be considered ideal (Ryan, 2008).
The fact that they pertain only to third-party lobbyists means that they are
aimed at only one element within the whole lobbying industry (Warhurst,

2008: 5). The code excludes the big companies, business associations and trade unions that lobby on their own behalf (Griffith, 2008: 26), as well as lawyers 'who make occasional representations to Government'.[110] As defined by the code, a government representative means a minister, parliamentary secretary, ministerial staff, public service employee or a member of the army.[111] The result is that the code, in concentrating upon the government rather than the parliament as a whole, is also missing out on a large section of the community that is the focus of lobbying activity.[112] For instance, the code does not relate to either MPs or senators, unless they are part of the government (Keane, 2008; Ryan, 2008). In fact, if Green Senator Robert Brown's private member's bill, the Lobbying and Ministerial Accountability Bill (2007), had become law, the result would have been a far more rigorous set of regulations for lobbyists to abide by (Griffith, 2008: 29). Brown's bill lapsed as the parliamentary session went into prorogation.

In conclusion, if the point of the Australian Government Lobbyists Register is to shed light upon those who seek to influence the government, then the federal lobbying code of conduct, as currently constituted, fails to fully do that. Many of the lobbyists active in Canberra, as well as many of those who are the focus of their lobbying, are being missed out entirely by the code, as it is currently constituted. This is evidenced by the fact that in May 2008 *The Australian* found there to be 706 holders of lobbyist passes, granting access to the Australian parliament,[113] while by the end of the year less than a third of this number had formally registered under the code of conduct.[114] This means that large amounts of lobbying activity are passing wholly beneath the regulatory radar. Whatever the objectives of the scheme, Warhurst (2008: 5) laments that 'whether the aim of the exercise is a more ethical industry or transparency in government or a level playing field in policy-making and politics, a limited scheme runs the risk of being set up to fail'.

Conclusion

This chapter has analysed the lobbying regulations in place in countries which have established them throughout the 2000s. In particular, it has paid attention to Lithuania, Poland, Hungary, Taiwan and Australia. Remarkable is the fact that five countries enacted lobbying laws in less than 10 years, whereas the previous century saw only four systems establish such legislation. This development points to the increasing significance states are attaching to lobbying regulations.

Taking together the countries presented in Chapter 2 along with those presented in this chapter allows us to pursue a comparative analysis of all of these regulations in order to see the similarities and differences between the jurisdictions. As such, Chapter 4 presents a theoretical classification of the different regulatory environments throughout the world. In particular, we will see which countries fall within what we outline as 'low-regulation', 'medium-regulation' and 'high-regulation' systems.

Notes

1 See http://www2.omnitel.net/ramunas/Lietuva/lt_history.shtml.
2 *Irish Times*, 24 December 2007, p. 15.
3 See www.alacrastore.com/country-snapshot/Lithuania.
4 The President is elected directly for a five-year term, with a two-term limit. See chapter 6, articles 77 and 78, 'The President of the Republic', constitution of the Republic of Lithuania (1992), available at http://www3.lrs.lt/home/Konstitucija/Constitution.htm.
5 See www3.lrs.lt/pls/inter/w5_show?p_r=3803&p_k=2.
6 See www3.lrs.lt/rinkimai/2004/seimas/index.eng.html.
7 See www.vrm.lt/index.php?id=808&lang=2.
8 *Ibid.*
9 *Ibid.*
10 *Ibid.*
11 See www3.lrs.lt/pls/inter/w5_home.home?p_kalb_id=2.
12 See www.eurofound.europa.eu/eiro/2004/12/feature/lt0412102f.htm.
13 See www.lpsk.lt/en.
14 See www.eurofound.europa.eu/eiro/2004/12/feature/lt0412102f.htm
15 The Law on Lobbying Activity is provided in English translation at www.oecd.org/dataoecd/18/15/38944200.pdf, p. 27.
16 *New York Times*, 7 April 2004, p. 5.
17 *Independent*, 8 January 2005, p. 32.
18 Baltic News Service, 27 March 2007; *Baltic Times*, 28 March 2007, for which see www.baltictimes.com/news/articles/17586.
19 Chapter 1, article 2, section 3, Law on Lobbying Activities 2000. See www.oecd.org/dataoecd/18/15/38944200.pdf, p. 27.
20 All the details of the COEC's duties and obligations, and its register of lobbyists, can be viewed at www.vtek.lt.
21 *Guardian*, 21 December 2007, p. 25.
22 *International Herald Tribune*, 19 June 2008, p. 11.
23 See www.poland.gov.pl/The,Prime,Minister,392.html.
24 The constitution of the Republic of Poland, 2 April 1997, is available in English translation at www.sejm.gov.pl/prawo/konst/angielski/kon1.htm.
25 See www.sejm.gov.pl/english/sejm/sejm.htm.
26 *Ibid.*
27 See www1.worldbank.org/publicsector/civilservice/rsPoland.pdf.
28 European Commission, Eurobarometer 65, Public Opinion in the European Union, *Poland*, spring 2006, p. 3. See http://ec.europa.eu/public_opinion/archives/eb/eb65/eb65_pl_exec.pdf. Macro-structural determinants of variations in legitimacy related to economic development, political system, degree of corruption and social structure (from the European Social Survey) are discussed by Domanski (2005).

29 See www.dbbakademie.de/fileadmin/dokumente/Tagungen/Korruption_2006/
    draft_abstract_Sitniewski_Perzanowska_ENG.pdf.
30 See www.unilob.pl/lobbying.htm.
31 *Ibid.*
32 Article 1, Act on Legislative and Regulatory Lobbying, www.olis.oecd.org/
    olis/2006doc.nsf/ENGDATCORPLOOK/NT00000D96/$FILE/JT00200198.
    PDF, p. 2.
33 See in particular article 8.1, *ibid.*, p. 4.
34 *Warsaw Business Journal*, 'Lobbying Goes Under the Table', 1 February 2007.
35 *Time International*, 27 November, 1989.
36 *Financial Post*, 2 July 1991, p. 11.
37 See www.heritage.org/Index/country.cfm?id=Hungary.
38 *Washington Post*, 26 September, 2006, p. A21.
39 See www.freedomhouse.org/inc/content/pubs/nit/inc_country_detail.cfm?page
    =47&nit=424&year=2007&pf.
40 See www.mkogy.hu/cgi-bin/insurl?/fotitkar/angol/general_info.htm#_
    Toc141002421.
41 There is a threshold stipulating that parties must achieve at least 5 per cent
    of the popular vote in order to gain representation within the parliament. On
    these points, see Kovács and Villányi (2007: 306) and www.freedomhouse.
    org/modules/mod_call_dsp_country-fiw.cfm?year=2006&country=6978.
42 See www1.worldbank.org/publicsector/civilservice/rsHungary.pdf.
43 See www.mkogy.hu/cgi-bin/insurl?angol/general_info.htm.
44 National Statistical Office, http://portal.ksh.hu/pls/ksh/docs/hun/xftp/gyor/gaz/
    gaz20606.pdf.
45 See www.eurofound.europa.eu/eiro/2002/06/inbrief/hu0206102n.htm.
46 See www.country-studies.com/hungary/trade-unions.html.
47 The act can be found at www.oecd.org/dataoecd/18/15/38944200.pdf.
48 See www.freshfields.com/publications/pdfs/2006/15472.pdf.
49 See www.gio.gov.tw/ct.asp?xItem=35606&ctNode=2584.
50 See www.ly.gov.tw/ly/en/01_introduce/01_introduce_02.
    jsp?ItemNO=EN020000.
51 See www.freedomhouse.org/template.cfm?page=22&year=2008&country=
    7500.
52 See https://www.cia.gov/library/publications/the-world-factbook/geos/tw.html.
53 See www.cepd.gov.tw/encontent/m1.aspx?sNo=0009648&key=&ex=%20
    &ic=&cd=.
54 *Time Magazine*, 8 September 1980.
55 *New York Times*, 14 March 2005.
56 See for example www.taiwanembassy.org/US/mp.asp?mp=12.
57 See http://web.worldbank.org/WBSITE/EXTERNAL/DATASTATISTICS/0,,co
    ntentMDK:20541394~menuPK:1277382~pagePK:64133150~piPK:641331
    75~theSitePK:239419,00.html#taiwan.
58 See www.gio.gov.tw/ct.asp?xItem=35598&ctNode=2584.
59 *Ibid.*
60 *Ibid.*
61 *Ibid.*
62 See www.ey.gov.tw/ct.asp?xItem=41251&ctNode=1327&mp=11.

63 *Ibid.*
64 See www.president.gov.tw/en/prog/news_release/document_ content.
    php?id=1105498690&pre_id=1105498701&g_category_
    number=409&category_number_2=373&layer=on&sub_category=455;
    see also the constitution of the Republic of China (Taiwan), chapter 6, 'Legis-
    lation', article 62.
65 See www.gio.gov.tw/ct.asp?xItem=35601&ctNode=2584.
66 See www.ly.gov.tw/ly/en/01_introduce/01_introduce_02.
    jsp?ItemNO=EN020000.
67 See www.president.gov.tw/en/prog/news_release/
    document_content.php?id=1105498690&pre_id=1105498701&g_category_
    number=409&category_number_2=373&layer=on&sub_category=455;
    constitution of the Republic of China (Taiwan), chapter 6, 'Legislation', article
    63.
68 See www.ly.gov.tw/ly/en/01_introduce/01_introduce_09.
    jsp?ItemNO=EN070000.
69 See www.freedomhouse.org/template.cfm?page=22&year=2008&country
    =7500.
70 *Time Magazine*, 13 January 2008.
71 *Time Magazine*, 22 March 2008.
72 *Ibid.*
73 Chapter 2, 'Rights and Duties of the People', article 14, of the constitution of
    the Republic of China (Taiwan). See:
    www.president.gov.tw/en/prog/news_release/document_content.php?id
    =1105498690&pre_id=1105498701&g_category_number=409&category_
    number_2=373&layer=on&sub_category=455.
74 See www.state.gov/g/drl/rls/hrrpt/2003/27767.htm.
75 See www.freedomhouse.org/template.cfm?page=363&year=2007&country
    =7283.
76 See www.state.gov/g/drl/rls/hrrpt/2003/27767.htm.
77 See www.tctu.org.tw/front/bin/ptdetail.phtml?Part=en001&Category=
    176367.
78 See www.freedomhouse.org/template.cfm?page=363&year=2007&country=
    7283.
79 The act is available at http://law.moj.gov.tw/Eng/Fnews/FnewsContent.asp?ms
    gid=3281&msgType=en&keyword=lobbying.
80 See www.cepd.gov.tw/encontent/m1.aspx?sNo=0010668&key=&ex=%20
    &ic=&cd=.
81 *Ibid.*
82 *Taipei Times*, 3 September 2008, p. 8.
83 *Taipei Times*, 3 September 2008, p. 3. See:
    www.taipeitimes.com/News/editorials/archives/2008/09/03/2003422113.
84 *Ibid.*
85 Central News Agency – Taiwan, 3 August 2008.
86 Central News Agency – Taiwan, 4 August 2008.
87 See www.gov.au.
88 See www.parliament.qld.gov.au/view/legislativeAssembly/introduction.asp.
89 See www.australia.gov.au/Local_Government_(Councils).

90 *The Economist*, 29 May 2007.
91 Reserve Bank of Australia, statement, August 2008. See:
    www.rba.gov.au/PublicationsAndResearch/StatementsOnMonetaryPolicy/
    statement_on_monetary_0808.html.
92 See www.economist.com/Countries/Australia/profile.cfm?folder=Profile-
    Forecast.
93 See www.aph.gov.au/PARL.HTM.
94 Commonwealth of Australia Constitution Act, chapter II. The constitution is
    available at http://australianpolitics.com/articles/constitution.
95 Commonwealth of Australia Constitution Act, chapter I, 'The Parliament',
    part V, 'Powers of the Parliament'.
96 See www.aph.gov.au/house/members/mi-state.asp.
97 See www.aph.gov.au/house/info/general/index.htm.
98 *Ibid.*
99 See www.aph.gov.au/Senate/general/index.htm.
100 See www.aph.gov.au/Senate/pubs/txtnov96.htm.
101 *Ibid.*
102 See http://australianpolitics.com/elections/features/compulsory.shtml.
103 Australian Government Lobbyists Register:
    http://lobbyists.pmc.gov.au/lobbyistsregister/index.
    cfm?event=whoIsOnRegister.
104 See http://lobbyists.pmc.gov.au/lobbyistsregister/index.cfm?event=contactWith
    LobbyistsCode.
105 Australian Government Lobbyists Register Office, communications with the
    authors, 25 September 2008.
106 See http://lobbyists.pmc.gov.au/lobbyistsregister/index.
    cfm?event=aboutRegister.
107 See for example Western Australia's 'Contact with Lobbyists Code',
    https://secure.dpc.wa.gov.au/lobbyistsregister/index.cfm?event=contactWith
    LobbyistsCode.
    On these points see Griffith (2008: 29, 30, 32).
108 Lobbying Code of Conduct, 10. Registration. See
    https://lobbyists.pmc.gov.au/lobbyistsregister/index.cfm?event=contactWith
    LobbyistsCode.
109 *Lobbying Disclosure Reform: Response to the Exposure Draft Lobbying Code
    of Conduct 2008*. See page 3 of:
    www.springboard.net.au/Assets/Lobbying%20Disclosure%20Reform.pdf.
110 Lobbying Code of Conduct, 3. Definitions. See
    https://lobbyists.pmc.gov.au/lobbyistsregister/index.cfm?event=contactWith
    LobbyistsCode.
111 *Ibid.*
112 *The Australian*, 16 May 2008, p. 7.
113 *Ibid.*
114 Australian Government Lobbyists Register,
    http://lobbyists.pmc.gov.au/lobbyistsregister/index.
    cfm?event=whoIsOnRegister.

4

Analysis of a quantitative index and the classification of regulatory regimes

Introduction

The objective of this chapter is to measure the relative strengths of lobbying legislation found throughout the world as presented in the previous two chapters and to use this as a basis to develop a theoretical classification of the different types of lobbying regulatory environments. This is achieved by using a method of analysis already established in the field which was developed by the Center for Public Integrity (CPI) in the US and which we ourselves have used in a previous study that examined developments in the US, Canada, Germany and the EP (Chari *et al.*, 2007). In so doing, we can gain an understanding of how the different systems throughout North America, Europe, Asia and Australia compare with each other from a theoretical perspective. It will be argued that, based on the analysis, there are three different regulatory environments for states that have lobbying legislation as previously discussed in Chapters 2 and 3: low-regulation systems, medium-regulation systems and high-regulation systems and we consider how each of the systems studied here falls within the different regulatory environments. We close the chapter by discussing which factors may help explain why there are different types of regulatory environment.

Measuring the strength of lobbying legislation using the Centre for Public Integrity Index

There are two measures of rigour in the literature which seeks to better understand how lobbying is regulated in the US. The first is Opheim's rating of the stringency of lobbying regulation in 47 states (Opheim, 1991: 405–421). Opheim's index consists of 22 separately scored items drawn from three different dimensions of lobbying regulation requirements. The dimensions were: (1) statutory definitions of a lobbyist (seven items); (2) frequency and quality of disclosure (eight items); and (3) oversight and enforcement of regulations (seven items). The values of the index ranged from a low of 0 for Arkansas to a high of 18 for New Jersey, Washington and Wisconsin. The second measure is Brinig *et al.*'s (1993: 377–384) rating of the restrictiveness of state lobbying laws. Rather than offer explicit coding schemes, their work highlights specific examples. They consider the frequency with which lobbyists are required to register and report, and their scheme emphasises the severity of penalties for violations of lobbying laws. The values of the index ranged from a low of 1 for Arkansas to a high of 14 for Alabama and Kentucky.

An extension of these methods of analysis has been pursued by the CPI in the US. The CPI is an organisation that, in its own words, produces 'original, responsible investigative journalism to make institutional power more transparent and accountable'.[1] One of its projects includes analysing lobbying laws in the 51 US jurisdictions that have lobbying legislation (the federal level and the 50 states). The objective of its analysis is to measure the effectiveness of lobbying legislation in terms of its transparency and accountability. The detailed and rigorous process of analysis that guides the CPI towards this objective is referred to as the 'Hired Guns' method, which results in what we refer to as 'CPI scores'. The CPI writes that:

> 'Hired Guns' is an analysis of lobby disclosure laws.... The Center for Public Integrity created a ranking system that assigns a score to each state (with lobbying legislation) based on a survey containing a series of questions regarding state lobby disclosure. The questions addressed eight key areas of disclosure for state lobbyists and the organizations that put them to work.[2]

These eight key areas are:

1 definition of lobbyist;
2 individual registration;
3 individual spending disclosure;
4 employer spending disclosure;
5 electronic filing;
6 public access (to a registry of lobbyists);
7 enforcement;
8 revolving-door provisions (with a particular focus on cooling-off periods).

Appendix A (p. 161) shows some sample calculations of CPI scores. As can be seen in example 1 in Appendix A, which analyses the state of Washington, there are a total of 48 questions for all eight sections of the index. Based on analysis of the legislation in place, each question is assigned a numerical (i.e. point) value according to the answer that is given.[3] In short, the more points that are given, the stronger is the legislation in terms of promoting concepts such as full disclosure, public access and transparency. The maximum score a jurisdiction could attain is 100 and the minimum score is 1 (a score of 0 would be given to a state where there is no lobbying legislation in place). According to the CPI, if a jurisdiction attains a score of 60 points or more it is deemed to 'pass', based on the grading system used in many US public schools. Regardless of the somewhat arbitrary rule of what constitutes a 'passing grade' or not, as a general rule one can argue that the lower the CPI score, the less robust is the lobbying regulation system in place.

Comparing the CPI method of analysis to others, one can see that the CPI's index goes well beyond the extent of Opheim's work, for example, by looking at individual lobbyist registration, electronic filing, public access and revolving-door provisions. On one level, this broader examination of lobbying regulations is a natural product of time and technological development. Electronic filing of returns by lobbyists and public internet access to detailed databases of lobbyists were far in the future in 1991, when Opheim was writing. But, on another level, the CPI's framework is more thorough than Opheim's in that it examines the issues of individual lobbying registration, public access to a directory of lobbyists and the revolving-door provisions, all of which Opheim bypassed. Thus, in expanding the range of lobbying regulations studied by Opheim, and setting out 48 separately scored items, as opposed to Opheim's 22, the CPI's framework constitutes a broader, and deeper, approach to analysing the rigour with which lobbyists are regulated.

Applying the CPI scoring system to other jurisdictions with lobbying laws

It should be noted from the outset that it is common in political science to apply a method of analysis used in one political system to other political systems, with the primary aim of gaining comparative insights. As a main objective of this study is to offer a comparative analysis of the lobbying legislation in place in different political systems in the world, it was felt that, given its robustness and detailed method of analysis, application of the CPI method would allow for greater insights into how the different countries studied compared and contrasted to each other. In other words, the fact that the CPI's framework was designed for an examination of lobbying regulations in the US should not render it inapplicable to other jurisdictions. As the framework is capable of taking account of the widely varying standards of lobbying regulation across all 50 American states, and at the federal level, it is also capable of taking account of lobbying regulations in other political systems. The use of the CPI method of analysis is justified not only because it offers a framework for comparative analysis, but also because it offers a rigorous examination based on 48 questions across eight different dimensions which are paramount in order to understand the nature of the lobbying regulations in place. In other words, the CPI checklist for evaluating the degree of stringency in registration requirements is useful because it gives a relatively objective point of reference for a comparison of various systems.

As such, we evaluate the CPI scores for all jurisdictions with lobbying legislation previously discussed in Chapters 2 and 3. As an illustration of how we arrived at our scores, example 2 in Appendix A (p. 164) shows the current scores of the states with the longest history of lobbying rules: the US federal (2007), Canadian federal (2008), the German and the EP legislation. For the purposes of contrast, example 3 in Appendix A (p. 169) presents the CPI scores of the earlier lobbying legislation in place in both the US and Canada. When the CPI scores of the earlier legislation in example 3 are compared with those for the present regulations in example 2, we see how with each iteration the legislation in both the US and Canada has become more rigorous over time. Example 4 in Appendix A (p. 172) presents the CPI scores for those states which have enacted lobbying laws in the 2000s, namely Lithuania, Poland, Hungary, Taiwan and Australia.

Table 4.1 summarises the CPI scores for the jurisdictions, in descending order.[4] Beyond the national-level regulation for all the countries, we include scores for those states and provinces which have lobbying laws in the US, Canada and Australia. Because *Länder*-level legislation is similar in all *Länder* to the German federal legislation, only the German federal level is reported. Even though the European Commission's scheme of 2008 is voluntary, the CPI score is nevertheless calculated in order to measure its comparative robustness. For illustrative purposes, and in order to understand how the different pieces of legislation may have changed when important amendments were made, we also calculated scores for the US federal acts in 1995 and 2007, as well as the Canadian federal acts in 1989, 2003 and 2008.

From an examination of Table 4.1, at least three observations can be made. First, over 50 per cent of US observations have scores of 60 or more. While the US federal legislation of 1995 had a score below all but two of the US states, it leaped ahead of many with its 2007 legislation, something which may be related to the Abramoff case (see Chapter 2, p. 23). Second, all Canadian observations have scores between 32 and 50. Similar to the US, the Canadian federal legislation of 2008 also gained strength from its previous value. In fact, one can see that throughout its three amendments Canadian federal legislation has become stronger with time. This helps illustrate that where the legislation is found on the scale between 1 and 100 can quite easily change with time. Those countries that developed legislation in central and eastern Europe (except Poland) hover within the same (40s) score range, while Taiwan and Australian observations are found within the same (30s) range. Finally, the lowest-scoring jurisdictions/institutions are the European Parliament, Germany, the European Commission and Poland.

Table 4.1 CPI scores (scale 1–100) of jurisdictions that regulate lobbying activity

Jurisdiction	Score	Jurisdiction	Score
Washington	87	Oregon	55
Kentucky	79	Vermont	54
Connecticut	75	Hawaii	54
South Carolina	75	Idaho	53
New York	74	Nevada	53
Massachusetts	73	Alabama	52
Wisconsin	73	West Virginia	52
California	71	Canada, federal, 2008	50
Utah	70	Pennsylvania	50
Maryland	68	Newfoundland	48
Ohio	67	Iowa	47
Indiana	66	Oklahoma	47
Texas	66	North Dakota	46
New Jersey	65	Hungary	45
Mississippi	65	Canada, federal, 2003	45
Alaska	64	Illinois	45
Virginia	64	Tennessee	45
Kansas	63	Lithuania	44
Georgia	63	British Columbia	44
Minnesota	62	Ontario	43
US, federal, 2007	62	South Dakota	42
Missouri	61	Quebec	40
Michigan	61	Taiwan	38
Nebraska	61	Western Australia	38
Arizona	61	New Hampshire	36
Colorado	60	US, federal, 1995	36
Maine	59	Nova Scotia	36
North Carolina	58	Wyoming	34
New Mexico	58	Australia, federal	33
Rhode Island	58	Alberta	33
Montana	56	Canada, federal, 1989	32
Delaware	56	Poland	27
Arkansas	56	European Commission	24
Louisiana	55	Germany	17
Florida	55	European Parliament	15

Sources: Chari *et al.* (2007), authors' present research and CPI research.

Threefold classification of regulatory systems

We now consider developing a theoretical classification system of the different types of lobbying regulatory environments. It is useful to note from the outset that theoretically classifying different systems is common in both the natural and the social sciences in order to gain a comparative view of the dynamics at play. For example, natural scientists studying chemistry make use of the periodic table in order to better understand common traits in certain elements, while biologists studying taxonomy group and categorise organisms by biological type, such as genus or species. Social scientists such as Esping-Anderson have used classification schemes in order to better understand, for instance, different categories of welfare system in the western world (Esping-Anderson, 1990). Clearly, such classification schemes will inevitably be debated and challenged: ideal types of systems, as discussed by authors such as Max Weber, are conceptualised based on the characteristics and elements of a given phenomenon, but they are not necessarily meant to correspond to all of the characteristics of any one particular case (Rogers, 1969; Weber, 1904). Nevertheless, a classification scheme serves as a basis for helping us understand common trends as well as differences, even if the concomitant conceptual apparatus does open up some debate.

Based on both the qualitative work done in Chapters 2 and 3 – the analysis of developments in the different political systems that established lobbying rules – and the quantitative work done in this chapter – the CPI data – we argue that there are three categories of lobbying regulatory systems: low-regulation systems, medium-regulation systems and high-regulation systems. Before we consider in detail below the common traits found in the systems, three points of clarification are in order.

First, reference is made below to each of these three categories being representative of legislation which falls within certain CPI point ranges. Thus, low-regulation systems have CPI scores which range from 1 to 29; medium-regulation ones range from 30 to 59; and high-regulation ones have a CPI score of more than 60 (which the CPI stated was a 'passing' grade in its view, as discussed above). These point ranges may be criticised for being somewhat arbitrary, but we have chosen them for both qualitative and quantitative reasons. Qualitatively, when we reanalysed the pieces of legislation found within each of these point ranges, we saw that they do have similar characteristics. Quantitatively, all three ranges are representative of almost equal distributions on the point scale. That is, low-regulation systems see a point range of 28 points (i.e. CPI scores between 1 and 29). Medium-regulation systems see one of 29 points (i.e. 30–59). High-regulation systems see a theoretical point range of 40 points (i.e. 60–100); yet, if we consider that the highest-ranking jurisdiction (Washington State) has 87 points, the range is effectively 27 points.

Secondly, as mentioned above, even though we are attempting to classify three different theoretical environments, all legislation for the individual jurisdictions should nevertheless be seen as representing a point on a continuum at any one time and different systems fall at different points on this continuum. As the Canadian and US federal legislation shows, where systems fall on the continuum may change over time and is not necessarily static.

Thirdly, when we use the three terms to describe these categories, we do not wish to normatively imply that 'high' is 'better', 'low' is the 'worst' and 'medium' offers a 'safe middle point'. We could have easily used terms such as 'gold', 'silver' or 'bronze', but these were probably even more likely to be misinterpreted. What we simply want to offer the reader is a classification scheme that helps us better conceptualise the common traits and rigour of different regulatory environments. Such a categorisation is constructed largely by analysing the robustness of the rules the lobbyist must follow when registering, the availability of the information to the public, the enforcement capability of the state, and the cooling-off period which the legislation requires. We believe that this conceptualisation is of particular relevance to all policy-making actors thinking either of developing such legislation or of amending existing legislation. Turning to the former, some may feel, for example, that developing a regulation scheme that is built on the medium-regulation category may serve the purpose intended; others may think that a low-regulation system is more desirable; while others may conclude that developing legislation that reflects the characteristics of a 'high-regulation' system serves their purpose.

Low-regulation systems

When turning to the first classification – the low-regulation systems – we see that this corresponds to states that attained CPI scores between 1 and 29. It includes Germany, the EP, the EU Commission's 2008 voluntary initiative, and Poland. Such a system has the following characteristics:

- Rules on individual registration exist, but few details have to be given.
- The definition of 'lobbyist' does not include those who lobby the executive branch of government, but only those who lobby the legislature.
- There are no rules on disclosure of the spending of the individual lobbyist or of employer spending (i.e. lobbyists and employers are not required to file spending reports).
- There is a weak system for online registration and registration includes having to do some form of 'paperwork'.[5]
- Lobbyist lists are available to the public, but not all details are necessarily collected or given (such as spending reports).
- There is little in the way of enforcement capabilities.
- No cooling-off period is mentioned in the legislation, which means that

legislators and members of the executive can register as lobbyists immediately on leaving office.

Medium-regulation systems

Medium-regulation systems correspond to those jurisdictions that attained a CPI score between 30 and 59 and include all the Canadian jurisdictions, several US ones and most of those countries which enacted lobbying rules throughout the 2000s – Lithuania, Hungary, Australia and Taiwan. The characteristics of this system include the following:

- Rules on individual registration exist and are tighter than they are in low-regulation systems (i.e. the lobbyist must generally state the subject matter/bill/governmental institution to be lobbied).
- In addition to legislative lobbyists, the definition of lobbyist extends to those who lobby the executive branch of government.[6]
- The regulations demand, though not necessarily complete, disclosure of and limits on individual spending (for example, gifts are prohibited and all political contributions must be reported, but there are clearly loopholes in this regard such as free 'consultancy' given by lobbyists to political parties).[7]
- There are no regulations for employer spending reports.
- There is a system for online registration (in some cases, such as Ontario, this is very efficient and effective, requiring low resources to use/update).
- The lobbying register is accessible to the public and is frequently updated, although spending disclosures are not in the public domain.
- In theory, a state agency can conduct mandatory reviews/audits, although it is infrequent that the agency will prosecute violations of regulations, because of a lack of resources and information (for instance, there is only one case on file in Canada, in Quebec in March 2006).
- There is a cooling-off period before legislators who have left office can register as lobbyists.[8]

High-regulation systems

The third category is high-regulation systems and this includes those jurisdictions that attained a CPI score of over 60, with the highest being obtained by Washington State, at 87. The jurisdictions found in this category correspond exclusively to more than 50 per cent of the US observations. Characteristics of this type of system include the following:

- Rules on individual registration exist and are the tightest of all the systems (for example, when registering, lobbyists must state not only the matter and/or institution subject to the lobbying but also the name of all employers; they must also notify the registrar almost immediately of any changes in the registration, and must provide a photograph of themselves).

- Similar to medium-regulation systems, the definition of lobbyist does extend to those who lobby the executive branch.
- Tight individual spending disclosures are required, in stark contrast to both low- and medium-regulation systems. Lobbyists must:
  * file a spending report,
  * report their salary,
  * account for and itemise all spending,
  * identify all people on whom money was spent,
  * report spending on household members of public officials, and
  * account for all campaign spending.

- Employer spending disclosure is also tight – unlike in low- and medium-regulation systems, an employer of a lobbyist is required to file a spending report and all salaries must be reported.
- A system for online registration exists.
- The lobbying register is accessible to the public and is frequently updated, including in relation to spending disclosures, which are also public (the latter of which is not found in the other two classifications).
- State agencies can and do conduct mandatory reviews/audits, and there is a statutory penalty for late and incomplete filing of a lobbying registration form.
- There is a cooling-off period before legislators who have left office can register as lobbyists.

Table 4.2 summarises the main elements of each of the different regulatory environments.

Understanding regulatory environments

This part of the chapter examines the different factors that may help explain why there are different types of regulatory environments found in the world. Here, we consider the different factors that may help explain why certain jurisdictions can be found within any one of the three classifications of regulatory environments and that can help explain their different points on the continuum. Table 4.3 serves as a summary of the main points of information found in Tables 4.1 and 4.2 and is useful in setting up an analysis of the different factors of importance.

In general, US jurisdictions are either high- or medium-regulation systems (many fall within the upper part of medium). It is impossible to accurately chart a trend in regional breakdowns in the US. Brinig *et al.* (1993) found wide variations in the regulation of lobbyists in 1993 and our data some 15 years later reflect similar disparities. We see that many states on the coasts and the mid-west are found in the high-regulation and the upper end of the medium-regulation range, such as Washington State,

Table 4.2 The threefold classification of regulatory systems

	Low-regulation systems	*Medium-regulation systems*	*High-regulation systems*
Registration regulations	Rules on individual registration, but few details required	Rules on individual registration, more details required	Rules on individual registration are extremely rigorous
Targets of lobbyists defined	Only members of the legislature and staff	Members of the legislature and staff; executive and staff; agency heads and public servants/officers	Members of the legislature and staff; executive and staff; agency heads and public servants/officers
Spending disclosure	No rules on individual spending disclosure, or employer spending disclosure	Some regulations on individual spending disclosure; none on employer spending disclosure	Tight regulations on individual spending disclosure, and employer spending disclosure
Electronic filing	Weak online registration and paperwork required	Robust system for online registration, no paperwork necessary	Robust system for online registration, no paperwork necessary
Public access	List of lobbyists available, but not detailed or updated frequently	List of lobbyists available, detailed and updated frequently	List of lobbyists and their spending disclosures available, detailed and updated frequently
Enforcement	Little in the way of enforcement capabilities are invested in the state agency	In theory, the state agency possesses enforcement capabilities, though these are infrequently used	The state agency can, and does, conduct mandatory reviews/audits
'Revolving door' provision	No cooling-off period before former legislators can register as lobbyists	There is a cooling-off period before former legislators can register as lobbyists	There is a cooling-off period before former legislators can register as lobbyists

Sources: Chari *et al.* (2007), authors' present research and Griffith (2008: 8).

Table 4.3 Jurisdictions found in each classification of regulatory environment

High-regulation jurisdiction	CPI score	Medium-regulation jurisdiction	CPI score	Low-regulation jurisdiction	CPI score
Washington	87	Maine	59	Poland	27
Kentucky	79	North Carolina	58	European Commission	24
Connecticut	75	New Mexico	58	Germany	17
South Carolina	75	Rhode Island	58	European Parliament	15
New York	74	Montana	56		
Massachusetts	73	Delaware	56		
Wisconsin	73	Arkansas	56		
California	71	Louisiana	55		
Utah	70	Florida	55		
Maryland	68	Oregon	55		
Ohio	67	Vermont	54		
Indiana	66	Hawaii	54		
Texas	66	Idaho	53		
New Jersey	65	Nevada	53		
Mississippi	65	Alabama	52		
Alaska	64	West Virginia	52		
Virginia	64	Canada, federal, 2008	50		
Kansas	63	Pennsylvania	50		
Georgia	63	Newfoundland	48		
Minnesota	62	Iowa	47		
US, federal, 2007	62	Oklahoma	47		
Missouri	61	North Dakota	46		
Michigan	61	Hungary	45		
Nebraska	61	Canada, federal, 2003	45		
Arizona	61	Illinois	45		
Colorado	60	Tennessee	45		
		Lithuania	44		
		British Columbia	44		
		Ontario	43		
		South Dakota	42		
		Quebec	40		
		Taiwan	38		
		Western Australia	38		
		New Hampshire	36		
		US, federal, 1995	36		
		Nova Scotia	36		
		Wyoming	34		
		Australia, federal	33		
		Alberta	33		
		Canada, federal, 1989	32		

Connecticut, New York, Massachusetts, California, Maryland, Virginia, Maine and Rhode Island (coasts) and Wisconsin, Ohio, Kansas, Michigan and Nebraska (mid-west). Many southern and western states can be found at lower levels, such as Louisiana, Florida, Idaho, Nevada, Alabama, Oklahoma and North Dakota. This may lead one to conclude that there is a general observation of differences being found between 'coastal and mid-west' versus 'south and west' states. Yet, there are also significant outliers to this general observation and this pertains, on the one hand, to those states that have high CPI scores, such as Kentucky, Alaska, Mississippi and Georgia, and, on the other, those that have lower scores, such as Illinois and Oregon. As such, this observation should be treated with some caution.

When turning to Canadian jurisdictions, we see that these can be found at different points within the medium-regulation range, ranging from the upper end (Canadian federal, 2008) to the lower end (as seen in the recent rules to be implemented in Alberta), with no discernable relationship to the province's physical location within Canada. European states range from around the middle of the medium-regulation system (Hungary and Lithuania), to the upper part (Poland) and medium part (Germany) of the low-regulation system. Both of the EU institutions are found within the low-regulation system. Taiwan is located towards the lower end of the medium-regulation range of jurisdictions, while Australian observations are found at the lower end of the medium range also.

Many readers may want to know at this point whether there is a relationship between perceived corruption levels in a country and the existence of stronger rules to regulate the behaviour of those who try to influence government, and whether or not this may serve as a factor to understand the overall trends of where states fit on the continuum. We have said that the goal of lobbying regulation is to add transparency and accountability to the policy-making process. But is there a relationship between where these countries are situated in terms of the different regulatory systems and levels of corruption in the country? One may reason that countries with stronger tendencies towards corruption may have stronger rules in place to stamp it out or, conversely, that countries with less corruption may have weaker rules because stronger ones are not needed. From this perspective, it is interesting to see if there is any type of discernable relationship between the perceived corruption levels in the country and the robustness of its lobbying legislation as measured by our work.

To this end, since the 1990s, Transparency International (TI) has developed what is referred to as the Corrupt Perceptions Index. In TI's words, the index:

> measures the perceived levels of public-sector corruption in a given country and is a composite index, drawing on different expert and business surveys.... [The scores are measured] on a scale from zero (highly corrupt) to ten (highly clean).[9]

Table 4.4 considers the TI's Corrupt Perceptions Index of 2008 and compares this with the various regulatory environments found in the different states (as no measurement is made by the TI for the political system of the EU, this information cannot be presented). The first column states the name of the country; the second, third and fourth, the TI's Corruption Perceptions Index, its confidence interval and its overall ranking in its 180-country analysis; and the fifth and sixth, the CPI scores and the classification of the lobbyists regulatory system (both of which are based on our evidence presented above).

Table 4.4 Perceptions of corruption and types of regulatory systems

Country	TI's Corrupt Perceptions Index, 2008	Confidence range of TI's scoring	Overall country rank by TI (in its 180-country analysis)	CPI values	Type of lobbying regulatory system
Australia	8.7	8.2–9.1	9	33–38	Medium
Canada	8.7	8.4–9.1	9	32–50	Medium
Germany	7.9	7.5–8.2	14	17	Low
US	7.3	6.7–7.7	18	34–87	High/medium
Taiwan	5.7	5.4–6.0	39	38	Medium
Hungary	5.1	4.8–5.4	47	45	Medium
Lithuania	4.6	4.1–5.2	58	44	Medium
Poland	4.6	4.0–5.2	58	27	Low

Sources: www.transparency.org/news_room/in_focus/2008/cpi2008/cpi_2008_table and authors' research presented above.

Table 4.4 suggests that, overall, there is no cogent relationship between perceptions of corruption and the types of regulatory systems that have been put in place in the different countries. When turning to 'clean' countries such as Australia, Canada, Germany and the US, which are in the top 20 of the 180 countries surveyed by TI, we see that they are representative of all three types of systems: low, medium and high regulation. Nevertheless, the data may shed some light on Australia: it may be the case that the lower end of the medium range – as opposed to a high-regulation system – was adopted in Australia in 2008 because of the rarity of corrupt practices between lobbyists and politicians. There may have been a perception that a robust regulatory system was not needed to stamp out corruption, as Australia is one of the top 10 cleanest countries in the world according to TI. There is some evidence of this in the passing of the federal bill, when Australian Senator Andrew Murray noted that 'he never experienced any corruption or misconduct from lobbyists' (Standing Committee on Finance and Public Administration, 2008: point 2.42).

When turning to the countries that fall in the middle of the TI index and that show signs of being 'half clean' (or 'half corrupt'), such as Poland, Lithuania, Hungary and Taiwan, we see that they are home to both medium- and low-regulation systems (however, it is interesting to note that none has a high-regulation system). The theoretical argument may be made that countries such as Hungary and Lithuania (but not Poland) have attempted to set up medium-regulation – as opposed to low-regulation – systems in order to help stamp out perceptions of corruption. But if this is the case, why not implement high-regulation schemes?

As such, based on all the observations in Table 4.4, and although there may be some insights that help explain Australia's point on the continuum, there is no firm, discernable relationship between perceptions of corruption and the nature of regulatory systems established throughout the world. With this in mind, one may argue that this does give some evidence that countries which have established more robust regulatory systems, such as the US and Canada, have done so in order to increase the public's awareness of links between policy makers and lobbyists, not simply to prevent corruption.

Taking all these points together, if we agree with the idea from Table 4.3 that North American jurisdictions, particularly US ones, have in general more robust regulatory systems in place than the European ones in particular, the question becomes: what other factors may help explain this? One may argue that there are at least two factors of importance: the historical importance of interest groups and civil society organisations (which have a longer history in North America); and the historical importance of highly visible scandals (again, which have a longer history in North America).

When turning to the first factor, the role of interest groups and civil society organisations in the US, as well as Canada, has been long established. Such groups have played an important part in the policy process in different areas, such as anti-tobacco policies and various environmental causes, for a significant amount of time. Given the importance of such groups, and their acceptance as policy-making actors in the process, they have been openly welcomed by government leaders to add expertise in the policy-making process. Yet, in order to prevent perceptions that such groups exercise undue influence in the policy process, state actors have ensured thorough, robust lobbying legislation is in place so that the public is aware of the links between policy makers and specific interests. Tusinski Berg (2009: 139) points out that the current lobbying regulation scene encourages interaction between lobbyists and state officials that is open and transparent and is a result of the significant impact of ethics legislation and the openness of state legislatures. Moreover, a critical, watchful press, which results in scandals being reported quickly and with lots of visibility, rapidly changing rules and ethics laws in a high-regulation environment has contributed to an increasingly professionalised lobbying industry over the past 20 years (Tusinski Berg, 2009: 139; Rosenthal, 2001).

This is related to the second factor: the importance of scandals in American politics. Many of the current lobbying regulations were produced in the mid-1970s, in response to scandals during the Watergate era. More recent scandals in Arizona, South Carolina and California led to a round of ethics reform in the early 1990s (Tusinski Berg, 2009: 139). This reinforces the view that policy makers believe that, in the wake of such scandals, transparency and accountability are ensured by strong lobbying legislation. As Tusinski Berg (2009) points out, MacKenzie's (2002) argument is accurate in that almost nothing in the Ethics in Government Act of 1978 which required financial disclosure for public officials and placed restrictions on the lobbying activities of former government employees would have prevented the crimes of Watergate. Nevertheless, stronger regulations in the guise of the Honest Leadership and Open Government Act were adopted in the US in 2007, after the Abramoff scandal, which saw the US federal lobbying legislation rise from a medium-regulation to a high-regulation system in our classification index. This new law not only enhanced the disclosure of lobbying activities, but also regulated some of the conduct of lobbying and lawmaking, such as requiring that campaign fundraising by lobbyists be disclosed to the public and posted on the internet, and prohibiting gifts and travel by lobbyists and lobbying organisations for lawmakers (Holman, 2009: 277–278).

When turning to these two factors and considering their importance in Europe, one can see that they are not as significant and can help explain why the regulatory systems in Europe are lower on the continuum of CPI scores. That is not to say that interest groups and civil society organisations do not exist. But in the case of central and eastern Europe, and even that of Taiwan, such groups have only recently had influence in the democratic policy-making process, after many years of communism, where the state was a significant driver of policy. In the case of Germany, a society which has a high corporatist ranking (Siaroff, 1999: 198), interest groups outside the capital and worker associations have seen fewer possibilities to access the policy-making process than their American counterparts. Nor have these jurisdictions in Europe seen the magnitudes of scandals seen in North America. As one EU official stated in interviews: 'Europe is not America: we have never seen cases like Abramoff here; we can have more trust in our lobbyists'.[10] This does not necessarily mean that scandalous events have not taken place in Europe between lobbyists and policy makers – it simply means that they have not been uncovered or achieved the same high profile in the media as in North America. Also, as we have seen in the case of the EU, Commission officials oftentimes rely on lobbyists to give technical expertise when developing policy and the relationship between the two is seen as symbiotic, where interest groups receive access to the policy-making process in return for their expertise. As such, in European states there has been a perception of 'less of a need' to provide rigid rules through which the public could gauge 'who is lobbying whom', given, on the one hand, the shorter history of interest group activity in some of the states and, on the other, the lack of highly visible 'scandals' in Europe when compared with North America.

Conclusion

This chapter started with an analysis of the comparative strengths of lobbying legislation throughout the world as discussed in Chapters 2 and 3. Based on the CPI's method of analysis, scores were presented for each jurisdiction. This was used as a foundation for a threefold classification of different regulatory environments: high regulation (found exclusively in the US), medium regulation (US, Canada, Hungary, Lithuania, Taiwan and Australia), and low regulation (Poland, Germany, the EP and the 2008 voluntary register of the European Commission). We then considered the different factors that may help explain why different jurisdictions have established different types of regimes. While (low) perceptions of corruption may shed some light in the case of Australia's less robust legislation of 2008, we argued that two other factors help explain the differences between the (stronger) North American and (weaker) European rules: the historical importance of interest groups in the policy-making process and the significance of scandal.

The next chapter pays attention to the attitudes of politicians, lobbyists and regulators in those systems which established rules throughout the 1900s. Here we seek to gain a better understanding of the effectiveness of lobbyist legislation and, of particular importance to many readers, how the different rules have affected lobbying behaviour.

Notes

1 See www.publicintegrity.org/about/about.aspx?act=mission.
2 See www.publicintegrity.org/hiredguns/default.aspx?act=methodology.
3 For discussion of the range of point values that can be assigned for each question, see www.publicintegrity.org/hiredguns/default.aspx?act=methodology.
4 CPI scores for the US are taken from the CPI website (www.publicintegrity.org), except for the 2007 federal legislation, which was calculated by the research team. The CPI scores for Canada, Europe (European Parliament and Commission, and countries), Australia and Asia were calculated by the research team using the CPI method of analysis. It is important to note that in the case of Polish, Hungarian, Lithuanian and Taiwanese legislation, the English-language versions of the lobbying legislation (as discussed in previous chapters) were the ones analysed to derive the CPI scores. We asked colleagues who spoke the native languages from these jurisdictions to compare the original version with

the English version and were satisfied from their comments that the documents were identical. Therefore, basing the scores on the English versions of these documents does not, in our view, constitute a source of error.

5 The exception to this is Poland and the European Commission's 2008 voluntary initiative.

6 The exception to this is Hungary, where the legislation does not recognise executive branch lobbyists.

7 The exception to this is the Australian federal legislation of 2008, where there are no individual spending disclosures.

8 Hungary is the exception here, as no cooling-off period is mentioned in its legislation.

9 See www.transparency.org/news_room/latest_news/press_ releases/2008/2008_09_23_cpi_2008_en.

10 Interview with Commission official, October 2008.

5

Examining findings from surveys and elite interviews in the four political systems with the longest history of lobbying regulation

Introduction

This chapter seeks to evaluate how effective lobbying rules have been in the different political systems with lobbying legislation and which are representative of the three classifications of regulatory systems discussed in the previous chapter.[1] We want to better understand the different actors' views of issues such as: how regulations may or may not foster transparency and accountability in the democratic process; the potential loopholes in the system; and how the rules have affected lobbyists' behaviour.

To this end, surveys were sent out in late 2005 to significant lobby groups (including professional lobbyists, in-house corporate lobbyists and NGOs), high-level politicians and senior public sector administrators in the US, Canada, Germany and the EP. We selected a purposive sample for two reasons. First, it simply would not be feasible to survey a truly representative sample of all lobbyists, politicians and administrators in the chosen jurisdictions. Secondly, this form of purposive sampling – expert sampling – is ideally suited to providing detailed information, as the sample can be selected on the basis of their possessing a wealth of in-depth knowledge in the area concerned.

Over 25 follow-up semi-structured interviews were performed with some of the survey respondents during the spring of 2006 as well as the autumn of 2008. We chose these jurisdictions because, as seen in Chapter 2, they are those which have the longest history of lobbying legislation, having established rules throughout the 1900s. Further, we felt that it was not unreasonable to assume that as the actors in these jurisdictions had the longest experience of having rules (compared with those in systems established in the 2000s), more reliable responses could be given in surveys and more cogent insights could be gained in interviews. Finally, the four jurisdictions were representative of high-, medium- and low-regulation systems, as discussed in the previous chapter.

Surveys were sent to actors: at the federal level in the US and a representative sample of US states – Washington, New York, California, Texas, Georgia, Colorado, Florida and Illinois;[2] at the federal level in Canada and in provincial jurisdictions that have lobbying legislation – Nova Scotia, Quebec, Ontario and British Columbia;[3] and at both the federal German level and the EP. For illustrative purposes, Table 5.1 summarises where surveys were sent while Appendix B, survey 1 (p. 178), shows the questionnaire sent out.

Table 5.1 Jurisdictions examined (rank order according to their CPI scoring)

High-regulation systems	*Medium-regulation systems*	*Low-regulation systems*
Washington State	Florida	Germany
New York	Canada, federal, 2003	EU Parliament
California	Illinois	
Texas	British Columbia	
Georgia	Ontario	
Colorado	Quebec	
	US, federal, 1995	
	Nova Scotia	

Source: authors' own research. Note that, as the surveys were sent out in 2005, the CPI scoring for the US federal system from 1995 and the Canadian federal system from 2003 is shown.

The total number of surveys sent by post between October and December 2005 to politicians, lobbyists and public sector administrators (generally lobbyist registrars or regulators) in these four political systems was 1,808, of which 1,225 were sent to lobbyists, 91 to public sector administrators and 492 to politicians, all of whose names were selected during the summer/early autumn of 2005 using the internet. Given that surveys sent out by email generally yield a lower response rate in past experience, a hard-copy survey was sent by post for this study.

Taking all four political systems together, a total of 140 surveys were completed: 6.5 per cent of all lobbyists, 19.8 per cent of all public sector administrators and 8.7 per cent of all politicians responded. In the US, 5.5 per cent of all lobbyists approached responded, while this figure was 11.4 per cent in Canada, 2.2 per cent for the EP and 5.5 per cent in Germany. In the US, 8.5 per cent of all politicians responded, while this figure was 6.8 per cent in Canada, 3.7 per cent for the EP and 7.6 per cent in Germany. Between 10 and 15 per cent of all public sector administrators (regulators) responded from all four political systems.

We were quite frankly disappointed with the overall (low) response rate. But, in hindsight, it may reflect how sensitive this issue can be. For example, several respondents did write back stating that although they were interested in the study, they did not want to, or claimed they were 'unable to', fill in the questionnaire: this in part can explain why the response rates were not higher, especially for politicians. As expressed to us later, in elite interviews, the subject matter was of some sensitivity and some potential respondents did not want to state their positions, even though anonymity was fully guaranteed throughout the process. Colleagues working in the area of lobbying regulations have also encountered the problem of low survey response rates: for example, Holman (2008: 5) found this when surveying lobbyists in Brussels and Washington, DC, in the summer of 2008. His experience points to the reluctance of lobbyists to involve themselves in research into their own industry. Another source of error which could explain why the response rate could have been higher is simply administrative: several respondents had moved, changed address, or (in the case of politicians) changed portfolios or retired from office. As can be seen in survey 1, reproduced in Appendix B, respondents were asked at the end of the survey form if they would be willing to take part in a follow-up interview with the authors. As such, we held over 25 on-site interviews in Canada and the US and held several telephone interviews with officials in Brussels and Germany in March and April 2006.

From a statistical perspective, the low response rate to our surveys means that no robust statistical analysis can be made and no firm correlations drawn. We recognise that, when compared with a large survey with a high response rate, the number of questionnaires dispatched, and returned, in this study was relatively small. Nonetheless, from the beginning, the objective of our study was to gain an indication of potential trends and relations, not to conduct a 'large N' study for its own sake. In this context, *it is important to note that our survey data are used for illustrative purposes only and are not to be taken as representative in the statistical sense.*

The remainder of the chapter thus turns to a deeper examination of the respondents' answers to the questionnaire, coupled with comments made during the later elite interviews, in order to gain some broad insights into the effectiveness of lobbying legislation across the systems studied, which fell into all three of the classifications. In the following section, we consider the knowledge of the respondents to the survey and then examine the actors' views on the relationship between accountability as well as transparency and lobbying regulation, potential loopholes in the regulations, and the impact of a register on citizen–representative relations. The penultimate section of the chapter offers insights based almost exclusively on the elite interviews on the financial costs to the state when regulations are pursued. This may be of particular interest to those readers who are state actors considering pursuing lobbying regulations. We also include in this discussion an analysis of the impact of different regulatory systems on the nature of lobbying, something particularly significant for all readers who seek to better understand the impact of regulations on the lobbyist profession.

Survey results

Setting the context: knowledge of respondents

We viewed it as important right from the beginning of the study to ascertain the knowledge of those whom we surveyed and later interviewed. The first 'main' question (question 6, survey 1 – see Appendix B) thus asked whether the respondents considered themselves to be knowledgeable on the legislation pertaining to regulation of lobbyists in their jurisdiction. Our survey results indicated that close to four-fifths of all respondents said they strongly agreed/agreed that they were knowledgeable. Around 15 per cent were 'neutral' and the remainder did not consider themselves knowledgeable. Of the three groups we surveyed, over 75 per cent of lobbyists agreed/strongly agreed with the idea that they were knowledgeable, while this proportion was well over 80 per cent for the other two groups (elected officials, 86 per cent; administrators, 83 per cent). Although the lobbyists represented the least knowledgeable group based on their self-assessment, overall figures indicate that our respondents had firm ideas of lobbying legislation in their jurisdiction. In the elite interviews we later held, almost all interviewees claimed to have a solid knowledge of lobbying rules. This latter finding is perhaps not much of a surprise: those we interviewed were self-selected, and it seems likely that those who knew more about the system of regulation would be more ready to be interviewed.

When the broad findings are viewed through the prism of the different types of regulatory environment discussed in Chapter 4, we see that around 9 out of 10 surveyed who stated that they had little knowledge about the legislation in their jurisdiction hailed from medium- or low-regulation environments. These illustrative data make some intuitive sense because if actors are in an environment where there are more robust 'rules', they will be more likely to feel they have the responsibility to learn what these rules are, as two interviewees from Canada stated. The opposite also makes some intuitive sense: the less robust the regulations, then the less likely it may be that respondents will feel full responsibility to learn about them, as their impact is probably minimal in any case.

Lobbying rules and accountability

As discussed in Chapter 1, according to deliberative democratic scholars, one of the main reasons for implementing lobbying legislation is that it promotes accountability. With this in mind, we asked three questions related to this idea:

- Do regulations help ensure accountability in your political system? (Question 7, survey 1)
- Does public access to an official list of lobbyists ensure accountability? (Question 12, survey 1)

- Do reviews or audits by state agencies of lobbyists ensure accountability?
  (Question 13, survey 1)

We consider the main findings for each in turn.

In relation to the first question, we found that, taking together all those surveyed, around seven-tenths felt that lobbying regulations helped ensure accountability in their political systems, just over a fifth were neutral, while the remainder disagreed. Thus, only one in ten respondents disagreed with the idea. When examining the different responses from the three groups, we nevertheless saw a slight divergence between them, as captured in Table 5.2. While over three-quarters of elected representatives and close to 7 out of 10 lobbyists felt regulations helped ensure political accountability, only half of all administrators agreed. Also, almost twice as many administrators as either of the other sets of respondents declared themselves neutral to, or openly disagreed with, the idea that regulations helped ensure accountability. This may suggest that, at least when compared with the other two groups surveyed, administrators remain somewhat more critical (or at least unsure) of the view that regulations help ensure accountability. Significantly, though, none of the respondents strongly disagreed with the proposition.

Table 5.2 Survey responses to the proposition that regulations help ensure accountability in the political system (percentage of sample responding)

Response	Politicians	Administrators	Lobbyists
Strongly agree	14	11.1	12.3
Agree	62.8	38.9	56.8
Neutral	16.3	33.3	19.8
Disagree	7	16.7	11.1
Strongly disagree	0	0	0

When deciphering the potential differences between the actors working in the three classifications of regulatory systems that were surveyed, there seems to be a more sceptical view from respondents in less robust regulatory systems: almost one-third of actors from medium- and low-regulation environments felt that the legislation did not necessarily produce accountability (almost 80 per cent of all respondents felt this way – indicating the low level of dissent in highly regulated environments). This again makes some intuitive sense, as more highly regulated systems openly promote accountability because the rules are more robust. On the other hand, with weaker rules there may well be an expectation that the system will have less effect in terms of promoting accountability.

Our second question on this theme asked whether public access to an official list of lobbyists would help ensure accountability. Overall, just

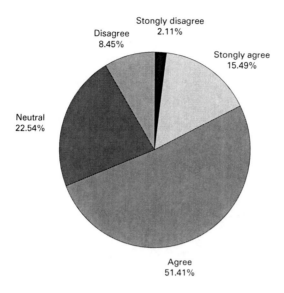

Figure 5.1 Survey responses to the proposition that public access to an official list of lobbyists ensures accountability (percentage of sample responding)

under 67 per cent of respondents felt access to an official list of lobby-ists ensured accountability (Figure 5.1), which is a similar figure to the percentage of respondents who felt lobbying regulations in general ensured accountability, as discussed above. A little more than 10 per cent disagreed, while a fifth were neutral. Thus, while two-thirds of respondents agreed, one-third did not.

On closer scrutiny, we find that around eight out of 10 administrators, seven out of 10 politicians, and six out of 10 lobbyists supported the idea that public access to an official list of lobbyists ensured accountability. Thus, while the majority of lobbyists still felt they should be listed for the public, almost four in 10 were neutral or disagreed.

We used a number of elite interviews to ascertain from those who answered negatively why they believed accountability was not attained by allowing the public access to a list of lobbyists. A common view was that, notwithstanding these lists, several private meetings still took place 'under the radar', particularly in the case of the EP. One interviewee spoke force-fully of the belief that simple lists of lobbyists' names, and the organisations or firms they represented, did not inform the public as to what legislation they sought to influence. Another was of the opinion that the register was little more than a marketing device for lobbyists. The majority of neutral and negative responses came from what we grade as low-regulation jurisdictions.

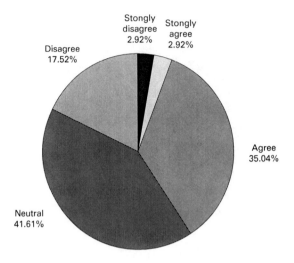

Figure 5.2 Survey responses to the proposition that reviews or audits by state agencies of lobbyists are effective in ensuring accountability (percentage of sample responding)

In that context, respondents from more highly regulated jurisdictions were more likely to believe that an official list did lead to more effective accountability. Again, this tallies with our earlier findings, as it is the highly regulated systems that are promoting such ideals of accountability.

Our third question on accountability sought to uncover respondents' attitudes towards an official agency being permitted to audit lobbyists. Slightly less than 38 per cent of all respondents strongly agreed/agreed that audits of lobbyists by state agencies would ensure accountability. Around 42 per cent were neutral, while roughly a fifth disagreed/strongly disagreed with the idea (Figure 5.2). Thus, fewer than four out of 10 respondents felt audits to be effective in ensuring accountability.

It follows that in none of the three groups was a majority in favour of the idea that audits of lobbyists might ensure accountability. Neutrality seems to have been the most common response to this proposition, with over 37 per cent of politicians, close to 60 per cent of administrators and 40 per cent of lobbyists taking this stance. Outright opposition was quite low, the highest opposition being 21.3 per cent, among lobbyists.

Our follow-up interviews helped shed some light on these figures. One respondent from a medium-regulation jurisdiction noted that information had not been filed for a number of years and lobbyists had not been contacted, never mind reprimanded, by the official auditing agency. The same respondent queried whether any increase in accountability was likely, given that the granting of audit powers to officials had not resulted in these powers actually being used. Another interviewee stated that in their jurisdiction the official agency had found abuses but seemed to view them as somewhat minor breaches and thus let them go unpunished. As in previous cases, most of those with negative views of state agencies employing audits were from medium- and low-regulation jurisdictions, with only just over 10 per cent from those areas we classify as highly regulated. Over 71 per cent of lobbyists from high-regulation jurisdictions believed that audits were effective in ensuring accountability. Thus, in environments where there are rigorous and seemingly effective rules in place, and where auditing powers are strongest, respondents felt these regulations had a positive influence on accountability.

Lobbying rules and transparency

One fundamental theoretical justification for the pursuit of lobbying legislation relates to the promotion of transparency, as discussed in Chapter 1. With this in mind, we asked respondents two questions related to transparency:

* whether or not they agreed with the idea that having specific rules on individual spending disclosures helps ensure that the process is more open (question 8, survey 1);
* whether or not they agreed that details of party campaigns should be available to the public (question 9a, survey 1).

With regard to the first of these two questions, slightly more than a quarter of all respondents strongly agreed and more than a half agreed, while the remainder either disagreed/strongly disagreed with or remained neutral to the idea that specific rules on individual disclosures help ensure transparency. This constitutes a strong response in agreement with the idea that spending disclosures help promote more openness and accountability.

When differentiating between the three groups of respondents (Table 5.3), over 90 per cent of politicians and slightly more than 75 per cent of lobbyists felt that the rules on spending disclosures helped ensure transparency. Although administrators were not as positively disposed to the idea as the other two groups, almost two-thirds were in favour. Interestingly, the only group where the combined percentages of neutrals and dissenters surpassed one-third was the administrators.

On the one hand, those from medium- and low-regulation environments made up around 80 per cent of all neutrals and dissenters. Yet, on the other, respondents from highly regulated jurisdictions expressed positive opinions on spending disclosure and transparency. However, it is significant to note that, of all systems, only the highly regulated ones have strong rules surrounding individual and employer spending disclosures, such as

Table 5.3 Survey responses to the proposition that specific rules surrounding individual spending disclosures help ensure transparency (percentage of sample responding)

Response	Politicians	Administrators	Lobbyists
Strongly agree	30.2	29.4	24.7
Agree	62.8	35.3	51.9
Neutral	2.3	29.4	17.3
Disagree	4.7	5.9	4.9
Strongly disagree	0	0	1.2

whether or not a lobbyist is required to file a spending report, whether salaries are to be reported by lobbyists in spending reports, and whether or not the recipient of the expenditure is required to be identified (see for, example, Appendix A, example 1, p. 161, for Washington State). Supplemented with interview data which suggest that respondents from highly regulated systems are satisfied with regulations surrounding individual spending disclosures, our interviews in low-regulation systems demonstrate two main views. Either interviewees not unreasonably want to see more rules surrounding individual and employer spending disclosures forming part of their legislation, as mentioned in our interviews with lobbyists and regulators in Canada, or they like the idea 'in theory', but do not want to see it form a full part of their legislation because, in the case of lobbyists, it would simply require more work.

The more normative second question on transparency sought to measure whether or not respondents felt that all party campaign contributions should be open to public scrutiny, thereby enhancing transparency in the political system. Regulation of contributions, whether by way of lobbying laws or other relevant legislation in the political system, and how these rules are enforced, is significant because it gives citizens further insights into connections between their public officers and those who lobby. It also has theoretical implications because regulations that appear rigorous may not necessarily be so.

Around 9 out of 10 respondents agreed or strongly agreed that all campaign contributions by lobbyists should be available to the public (Figure 5.3). Most of the remainder were neutral, while the percentage of dissenters was very small. Consistent with the above observation, there was very little difference between the three groups: 88 per cent of politicians, 94 per cent of administrators and 86 per cent of lobbyists agreed or strongly agreed that lobbyists' campaign contributions should be available for inspection. What minor dissent there was came from jurisdictions classified as low regulation.

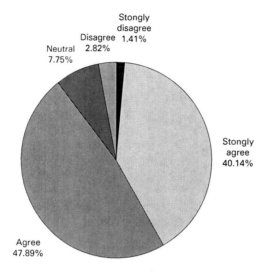

Figure 5.3 Survey responses to the proposition that details of all political party campaign contributions by a lobbyist should be available to the public (percentage of sample responding)

Loopholes

We stated in Chapter 1 that lobbying is a legitimate political activity pursued throughout democratic world. Yet, there is no doubt that, especially after the Abramhoff scandal in the US, publics across the world have become increasingly preoccupied with the 'sleaze' associated with the lobbying industry. Question 9b of survey 1 thus sought to show whether or not policy makers agreed that there were loopholes in the system permitting lobbyists to give gifts, regardless of the legislation in force.

An intriguing finding was that over 35 per cent of respondents agreed there were loopholes in the regulations which allowed lobbyists to give 'gifts'. Significantly, only around 28 per cent of actors disagreed with the proposition, with the remaining 36 per cent neutral. Thus, less than one-third of respondents seemed convinced about the absence of loopholes (Figure 5.4). Around a third of politicians, a fifth of administrators and around 40 per cent of lobbyists felt there were loopholes allowing lobbyists to give 'gifts' regardless of the legislation.

In the elite interviews, we also found that the ones most likely to know of the loopholes and readily talk about them were lobbyists. While most who affirmed the existence of loopholes in the regulations came from low- or medium-regulation jurisdictions, about one in three whom we interviewed came from what we classify as high-regulation jurisdictions.

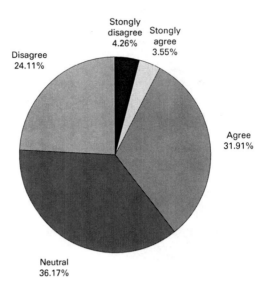

Figure 5.4 Survey responses to the proposition that there are loopholes in the system that allow individual lobbyists to give 'gifts' regardless of the legislation in force (percentage of sample responding)

One interviewee in a low-regulation system claimed that meals and tickets could be easily given to lobbyists. A lobbyist from a medium-regulation jurisdiction even stated that one form of a gift that they had heard of was flying a politician to Turin for the 2006 Winter Olympic Games.

High-regulation jurisdictions would not seem to be immune, however, from such behaviour, with some politicians and administrators from these areas observing that, given that human nature is what it is, it would be likely that at least a few of their colleagues do not declare the gifts they receive. For example, even in Washington State, the most regulated jurisdiction in the entire study, and commonly seen as a model of regulatory behaviour, a CPI report in August 2005 found that the spirit of the state's exemplary disclosure law was being undermined by lobbyists reporting their clients' purposes on disclosure forms in vague, non-descriptive terms (Gordon, 2005). This view was reiterated by both lobbyists and regulators in inter-views held in Olympia, Washington State, in March 2006, and has also been a hot topic of debate in the Seattle press as recently as October 2008.[4] A senior official of the Public Disclosure Commission (PDC) in Washington State was of the view that while the vast majority of lobbyists, and those whom they lobby for, were happy to abide by the rules, there were always a few who would try to find ways around them.[5] Further north, in Canada, to offer another example, the legislation states that only $1,000 can be given to any political party during an election campaign. Nevertheless, a number of lobbyist interviewees pointed out that there were any number of ways of getting around this, including free consultancy work for a political party during an election with the view of attaining certain favours if that party gets elected; or helping to 'fundraise' for a political party by holding special private events.

Loopholes in essence relate to the problem of how rules and regulations are enforced. Although there is little enforcement capability in low-regulation systems, most legislation in high- and medium-regulation jurisdictions encompasses a system of financial fines and even possible imprisonment if a lobbyist breaks the rules. Yet the key question is, how effective are the regulators in ensuring that lobbyists register? In interviews with a number of Canadian regulators, a common refrain was that there probably were, albeit just a few, lobby groups that had not registered. As one interviewee noted:

> Some lobby groups are not registered because they are ignorant of the rules. Others, such as some lawyers, don't realise that they are lobbyists. If I receive a complaint from a third party, I investigate it ... but I have usually found that 'human error' is the reason for not having registered [there is no maliciousness].... Registering helps increase the credibility and trust that citizens have in lobby groups and politicians alike.[6]

A similar point was made by the PDC in Washington State, which viewed non-registration for the most part as more due to innocent human error rather than anything more sinister. In interviews with regulators and lobbyists in Washington State, what quickly became apparent was the widespread credibility that the registration system had gained in a short period of time. This was because the PDC spent much time and effort in explaining not only how the system worked to both lobbyists and organisations that wanted to lobby government, but also why it was being implemented, leading to a situation where those who hire lobbyists demand that their lobbyists be registered.[7] Thus, it is clear that many lobby groups in jurisdictions such as Washington State do register, not only because it is compulsory, but also because it is manifestly in their interests to do so.

The impact of a register on citizen–representative relations

As mentioned in Chapter 1, one of the theoretical reasons against having a lobbyist register, perhaps best expressed by the British Committee on Standards in Public Life, more commonly known as the Nolan Committee, is that it creates a barrier to entry, especially if citizens feel that they could not approach a politician without a lobbyist acting on their behalf (Nolan Committee, 1995). We therefore asked in the survey whether a register of lobbyists makes citizens feel inhibited from approaching their representatives alone (question 10, survey 1). Overall, we found that only around 10 per cent of respondents felt such a register of lobbyists would make citizens feel inhibited from approaching their representative and a similar percentage expressed neutrality. Over 80 per cent of respondents disagreed, and of these around three out of ten strongly disagreed that a register would interfere with the citizen–representative relationship. These findings suggest that having a register would not in any way make voters wary of meeting a politician without a lobbyist.

Analysing the differences between the three groups surveyed (Table 5.4), while 14.0 per cent of politicians felt a register would make citizens feel inhibited from approaching them alone, only 8.6 per cent of lobbyists expressed a similar opinion, and no administrator did. There was not one respondent who strongly agreed with the idea. Over three-quarters of all groups of actors, and almost nine-tenths of administrators, felt a register would have no impact on the relationship citizens have with their politicians. Almost all of the (few) respondents who did believe that a register would interfere in the citizen–representative relationship came from medium- or low-regulation jurisdictions. Almost no politicians, lobbyists or administrators from the six jurisdictions where regulations are most stringent felt this way.

Table 5.4 Survey responses to the proposition that a register of lobbyists makes ordinary citizens feel inhibited about approaching their local representatives alone (percentage of sample responding)

Response	Politicians	Administrators	Lobbyists
Strongly agree	0	0	0
Agree	14.0	0	8.6
Neutral	9.3	11.1	8.6
Disagree	55.8	66.7	50.6
Strongly disagree	20.9	22.2	32.1

The evidence here is clear cut: a large majority of those who completed the questionnaire, along with the actors we interviewed, felt that a register of lobbyists would not affect how citizens related to their representatives. This contradicts the arguments put forward by the Nolan Committee. The Nolan Committee, which reported in May 1995, did not propose a mandatory register of lobbyists, on the grounds that such a register would confer formal status on lobbyists and potentially give the impression that the only successful way to approach MPs or ministers in the British case was through a registered lobbyist. Nolan stated:

To establish a public register of lobbyists would create the danger of giving the impression, which would no doubt be fostered by lobbyists themselves, that the only way to approach successfully Members or Ministers was by making use of a registered lobbyist. This would set up an undesirable hurdle, real or imagined, in the way of access. We commend the efforts of lobbyists to develop their own codes of practice, but we reject the concept of giving them formal status through a statutory register. (Nolan Committee, 1995: 36)

In our interviews, we found that the US respondents were particularly disdainful of Nolan's view. There was one notable case during an interview with a senior legislative aide in Pennsylvania, at the time the only US state without lobbying regulation. The interviewee greeted our initial question on a register inhibiting citizens with the words 'You're joking, right?' But, when informed that this was indeed what the Nolan Committee had recommended in Britain, he smiled and stated that in the American system if a constituent banged on a legislator's door and the said legislator was with a lobbyist, the lobbyist would be 'put out on his ear' and told to wait. While there might be an element of wishful thinking in this, it does reflect the importance of the constituent, and the 'every vote counts' principle in US politics. While the culture of lobbying is enormously strong, as outlined in Chapter 2, the culture of constituents approaching their representatives is equally strong and there is no evidence to suggest that any lobbying legislation has inhibited ordinary citizens from going to see their representatives about ordinary issues.[8]

Beyond the survey questions – financial costs and how have the rules affected lobbying?

A significant question that many practitioners would like answered is, how has lobbying legislation affected lobbying? The elite interviews revealed that lobbyists do, indeed, have to dedicate some time to registering, and thus it does represent something of a 'burden' if one agrees with the idea that 'time is money'. In short, lobbyists must spend the time necessary to fill out the forms required by the jurisdiction wherein they are lobbying. They also must ensure that they have not given incorrect information. And in some cases, especially in highly regulated systems, lobbyists have to give significant information, which may require extra staff time and resources of their company.

Overall, in our interviews we did find a direct relationship between the robustness of the legislation and the time needed by lobbyists to register: fewer details are required in low-regulation systems, such as Germany and the EP, where usually a one-off registration process gathers the details relatively easily; medium-regulation systems, as seen in Canada, require more time; and high-regulation systems, such as those in the US, require the most time, especially in relation to the provision of individual and employer spending reports, as well as updating information. One lobbyist working in several high-regulation jurisdictions even said that his group struggled to find the staff time necessary to register in all jurisdictions. In some cases, this means that some (albeit very few) organisations in medium- and high-regulation systems feel that updating their registration profile has not always been possible, even if they were breaking the law by not updating at the intervals required by the legislation. The obvious need to devote time and resources to registering, in direct proportion to the strength of the regulatory environment, means that lobbyists have less time to devote to actual lobbying. Further, the more frequently the legislation requires them to update their profiles, the more time and resources have to be earmarked.

The corollary to this is the financial cost to the state in terms of implementing a meaningful regulatory system. One of the reasons for having no lobbying regulation or for a low-regulation system relates to the potential high costs to the state of setting up a registration system. There is no doubt that having any regulatory system in place is going to have financial implications for the political system. For example, in the case of the Ontario government, the development of software required to keep and monitor the register had an estimated one-off cost of $50,000. However, if the technological system in place is strong, as is the case in Ontario, few administrators are required to monitor it. But this does not mean that having a system in place can be done without any administrators: if it is to be effective, public sector administrators have to be devoted to the task. According to the different types of regulatory systems in place, there may be from at least one to two people working at the registry (in low-regulation systems), to 25, as seen in the highly regulated system of Washington State. In 2008, Washington State was ranked first in the US in campaign finance disclosure for the fifth consecutive year, with the Public Disclosure Commission's electronic filing process and the accessibility of campaign finance data rated the best in the country (Public Disclosure Commission, 2008). Notwithstanding the financial costs involved when running a lobbying register, many respondents repeated in interviews that the obvious benefit is increased accountability in the political system. This can be seen by the position of Washington State in the CPI rankings and was reinforced strongly by officials in Washington State during a series of interviews carried out there. There may, of course, be a type of wishful thinking among officials here in justifying the spending on their regulatory offices. The costs of the regulatory framework in each state varies considerably, as the states themselves vary in relation to their legislation. As one Wisconsin lobbyist noted: 'The individual states vary all over the lobbying map on lobbying regulation. Wisconsin is very strict in its ethics laws. Reporting requirements are onerous' (Newmark, 2009: 93). Clearly, the more a state or legislature is worried about transparency, the more it will be willing to spend on a robust regulatory framework. Thus 'larger states or states that have been rocked by scandal may adopt stricter laws because they are necessary in the eyes of the public' (Newmark, 2009: 94). This is what happened in Washington State in the early 1970s. In that context, states will literally pay the price if they feel it is worth it in terms of public perception.

If the first impact that regulations have had relates to the time and resources required by lobbyists to register (which is directly related to the robustness of the regulatory regime), the second impact is that, particularly in high- and medium-regulation systems, gone are the days when a lobbyist can just show up at a politician's office. We need to be clear on something important here, however: lobbying legislation imposes virtually no burdens on politicians whatsoever. In principle, politicians are *not* responsible for making sure lobbyists are registered. Nor do they have to keep a record of whom they have talked to. Nor can they be fined if a penalty is incurred by a lobbyist who, for example, has not registered. However, from our interviews, particularly in high- and medium-regulation systems, it was apparent that several politicians will nevertheless make sure that a lobbyist they are going to talk to is registered, and if not they will not make or will cancel the appointment immediately. In some cases where this has occurred, as mentioned by Canadian interviewees in particular, politicians will indirectly put the lobbyist's name on a black-list and tell colleagues and other state officials about it. In the case of low-regulation jurisdictions, most politicians are not really too concerned about whether the lobbyist they are meeting is registered, which results in more 'freedom' for lobbyists to show up at the politician's door (or, as in the case of the EP, simply meet outside the Parliament building without registering in the first place).

A third impact of the regulations is what we refer to as the 'positive kick-back' dynamic for lobbyists. While this may not be as apparent in low-regulation systems, virtually all of those interviewed in medium- and high-regulation systems stated that the registration process was worth it, regardless of the time burdens it may impose, because of four positive kick-backs.

- Lobbyists can see what competitors' lobbying strategies are. From a lobbyist's point of view, having a public registry helps ensure transparency in terms of 'who is talking to whom' and most lobbyists feel that they benefit the more transparent the overall process is. In fact, several stated that, at the beginning of the working week, they religiously inspect the lobbyist register in order to see what other interest groups are doing. In high- and medium-regulation systems, if lobbyists by word of mouth realise that someone attempting to lobby has not registered, they do not hesitate in lodging a third-party complaint to the registrar's office. This adds strength to Thomas and Hrebenar's observation (1996: 29) that lobbyists themselves are major consumers of the information provided on these lists.

- Lobbyists can show clients or members of the organisation what they are working on in trying to influence the government. As seen in interviews with in-house corporate lobbyists, professional consultancies and NGOs, a register allows corporate bosses, clients of consultancy firms and members of civil society organisations to see what the lobbyist acting on their behalf is actually doing. As one NGO interviewee in a medium-regulation jurisdiction in Canada stated, 'We can tell our members, "Do you want to see what we've been doing?" Well, there it is: check out the registry!'
- Citizens as a whole can see that lobbyists are professional and legitimate policy-making actors; this allows lobbyists to be 'proud' of what they do and helps cement their role as policy-making actors. With registration, citizens can readily see what lobby groups are doing and whom in government they are talking with, meaning that, over time, citizens become less cynical about the work and nature of lobby organisations. All this helps increase perceptions among the public that lobby groups are 'professionals'.
- Politicians, too, can openly state that they are meeting with lobbyists and, by so doing, indirectly decrease citizens' perceptions that 'backroom deals' are taking place. As above, a register professionalises the activity of lobbyists. Consequently, as many politicians in Canada and the US we interviewed stated, if a constituent has a question regarding which lobbyists are trying to influence government decisions in a specific policy area, politicians can simply state that this information is on the register. This decreases public misperceptions with regard to whom the government is being lobbied by.

We close with a word of caution: when we are referring to 'positive kickbacks', we are looking at survey responses and comments made in interviews from actors in high- and medium-regulation systems in North America. The question that one may have is, would actors in all medium-regulation systems throughout the world that established lobbying rules in the 2000s believe that these 'kick-backs' are more important than potential costs? Judging from some of the information presented in Chapter 3, it appears that not all lobbyists in central and eastern Europe have actually registered. This may be because these registers have only recently been set up (in the 2000s) and, with time, many more lobbyists may sign up. Nevertheless, it may also point to the idea that lobbyists from this part of the world have not embraced the benefits of lobbying rules, or to see how a register could inform their lobbying strategies as fully as their North American counterparts. While it is beyond the scope of this book to examine the attitudes of actors from all areas of the world where there is lobbying regulation, in a longer-term future project we hope to be able to send surveys and perform interviews with actors in Lithuania, Poland and Hungary and use this as a basis to update this edition of the book and gain insights into actors' views on lobbying in central and eastern Europe. Something to be pondered on while the evidence is being gathered, however, is the question of whether it is valid to believe that lobbyists in these countries do believe that the costs outweigh the benefits, as reflected in the fact that they are not signing on in droves to the register. One variable that may explain this is the 'political culture' in these states and in North America. That is, lobbying may still be seen as a negative activity in society's eyes and lobbyists are reticent to admit that they are actively doing it. Further, as there may be no strong history of enforcing (or even playing by) the rules, because they have only recently been established, lobbyists in these countries may not fear any penalties if they do not register, even if the environment they find themselves in can be classified as falling within a medium-regulation system.

Conclusion

This chapter has analysed the attitudes of politicians, administrators and lobbyists towards lobbying regulations in the US, Canada, the EP and Germany, through a questionnaire survey and follow-up elite interviews with a self-selected sample of the survey respondents. We first noted that, given the small number of surveys returned, our analysis could not offer a robust statistical analysis. Nevertheless, the surveys were used for illustrative purposes and, when supplemented with the interviews we conducted, offer insights into the effectiveness of the world of regulated lobbying in jurisdictions that established such rules throughout the twentieth century.

All three types of actor surveyed – politicians, administrators and lobbyists – were generally in favour of lobbying rules, and pointed to the increased accountability and transparency which are generally associated with them. The evidence suggests that actors in high-regulation jurisdictions, as opposed to medium- and low-regulation jurisdictions, showed more robust support for certain aspects of the regulatory regime, such as the effectiveness of individual spending disclosures in helping to ensure transparency. Yet even respondents from medium- and low-regulation jurisdictions broadly supported the regulations governing their activities. In line with various theoretical predictions, respondents held that the regulation of lobbying offers distinct advantages to them as actors within the governmental system, their political system as whole and the public's attitude to politics in general. The more stringent the regulatory legislation, and the more thoroughly it was applied, and crucially seen to be applied in a fair and equitable manner, the more knowledgeable actors were of these regulations, and the more open, transparent and accountable they regarded their political system as being. Nevertheless, one significant finding of the survey was that, regardless of the regulatory environment in place, loopholes can be found and, unfortunately, can be exploited.

Finally, the interviewees gave us insights into how the rules have affected the behaviour of lobbyists. We argued that the more the system is regulated, the more time and resources it demands of lobbyists to comply with it. This means that time must be invested before lobbyists can actually start their job of influencing the government and, even once they have started, must be invested in updating their registration profile. Further, we noted that in high- and medium-regulation systems, lobbyists must ensure that they are registered before they approach a public official, or they run the risk of being altogether alienated from the politician being lobbied. Regardless of costs to the lobbyists, however, we noted that a registration system, particularly in more robust regulatory environments, had four positive kick-backs: lobbyists can see what competitors are doing and subsequently use this as a basis to change lobbying strategies in order to make a more convincing case when influencing government; lobbyists can 'legitimise' themselves and use the register to show clients or members of an organisation how they are trying to exercise influence; citizens can see that lobbyists are professional and legitimate policy-making actors; and by openly stating that they are meeting with lobbyists, politicians can indirectly decrease citizens' perceptions that 'back-room deals' are occurring.

Notes

1 The findings presented in this chapter build on work presented at the Canadian Political Science Meetings in June 2007, the Political Studies Association of Ireland Annual Meeting in October 2007 and the European Centre for Public Affairs Annual Meeting in October 2008, as well as Chari *et al.* (2007) and Murphy *et al.* (2009).
2 If one examines Table 5.1, it can be seen that these states are a representative sample of different states along the range of CPI scores for the US.
3 Given that Newfoundland implemented legislation only in late 2005, no surveys were sent to this jurisdiction.
4 See for example a report dated 15 October 2008 on the Seattle pi news website, http://seattlepi.nwsource.com/local/383482_campaignfinance15.html.
5 Interview with a senior official in the Public Disclosure Commission, Olympia, Washington State, 28 March 2006.
6 Comments made by an interviewee in Canada, March 2006.
7 Interview with a senior official in the Public Disclosure Commission, Olympia, Washington State, 28 March 2006; also, interview with a number of lobbyists in Washington State on 28 and 29 March 2006.
8 Interviewees in Washington State, Pennsylvania and Washington, DC, all affirmed this view.

6

Examining the opinions of actors in unregulated jurisdictions

Introduction

As discussed in Chapter 1, the lobbying of government by various interests is regarded as central to the democratic process. Deliberative democratic theorists tell us that the regulation of lobbying has a positive effect on both political systems and the behaviour of those within them. Yet, only the small number of democracies examined in the previous chapters have implemented legislation regulating lobbyists. Even in the countries that are regulated at the federal level, such as Australia and Canada, some state/provincial jurisdictions still have not enacted lobbying regulations. This is also the case in the EU. This chapter examines the attitudes of actors towards lobbying legislation in such unregulated provinces, states and institutions which exist in political systems where lobbying rules are otherwise in force.[1] The actors we deal with here have knowledge of lobbying regulations, and what these regulations entail, as well as the consequences of the absence of such regulations for their jurisdictions. Our objective is to discover whether these actors see benefits in the introduction of lobbying legislation, as is suggested by deliberative democratic theory, or whether they are satisfied that their jurisdictions operate without lobbying regulations. The findings are presented here in order to provide some insight into, as well as indications of, how the rest of the unregulated democratic world regards the issue of lobbying regulation.

To regulate or not to regulate?

Ainsworth (1997) argues that, in regulated jurisdictions, the position of legislators in relation to the formulation of lobbying rules allows them to structure their relationship with lobbyists. The Citizens' Conference on State Legislatures, as early as 1971, stated that the rigour of lobbying regulation indicated a state's legislative independence (Citizens' Conference on State Legislatures, 1971). In Chapter 5 we found that actors in what were classified as high-regulation jurisdictions were more likely to agree that regulations helped ensure accountability in government than were actors in either the medium- or low-regulation environments. The conventional logic tends to be that the stronger the rules governing lobbyists, the more accountable the political system will be.

Thus, while many studies have examined lobbying legislation, and the attitudes of actors within regulated environments, few have sought to uncover attitudes towards lobbying regulations in unregulated jurisdictions/ institutions. Yet, these unregulated jurisdictions make up the great majority of democracies. Various scandals, questions as to accountability and transparency in government, and ease of access to legislators have led to the lack of regulations being questioned in a number of countries. France, Ireland, Italy, Latvia and the UK have all considered implementing lobbying regulations at one stage or another, but, for a variety of reasons, have still not done so. However, Lithuania, Poland, Hungary, Taiwan and Australia have all introduced lobbying regulations throughout the first decade of the twenty-first century.

As discussed in Chapter 1, according to deliberative democratic theory, the introduction of lobbying regulations should be beneficial. As a result, we set out to discover whether, in jurisdictions without lobbying regulations, significant support exists for the argument that lobbying regulations promote transparency and accountability in government. Absent in the literature is any study which has sought: to gauge attitudes towards lobbying regulations in unregulated jurisdictions; to offer a comparative analysis of overall attitudes towards lobbying legislation in these jurisdictions; and to analyse and compare the views of key agents – politicians, administrators and lobbyists – towards regulations in unregulated jurisdictions. The findings presented in this chapter should provide valuable insights into how the issue of lobbying regulation is regarded by those living in unregulated jurisdictions.

Overview of jurisdictions examined

By studying a number of cases, we can discover trends and achieve an understanding of the broader characteristics within a political environment (Blondel, 1995: 3). The value of selecting numerous cases for examination here is the perspective offered, and the hope of building a body of increasingly complete explanatory theory (Mahler, 1995; Mayer *et al.*, 1993).

While many democracies have freedom of information (FOI) legislation, few have implemented lobbying regulations. This disparity may be due to states regarding strong FOI legislation as sufficient to ensure both transparency and accountability. However, Bertók (2008: 18) argues that lobbying regulations are vital in enabling the public to exercise, in conjunction with FOI legislation, their right to know who is attempting to influence political decisions. At the time when we began this research, in late 2005, three jurisdictions with lobbying legislation in place, Canada, the US and the EU, all had provinces, states or institutions without such regulations.[2] As such, these unregulated jurisdictions provided an ideal environment in which to examine actors' attitudes towards regulations.

As we have seen, up to January 2007, 49 of America's 50 states had legislation regulating lobbyists. The sole outlier in this regard was Pennsylvania. Pennsylvania originally introduced legislation regulating lobbyists in 1998. However, in 2000, the Pennsylvanian Supreme Court struck this legislation down, stating that Pennsylvania's efforts to monitor the activities of lobbyists amounted to illegal regulations on the practice of law. Two years later, the court reaffirmed its earlier ruling. However, over the next few years demands to bring Pennsylvania back into line with all the other states led eventually to the adoption of a lobbying disclosure act, signed by Governor Ed Rendell in November 2006 and enacted two months later (in January 2007). Nevertheless, we were able to glean valuable insights into the attitudes of actors without lobbying regulations through our questionnaire and a number of elite interviews in Pennsylvania in the spring of 2006.

In Canada, the situation is somewhat different. Canada introduced lobbying regulations initially at the federal government level in 1989, and from there lobbying regulation has gradually trickled down to the provinces over the last 20 years. This is in contrast to the US, where lobbying regulations existed at the state level as early as the 1890s before gradually finding their way to Washington, DC. The unregulated Canadian provinces we focus on here to gain our insights into attitudes towards regulation are Prince Edward Island, New Brunswick, Manitoba, Saskatchewan and Alberta. As pointed out in Chapter 2, while Alberta passed a lobbyists act in 2007 providing for the establishment and maintenance of a lobbyists registry, the legislation had not been enforced at the time of writing.

Until recently, the only EU institution to have lobbying regulations in place was the EP. This changed in mid-2008, when the Commission introduced its voluntary register of interest representatives. Thus, our research was conducted at a time when two of the three main EU institutions were without any form of lobbying regulations, either compulsory or voluntary. The Council still operates free from any form of lobbying regulations.

Research approach

This chapter examines the attitudes of politicians, administrators and lobbyists in states, provinces and institutions that do not have lobbying legislation, but which exist in political systems where such legislation is in force. Thus, we examine the one American state, the five Canadian provinces and the two EU institutions which, when this research was carried out, were unregulated jurisdictions.

This approach fulfils a basic research requirement of having a range of 'most similar' and simultaneously 'most different' cases to examine.

By 'most similar' we mean that all cases are selected from longstanding western democracies. By 'most different' we mean that while one of the cases is a state legislature, others are provincial legislatures, while others still are supranational institutions – the EU Commission and the Council. The 'most similar' criterion ensures like is compared with like and that 'the context of analysis [is] analytically equivalent, at least to a significant degree' (Collier, 1997: 2). At the same time, the 'most different' criterion 'places parallel processes of change in sharp relief as they are operating in settings that are very different in many respects' (Collier, 1997: 2). In other words, diverse circumstances should enable the identification of appropriate explanatory factors.

To investigate actors' attitudes, as in the previous chapter, a combination of semi-structured in-depth interviews and non-probability expert sampling was employed. Due to the impracticality and expense of attempting to survey a representative sample of politicians, administrators and lobbyists in the chosen jurisdictions, a sample of actors was selected for their in-depth knowledge in the area examined. In this instance, the expert sample size was 460. However, we recognise that by employing a non-probability sampling technique we cannot generalise from our findings to the larger population. All findings gleaned from the questionnaire used for this part of the study (see Appendix B, survey 2, p. 181) will be mediated through our findings from subsequent interviews (see below) and the broader literature.

These expert surveys were sent between September 2005 and January 2006. The overall response rate was approximately 10 per cent, with politicians responding at 8.3 per cent, administrators 18.3 per cent and lobbyists 5.3 per cent. There was some variation in response rates across jurisdiction. As in the case with regulated jurisdictions, our survey data were supplemented with 18 in-depth, semi-structured interviews, held between March and July 2006, with elected representatives, administrators, lobbyists and academics in the unregulated jurisdictions studied. The survey findings are examined in conjunction with the material obtained from the in-depth interviews.

Respondents and interviewees from these jurisdictions and institutions should provide informed insights into the world of unregulated lobbying. They work in unregulated environments, but are also aware of the existence of lobbying regulations in neighbouring jurisdictions and institutions. The fact that these actors have knowledge of legislation enacted elsewhere means we avoid the problems of having to define 'lobbying' and 'regulation' for them, something that Greenwood and Thomas (1998: 489) point out is critical.

We examine our findings in relation to politicians, administrators and lobbyists from Pennsylvania and the five Canadian provinces without lobbying legislation. Because the European Council and European Commission are unelected bodies, only EU lobbyists and EU administrators (including those working within the various Directorates General in the EU Commission, as well as those in permanent representations of the member states in the EU) were questioned. As certain jurisdictions and institutions with which the above share sovereignty have lobbying regulations, the actors questioned and interviewed all possessed some knowledge of lobbying regulations and what these entail. It must be noted that the material presented can be considered only a snapshot of attitudes towards lobbying regulation, in the selected jurisdictions, in the winter months of 2005/6. As above, since this research was undertaken, three of the jurisdictions examined now have some form of lobbying rules in place: Pennsylvania introduced lobbying regulations in early 2007, voluntarily regulations came into operation at the EU Commission in mid-2008, and lobbying legislation was passed in Alberta in December 2007, and was due to come fully into force in 2009 but had not done so by July of that year.

Examination of attitudes towards the regulating lobbying in unregulated jurisdictions

Reasons for the absence of legislation

The most favoured reason for an absence of lobbying legislation among elected representatives was that it was unnecessary, as they believed that there was little lobbying in their jurisdictions (Appendix B, survey 2, question 6). A representative from a small Canadian province commented that the province was so small everybody knew whom politicians were meeting with. As a result, they saw no need for formal regulations. Clearly, some actors do not see the need for the increased publicity that lobbying regulations promise (Naurin, 2007). A small survey of MPs in Denmark produced similar findings, and the author concluded 'that most were aware of who was lobbying them and why' (Rechtman, 1998: 584).

Arguing against the need for regulations, two high-ranking politicians from Canada stated that the monitoring of lobbyists had never been an issue in their jurisdictions. But at what stage does the regulation of lobbyists become an issue? Just because lobbying is not in the public's consciousness does not mean it is not going on, nor that the amount of lobbying activity is insignificant. This then leads to the next logical question – what type of regulations would be required to deal with the lobbying? In Chapter 4 we theorised the existence of different regulatory environments, ranging from high regulation, through medium regulation to low regulation. However, another reason put forward by politicians for the absence of legislation was that they were simply opposed it. Their opposition to lobbying regulations ranged from regarding them as additional unnecessary bureaucracy to the fact that there was no public demand for them.

A majority of administrators and almost half of lobbyists put the absence of regulations down to the fact that they considered the self-regulation of lobbying and lobbyists to be adequate (question 6). This was something that very few politicians agreed with. Nevertheless, it explains some of the very tentative steps adopted by certain jurisdictions in their efforts to shed some light into the 'black box' of lobbying activity. For instance, in the EU, the Commission had, until mid-2008, sought only to encourage self-regulation among lobbyists (Greenwood, 1998: 588). Self-regulatory regimes are 'relatively popular instruments to apply to the activities of lobbyists … amongst those who are the targets of regulation' (Greenwood and Thomas, 1998: 493–494). The issue of the increasing levels of red tape associated with lobbying regulation was another source of the lobbyists' opposition to lobbying legislation.

From Table 6.1, it is clear that only a small minority of respondents put the blame for the absence of lobbying legislation on the opposition of both politicians and lobbyists (question 6). Administrators and lobbyists from Europe were more inclined than their North American counterparts to blame the absence of legislation on the opposition of politicians and lobbyists. The primary reason put forward for the absence of lobbying legislation by the majority of respondents from Brussels was that they did not see the need for it – arguing that self-regulation was sufficient. Some argued that the EU was bureaucratic enough, without lobbyists having to register with an official body, fill out regular reports and frequently update their details. That there are over 15,000 lobbyists active in Brussels raises the question, at what stage does regulation become an issue?

Table 6.1 Main reasons perceived for absence of lobbying legislation (percentage of sample responding)

Reason endorsed	Politicians	Administrators	Lobbyists
Politicians opposed	18.2	0	9.1
Lobbyists opposed	9.1	14.3	0
Self-regulation sufficient	9.1	57.1	45.5
Lobbying minimal	36.4	4.8	9.1
Politicians and lobbyists opposed	0	0	9.1
Other	27.3	23.8	27.3

Requirements to register and report spending

When asked in interviews and questionnaires (question 7, survey 2), a majority of politicians and administrators agreed that lobbyists should have to register when engaged in lobbying activity (Table 6.2). There was near universal support for this idea from EU respondents. This was despite the fact that these same respondents had stated that the main reason for the absence of regulations in the EU was that self-regulation was sufficient.

This suggests that the European Commission's new voluntary scheme is actually a less preferred option than mandatory registration. Some administrators also pointed out that there were loopholes in political systems created by the absence of a register of lobbyists.

A majority of lobbyists also felt that a register should be put in place. In this case, a similar level of support for a register was found among lobbyists in both North America and Europe. The former Speaker of the Danish parliament, Erling Olsen, advocates 'strict rules on lobby activities and registration in order to secure transparency' (Rechtman, 1998: 583). Jordan (1991) argues that it is common sense that if a government demands driving instructors, and various other professions, to be registered, why should the public not be protected from unscrupulous lobbyists?

Table 6.2 Survey responses to the proposition that lobbyists should be required to register when lobbying public officials (percentage of sample responding)

	Politicians	Administrators	Lobbyists
Strongly agree	27.3	36.4	9.1
Agree	36.4	36.4	45.5
Neutral	36.4	9.1	27.3
Disagree	0	9.1	9.1
Strongly disagree	0	9.1	9.1

All politicians were of the opinion that lobbyists should be required to report their spending activities (question 8, survey 2). The only differences among them concerned how regularly these reports should actually have to be filed. Some politicians were in favour of lobbyists filing annually, while other preferred six-monthly or even quarterly filings. The majority of administrators expressed similar opinions to those of politicians. Interestingly, most lobbyists also supported the idea of their having to file spending reports. Those lobbyists who opposed the filing of spending reports did so as they regarded it as needless, or they opposed the bureaucratic hassle it would involve. However, if lobbyists, like lawyers, are billing clients by the hour, and keeping detailed accounts of these billings, then it is hard to understand how an annual, semi-annual or even quarterly summation of their expenditures should be difficult for them to produce. Thus, politicians, administrators and lobbyists largely felt lobbyists should be required to file spending reports regularly, at least annually. They were also in agreement that the political campaign contributions by lobbyists should be available for public scrutiny. As Jordan (1998: 534) argues, registration should not be about recording and identifying who is active, but should reveal qualifications and enforce a code of good practice.

Elected representatives overwhelmingly agreed that lobbyists' political campaign contributions (question 9, survey 2) should be openly available for public scrutiny. Most administrators agreed with the politicians that lobbyists should have to reveal their campaign contributions. In fact, what dissent there was among administrators came from respondents in the EU who expressed neutrality, or disagreement, on this issue. Interestingly, nearly all lobbyists also agreed that their political contributions should be available for public inspection.

Lists of lobbyists and their expenditures
All politicians, and a majority of administrators, felt that a list of lobbyists, and their lobbying expenditures, should exist for public scrutiny (question 10, survey 2). From Table 6.3 it is clear that most representatives expressed the view that this list should be a legal requirement, be available at all times and be accessible online for anyone to access and examine at any time. However, administrators were less supportive of the idea that lobbyists should be required by legislation to reveal information about both themselves and their business activities. A majority of EU administrators favoured a list of lobbyists being created on a voluntary basis, whereas their North America counterparts supported the idea of a list being a legal requirement. Over one-third of lobbyists advocated legislation requiring a list of lobbyists, and their expenses, to be available to the public. The lobbyists were equally divided between a list required by law, but available only upon request, and a list being provided entirely on a voluntary basis. However, very few of the lobbyists we spoke with, or who responded via questionnaire, voiced outright opposition to the idea of a list. Overall, politicians, administrators and lobbyists were largely proponents of regulation, expressing views similar to those discovered by Gray and Lowery (1998).

Table 6.3 Survey responses to the proposition that a list of all lobbyists (and their expenditures) should be freely available to the public (percentage of sample responding)

	Politicians	Administrators	Lobbyists
By law, at all times, for example on a centralised website	63.6	40.9	36.4
By law, upon request to the state or a lobby group	27.3	27.3	27.3
On a voluntary basis	9.1	27.3	27.3
Never	0	4.5	9.1

Although a majority of lobbyists supported 'by law' options, including the idea of a register, the filing of spending reports and the provision of

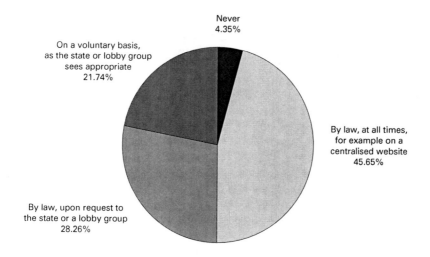

Figure 6.1 Survey responses to the proposition that a list of lobbyists and amounts spent on lobbying activity should be freely available to the public (percentage of sample responding)

details on political contributions, nevertheless over a third were opposed to mandatory legislation compelling the provision of such information to the public. They favoured non-compulsory regulations, akin to those found in what we refer to as medium- or low-regulation environments as discussed in Chapter 4. They clearly preferred the idea of having some control over the information they provided. Lobbyists were not opposed to providing information when asked to do so, or when they felt like it, as opposed to being compelled to do so. This is not that surprising, when it is recognised that all of the actors (apart from those from Pennsylvania) come from jurisdictions or institutions bordering upon, or sharing sovereignty with, medium- or low-regulation lobbying environments.

Overall, almost half of all respondents felt that a list of lobbyists, and their expenditures, should be required by law to be available to the public via the internet (Figure 6.1). Close to 30 per cent of respondents were of the opinion that these lists of lobbyists and their expenditures should be available upon request, and that this availability should be guaranteed by legislation. One-fifth of respondents thought the list should be provided only on a voluntary basis. Significantly, less than one in 20 respondents opposed the idea of providing such information to the public under any circumstance. Thus, the real issue was not whether a list of lobbyists, and their expenditures, should exist, but under what conditions this list should be provided to the general public. These findings generally fit with Largerlof and Frisell's (2004) argument that a requirement for lobbyists to register should contribute towards greater transparency.

The consequence of a register for citizens

We also asked respondents if they thought that a register would inhibit citizens from approaching their representative (question 11, survey 2). Taking all the responses together, a majority of close to 70 per cent felt a register would not negatively affect how citizens related to their political representatives. The significance of this finding is that it contradicts the arguments put forward by the Nolan Committee (1995) in the UK, as alluded to in the last chapter, and that it also contradicts Brinig *et al.*'s (1993) contention that a register of lobbyists could be considered a barrier to entry. When attempting to see differences between the groups surveyed, only a small minority of politicians felt a register would inhibit citizens from approaching them alone, that is, without the support of a lobbyist. The administrators' views on this were almost identical to those of the politicians. The few administrators who felt that a register might be detrimental to relations between citizens and their public representative were mostly from the EU. However, the attitudes of lobbyists diverged significantly from those of the other two groups, in that more of them felt a register would inhibit citizens from approaching their politicians alone. Despite this, a slight majority of lobbyists (mostly through responses from North America) believed that a register would not affect the citizen–representative relationship.

The auditing and penalisation of lobbyists

The monitoring of lobbying is crucial in preventing corruption (Campos and Giovannoni, 2006: 22). When asked if an independent agency should have unrestricted powers to conduct audits of lobbyists (question 12, survey 2), only a minority of politicians and administrators agreed (Table 6.4). Many more favoured audits of lobbyists only when 'deemed necessary', while a smaller number of politicians and administrators felt that an independent agency should never be permitted to audit lobbyists. An interesting contrast here is that, whereas some EU administrators favoured an independent agency having unrestricted powers to audit lobbyists, no Canadian administrators did. For Canadian administrators, the idea of audits being conducted by an independent agency was acceptable only when those audits were deemed necessary. In this case, audits could take place only when this independent agency (the lobbying registrar) felt that there were genuine grounds for conducting an audit of the lobbyist in question. Thus, in these circumstances, the state agency would be expected to provide something akin to the American legal concept of 'probable cause' before conducting the audit.

Table 6.4 Survey responses to the proposition that an independent agency should be allowed to pursue mandatory audits of lobbyists (percentage of sample responding)

	Politicians	*Administrators*	*Lobbyists*
Always	27.3	20	9.1
Only when deemed necessary	54.5	55	45.5
Never	18.2	25	45.5

Very few lobbyists were of the opinion that an independent agency should have the power to pursue mandatory audits. Almost half felt the agency should have this power only when deemed necessary, while nearly half argued against ever granting an independent agency auditing authority. Most of the lobbyists who opposed audits were from the EU. It is clear that lobbyists' opinions were at variance with those of the other two groups of actors, in that nearly twice as many lobbyists as either politicians or administrators expressed outright opposition to an independent agency being allowed to pursue audits. This finding might reflect a deep-seated desire among lobbyists to maintain the independence from audits that they presently enjoy in their unregulated jurisdictions.

In politics, as in business, principals must be able to compel their agents to provide clear reasons for their actions (Gutmann and Thompson, 2004; Schelder, 1999). 'In order to affect agency behaviour the principal must also have some kind of sanctioning mechanism in its hands – i.e. a possibility of accountability' (Naurin, 2006: 91). The making public of lobbyists' activities through the requirement for transparency is not enough to deter corruption (Lindstedt and Naurin, 2006). Therefore, would the penalising of certain lobbying behaviours (giving excessive campaign contributions, providing prohibited gifts, the incomplete filing of reports to a registrar, or deliberately not registering at all) deter such actions? By 'penalisation' we mean imposing the standard form of penalties for illegal lobbying that can be found in Canada, the US, Hungary or Poland, which can involve fines in the tens of thousands of dollars or, in extreme cases, up to five years' imprisonment.[3]

Responses to question 13 (survey 2) reveal that a majority of politicians were of the opinion that penalising unprofessional lobbying would act to deter it (Table 6.5). The imposition of penalties, and the naming and shaming that would inevitably follow, would mean that clients of lobbyists might take their business elsewhere. All of the Pennsylvanian actors we spoke with stressed how embarrassed they were that their state (at the time) was the only one in the Union without lobbying regulations and, hence, unable to impose penalties on lobbyists who were potentially rule

Table 6.5 Survey responses to the proposition that penalising unprofessional lobbying behaviour acts as a deterrent against such behaviour (percentage of sample responding)

Response	Politicians	Administrators	Lobbyists
Strongly agree	27.3	13.5	22.2
Agree	36.4	50.0	44.4
Neutral	18.2	13.6	33.3
Disagree	18.2	18.2	0
Strongly disagree	0	4.5	0

breakers. Most administrators expressed opinions akin to those of the politicians. However, more than a fifth of the administrators questioned did not believe penalising unprofessional lobbying behaviour would act as a deterrent. While all North American administrators approved of penalties for lobbyists, only two-thirds of their EU counterparts did likewise. Somewhat surprisingly, in light of their relative reticence on the issue of an independent agency conducting mandatory audits, lobbyists were the ones who most strongly agreed that penalties would deter unprofessional behaviour. This finding highlights how significant the issue of being penalised for misconduct was for lobbyists.

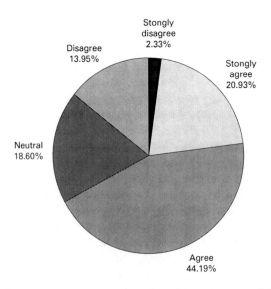

Figure 6.2 Survey responses to the proposition that penalising unprofessional lobbying behaviour acts as a deterrent (percentage of sample responding)

Overall, almost two-thirds of all actors felt that penalising unprofessional lobbying behaviour would work to deter it (Figure 6.2). Lindstedt and Naurin (2006) argue for the need for both sanctions and transparency. Overall, only 16 per cent of actors felt that penalties would not work, while almost one-fifth were neutral. However, for penalties to work they must be enforced. Otherwise, both the penalties and the regulations they are derived from will come to be disregarded (Rush, 1998: 522). Thus, there must be an independent agency capable of conducting audits and of imposing penalties for any transgressions of the regulations (Holman, 2008: 39).

Lobbying regulations and transparency, accountability and effectiveness
A crucial issue that needs to be addressed here is whether the actors felt that transparency, accountability and effectiveness in policy making would be improved if legislation regulating lobbying were to be implemented (question 14, survey 2). This question seeks to tie together the deliberative democratic principles with the reality of lobbying regulation on the ground.

Table 6.6 Survey responses to the proposition that if legislation regulating lobbying were implemented, then transparency, accountability and effectiveness in policy making would be improved (percentage of sample responding)

Response	Politicians	Administrators	Lobbyists
Strongly agree	18.2	15.8	8.3
Agree	54.5	31.6	58.3
Neutral	9.1	31.6	27.3
Disagree	18.2	15.8	9.1
Strongly disagree	0	5.3	0

From Table 6.6 we can clearly see that a majority of politicians felt transparency, accountability and effectiveness in policy making would be improved if legislation regulating lobbying were implemented. Some politicians felt that while the decision-making process was very open in their jurisdictions, the issue of transparency needed to be addressed through legislation regulating lobbying.

Almost half of the administrators agreed that implementing lobbying legislation would improve transparency and accountability. However, we did encounter a number of administrators who did not believe that legislation ensuring transparency and accountability was necessary, as they felt lobbyists did not possess the influence over policy making that they liked to 'pretend they had'. One administrator, in particular, stated that the 'primary responsibility for transparency has to remain with the lobbied', as opposed to those who lobby. Thus, the behaviour of politicians, as opposed to that of lobbyists, should be the focus of regulation.

Two-thirds of lobbyists held the view that regulatory legislation would improve transparency and accountability in government. That only half as many lobbyists as either politicians or administrators 'strongly agreed' with the proposition suggests less conviction on the issue, however. The level of dissent among EU lobbyists was twice as high as among their North American counterparts. One Canadian lobbyist suggested that the legislation, in addition to dealing with transparency and accountability issues, should also place a cap on lobbyists' expenditures.

The perennial outlier here is Pennsylvania. Politicians, legislative aides, government officials and lobbyists from Pennsylvania all insisted on the need for lobbying disclosure legislation in their state. Two primary reasons were provided: first, without legislation, Pennsylvania was seen as a 'laughing stock' in the US; secondly, 'while no one is openly opposed to it [regulation], there is a view that it obviously suits some people and groups, and in that context the sooner Pennsylvania gets constitutional legislation the better to level the playing pitch'.[4]

It is clear from Figure 6.3 that just over 60 per cent of all respondents were of the opinion that transparency, accountability and effectiveness

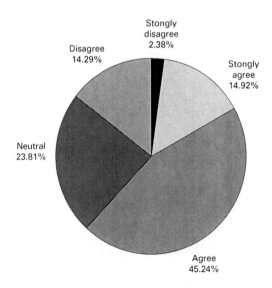

Figure 6.3 Survey responses to the proposition that if legislation regulating lobbying activity were implemented, then transparency, accountability and effectiveness in public policy making would be improved (percentage of sample responding)

in policy making would be improved by the introduction of legislation regulating lobbyists. This finding is close to Thomas and Hrebenar's (1996) contention in relation to the views expressed by proponents of lobbying regulation. Just over a fifth of actors expressed themselves to be 'neutral', while the remaining 17 per cent were of the view that lobbying legislation would not improve the policy-making environment. These findings confirm the hypothesis that in unregulated jurisdictions significant support exists for the transparency and accountability lobbying regulations offer. Thus, even those who will have to bear the burden of lobbying regulations recognise the benefits that these offer to society in general.

The North American and EU lobbyists' largely positive response to regulations discussed here contrasts sharply with the opposition voiced by the Scottish lobbying industry to the prospects of regulations being introduced in the Scottish Parliament (Dinan, 2006: 64). While Dinan (2006) uncovered disparities between Scottish lobbyists' views in public and in private, we found consistency between the questionnaire responses and what we found through our follow-up interviews. This contrast between our findings, and those of Dinan, may be due to the 'aversion to public scrutiny in British political culture' (Dinan, 2006: 65).

Conclusion

The vast majority of democracies in the world have yet to implement lobbying regulations. Using the central presuppositions of deliberative democratic theory, we hypothesised that there should exist in unregulated jurisdictions significant support for the transparency and accountability offered by lobbying regulations. A combination of in-depth interviews and purposive sampling was utilised to gauge attitudes towards lobbying legislation among actors in unregulated jurisdictions. While we were unable to take the survey data as representative in the statistical sense, we were able to mediate it through our findings from the in-depth interviews. Indeed, a significant lesson that can be taken from our research experience into lobbying regulation is that the reluctance of actors to participate in a sensitive area can prove a big obstacle in itself. Future research in this area might best be served by combining email questionnaires, online questionnaires and hard copies dispatched by post as a means of grabbing the attention of respondents while providing them with the broadest possible means of reply.

Our findings showed that the majority of interviewees and survey respondents put the absence of lobbying regulations down to self-regulation being sufficient, or that too much bureaucracy resulted from official regulations. Nevertheless, some respondents believed that the absence of a register resulted in loopholes. Almost two-thirds of actors believed lobbyists should have to register, although lobbyists themselves were a little less supportive of this idea than either politicians or administrators. A majority of actors were of the opinion that lobbyists should file annual spending reports and that their political party contributions should be in the public domain. Most also believed that the public should have access to a list of lobbyists and their expenditures. Interviewees and respondents also felt that the relationship between citizens and their representatives would not be negatively affected by requiring lobbyists to register. However, there was a greater degree of reticence on the possibility of an independent agency having the power to conduct mandatory audits of lobbyists. Most of the actors approved of the idea, but with the requirement that these reviews take place only when 'deemed necessary'. The findings are in line with what deliberative democratic theory predicts in relation to greater transparency: a higher level of public confidence in political institutions and a positive impact upon the policy-making process.

For a majority of actors, the prospect of penalising unprofessional lobbying activity was seen as a deterrent to such behaviour. In line with deliberative democratic theory's argument that exposure is purifying, a majority of interviewees and respondents felt that transparency, accountability and effectiveness in policy making would be improved if legislation regulating lobbying were introduced. These findings hold with the hypothesis that if deliberative democratic theory is correct, then significant support should exist for the transparency and accountability offered by regulations, even in jurisdictions without such regulations currently in place.

As events in the last decade reveal, the regulation of lobbyists is continuously evolving. The findings presented here captured the attitudes and opinions of actors only at a point in time. Since this research was conducted in 2005, Pennsylvania, Hungary, Australia and Taiwan all introduced mandatory lobbying regulations, Alberta is in the process of so doing, and the European Commission has set up a voluntary registry. Fascinatingly, the findings presented here are consistent with these changes: there is a strong undercurrent of support to pursue lobbying regulations in unregulated jurisdictions.

Notes

1 The findings presented in this chapter build on work that was presented at the meeting of the American Political Science Association in August 2008, and Hogan *et al.* (2008).
2 The Bundestag has specific rules regulating lobbyists. Each *Landtage* (state legislature) has similar codes. Thus, there is no jurisdiction in Germany which does not have lobbying legislation in place.
3 See http://laws.justice.gc.ca/en/ShowFullDoc/cs/L-12.4///en; and http://frwebgate.access.gpo.gov/cgi-bin/getdoc.cgi?dbname=110_cong_public_laws&docid=f:publ081.110.pdf; www.oecd.org/dataoecd/18/15/38944200.pdf.
4 Interviews in Pennsylvania were carried out on 30 and 31 March 2006.

7

Conclusion

Overall scope

Our aim in writing this book has been to show how lobbyists are formally regulated in some political systems. Interestingly, this is an issue that, for whatever reason, has largely been ignored by much of the lobbying/interest group literature up until now. Thus, this is the first major work of political analysis to offer an in-depth interrogation of this phenomenon from a global comparative perspective. This involved analysing regulatory developments in North America, Europe, Asia and Australia. Additionally, we have sought to uncover why many jurisdictions have yet to implement lobbying laws, despite the existence of such laws in neighbouring states, provinces and institutions.

In comprehensive terms, the book identified, and sought to correct, a fourfold void in the academic literature on this subject. First, it provided a broad overview of the historical development of lobbying regulations in every country that has introduced such laws. Secondly, it provided a comparative analysis of the types of laws and regulations in place within these countries. Thirdly, it provided a comprehensive examination of the views of the figures central to the process – lobbyists, administrators and politicians – from across these countries. Finally, it addressed the issue of assessing attitudes towards lobbying regulations in jurisdictions without any such regulations currently in place.

Thus, the book has taken a comprehensive, and comparative, look at lobbying regulations across the globe, as they stand at the end of the first decade of the twenty-first century. In particular, we wanted to understand actors' opinions on issues such as how regulations may or may not foster transparency and accountability in the democratic process. Thus, the book moved beyond theory, and what theory has told us are the benefits of lobbying regulations, and provided a range of findings from the practical realm of the lobbying world.

The research approach adopted was a mixed-methods one which combined textual analysis, surveys and in-depth interviews. Such a combination of qualitative and quantitative methods is well suited to the gathering of information at both the macro and micro levels. By adopting such an approach we gained an understanding of the legislation, but also of how those who work and operate under its rules regard such legislation. We developed a framework of analysis that categorised lobbying systems as low, medium or and high regulation. In that context, the use of 'thick' description and analytical narrative permitted us to integrate all of our findings into a seamless account.

Transparency and accountability

In general, 'sunshine' laws are seen to be of growing importance, and prevalence, in democracies today. While FOI legislation and lobbying regulations have existed for a long time, their implementation by democracies has been relatively recent. This is partly because only about half the countries in the world are democracies, and only 30 years ago this figure was half of what it is today. But over the past decades we have seen the gradual spread of sunshine laws. FOI legislation has been to the forefront in this regard, with lobbying regulations tending to trail in its wake. This can been seen by the fact that while 86 political systems currently have FOI legislation, of one form or another (Vleugels, 2008), only nine have lobbying regulations. Nevertheless, even this small number of countries with lobbying regulations constitutes an increase of over 100 per cent on the number of countries with such regulations in force at the close of the twentieth century. Between 2000 and 2008, Australia, Hungary, Lithuania, Poland and Taiwan all joined the ranks of states that regulate lobbying.

While many of the states that have FOI legislation do not have lobbying regulations, most of the countries that have lobbying regulations operate these in conjunction with FOI legislation. Nevertheless, sunshine laws need not be treated as discrete entities, and certainly the implementation of either FOI legislation or lobbying regulations should not be seen as mutually exclusive options. In fact, transparency is enhanced by implementing such legislation in concert.

We argue that the introduction of lobbying regulations can bring transparency and openness to the policy-making process. The fact that such regulations are often administered by independent agencies, established by statute, serves to guarantee a level of impartiality and propriety in the process of regulation. Where these agencies can impose fines for infraction of the regulations and, in conjunction with justice departments, bring criminal proceedings for the flouting of the regulations, then, in addition to transparency, accountability is integral to lobbying regulations. With such regulations, the 'black box' of policy making is no longer so dark, as certain of the information asymmetries inherent in the lobbying process are negated. The regulations also place the public's interest above those of special interests, or those of the representatives placed in a position of trust by the public. Thus, the issue of regulating lobbying relates directly to the principal agent problem, but while industry has long sought to address this problem, it is something that only a minority of democracies have yet confronted, for reasons associated with the burdens regulation imposes on politicians and lobbyists alike and with potential financial costs to the state.

Evolution of lobbying regulations

One of the aims of the book has been to capture the history, and evolution, of lobbying regulations, with an in-depth analysis of the state of play in terms of existing regulation. Comparative analysis of extant regulation permitted us to see how regulations vary both across countries and within countries. This analysis also permitted us see how high-, medium- and low-regulation systems compare with each other. Thus, we were able to rank jurisdictions by the rigour of their regulations.

We first examined the history of lobbying regulations in the US, Canada, the EU and Germany. This examination primarily focused upon regulatory developments in these jurisdictions during the twentieth century. However, in the case of the US, we also discussed the development of lobbying regulations at state level in the latter half of the nineteenth century, while in the case of Canada we examined certain provincial regulations that have come into existence during the early twenty-first century. We then turned our attention to the regulations that have come into existence exclusively in the twenty-first century, in Lithuania, Poland, Hungary, Taiwan and Australia.

We then examined how the different types of systems established throughout the world can be clearly classified. This classification crucially enabled us to see which jurisdictions are highly regulated, which are not, and what it is that differentiates one from the other. We also examined the effectiveness of the regulations, in terms of transparency, accountability, the presence of potential loopholes and the burdens in terms of bureaucratic red tape that the regulations impose upon both politicians and lobbyists alike. We discussed the costs of imposing such regulations, as well as their enforceability. Thus, the book provides a thorough examination of extant lobbying legislation and how rigorously these laws are formulated and implemented. As we have shown, the actual implementation of the regulations on the ground is as important as what the establishing act, or resolution, actually states.

Interestingly, the only national-level system that can be classified as highly regulated is that of the US, based on the 2007 Honest Leadership and Open Government Act. Prior to this, the US federal regulations, along with Canada's federal regulations, were both classified as medium-regulation jurisdictions. Canada, despite its Lobbying Act, introduced in 2008, is still classified as a medium-regulation environment, albeit with a slightly higher CPI score than before. Australia, Hungary, Lithuania and Taiwan are all also rated as medium-regulation jurisdictions, while Germany, the EP, the European Commission and Poland are all rated as low-regulation jurisdictions. It is noteworthy that in the cases of both the US and Canada, with each iteration federal legislation underwent it became more rigorous. However, this can be a (painfully) slow process, especially in the case of the US, where federal lobbying regulations had been regarded as weak ever since they were first introduced in 1946. At the state level, in the US, we saw examples of highly regulated jurisdictions, with 25 of the 50 states placed in the high-regulation category, while the other 25 states were deemed to be medium-regulation environments. All Canadian provinces with lobbying regulations were assessed as medium-regulation jurisdictions.

Given the low response rate to our questionnaires by politicians, administrators and lobbyists, our analysis could not be seen as robust statistically. However, when used for illustrative purposes these surveys served to supplement the findings from the in-depth interviews and textual analysis. Our overall findings showed that politicians, administrators and lobbyists were favourably disposed towards the regulations governing lobbying in their respective jurisdictions. Support for lobbying regulations was clearly stronger in high-regulation jurisdictions than in medium- and low-regulation jurisdictions. As theory predicts, respondents held that regulations provided advantages to themselves, to their political systems and to the general public as well. The more stringent the regulatory legislation, and the more thoroughly it was applied, the more knowledgeable actors were of these regulations, and the more open, transparent and accountable they regarded their political systems to be. Hand in hand with more stringent regulation, and greater transparency, went a kind of pride among the actors in relation to their democratic openness.

Finally, we also examined attitudes in institutions, and other sub-national jurisdictions in the US (when Pennsylvania was an outlier), Canada and the EU that do not have lobbying regulations in place. This exploration was driven by deliberative democratic theory, which, by extension, would hold that even in jurisdictions without lobbying regulations, significant support should exist for the transparency and accountability offered by such regulations. This examination provided an insight into why lobbying regulations had not been implemented in these jurisdictions, despite lobbying regulations being in place in nearby states or provinces or institutions, as well as at the federal level. A majority of surveys from these jurisdictions, in addition to a majority of those interviewed, felt that penalising unprofessional lobbying would serve to deter such activity. In line with deliberative democratic theory, and the view that exposure has a purifying effect on politics, a majority of interviewees and respondents believed if legislation regulating lobbying were introduced, transparency, accountability and effectiveness in policy making would be improved. While this was only a very small sample, and no broad conclusions could be drawn from these findings, it nevertheless suggested that an undercurrent of support, as predicted by deliberative democratic theory, exists for the assertion that lobbying regulations offer greater transparency and accountability.

The regulations on the ground

In low-regulation jurisdictions, rules on individual lobbyist registration exist, but few details beyond registering as a lobbyist are required. Moreover, while lists of those who have registered as lobbyists are available for public scrutiny, details are not, such as the amount they spend on their lobbying activities, whom they lobby and, often, whom they are lobbying for, and the subject matter they are lobbying on. The regulations usually ignore lobbyists who attempt to influence the executive. Also, there is usually no cooling-off period required before a legislator can become a lobbyist.

The main advantage of low-regulation systems is that they at least provide for a minimum standard of registration for lobbyists. Although there is a central register in such jurisdictions, lobbyists are in many respects expected to self-regulate. The result tends to be a situation where one does not have a sense that the independent monitoring agency is constantly watching the behaviour of lobbyists to ensure they conform with the rules laid down by legislation. In general, the lobbyists working in these low-regulation environments are not necessarily against the existence of a register. The bureaucratic red tape involved is relatively minor, and the maintenance of such a register and the issuing of passes for lobbyists are not overtly burdensome upon the state.

If lobbying is about gaining access to decision makers, and ultimately influencing them, one of the disadvantages of low-regulation systems is that they tell the public very little about what type of influence lobbyists have on politics in general. While having a register of lobbyists tells the public who lobbyists are, by not making them reveal whom they are lobbying, or what issue they are lobbying on, the public is none the wiser as to the influence and pressure being brought on decision makers by paid lobbyists. Accordingly, both transparency and accountability are less likely to be ensured in low-regulation systems.

In medium-regulation jurisdictions, lobbyists must not only register themselves, but also state the institutional actors that they are lobbying and the subject matter that they are lobbying on. Some regulations exist surrounding individual spending disclosures, and in-house lobbyists are included within the legislation. Gifts are prohibited and all political contributions must be reported, but there are no regulations on employers' spending reports, and lobbyist spending disclosures are not available for public scrutiny. Moreover, medium-regulation jurisdictions do not require lobbyists to provide full details of their employers. However, in these jurisdictions the 'revolving door' for legislators is largely closed.

The main advantage of medium-regulation systems is that they provide the public with access to a register of lobbyists, and those who are lobbied, by requiring lobbyists to provide information on whom they are lobbying within government, whether elected representatives or public officials. While more information must be provided to the central register, resulting in more work, nonetheless in our elite interviews with actors in such systems the overriding view was that, once such a system had been set up, both lobbyists and administrators found it easy to deal with and quickly became accustomed to it. Online registration, such as that which exists in the Canadian province of Ontario, which is clearly efficient and effective, requiring little effort to use and update, would seem to be the way forward in this regard.

The main disadvantage of medium-level regulations is that, from a transparency perspective, lobbyists do not have to declare full details of who their employers are, and complete spending disclosures are not in the public domain. In that context, while the public can see who is the lobbyist, who is the lobbied, and what issue the lobbying is on, they cannot get a complete picture of those employing the lobbyist. Thus, the ultimate objective behind approaching the political establishment remains somewhat hidden from view. This can clearly lead to loopholes within such systems, whereby, for instance, lobbyists can provide so-called 'free consultancy' to political parties.

The main requirement of lobbyists in high-regulation systems is that they must disclose full details of their employers, as well as the institutional actors they are lobbying, and the subject matter they are engaged in lobbying on. Tight individual spending disclosures are required of lobbyists and, crucially, the employers of lobbyists. Scrutiny of spending disclosures is open to the public. The law is rigorously enforced and penalties for breaches of the law are far more severe than those found in the low- or medium-regulation jurisdictions.

The main advantage of high-regulation systems is that, from a public probity perspective, they offer the most comprehensive solution to ensuring that lobbyists cannot unduly influence elected representatives or public officials. By disclosing the lobbyist, the actor lobbied and full details of those employing the lobbyist, there is very little scope for malfeasance in public policy making through the lobbying process. Moreover, having mandatory spending disclosures, and significant reviews or audits of lobbyists, further limits the potential for lobbyists to engage in illegal acts, simply because it is very difficult to do so. While, as the Abramoff scandal in Washington, DC, showed, it is practically impossible to outlaw illegal acts if certain individuals are committed to engaging in them, having a comprehensive system of lobbying regulation, and spending disclosure, should reassure the public that lobbyists are not able to have improper influence on the political system. The obvious benefit therefore is increased transparency and accountability in the political system.

The main disadvantage of a high-regulation system is that by imposing such comprehensive regulations doubt can be cast in the minds of both lobbyists and those that are lobbied as to where the dividing line lies between what is legal and illegal in the terms of the lobbying relationship. Lobbying is a central element of political life in liberal democracies today. By imposing such tight rules, and what one may even consider to be a 'burden' on lobbyists, governments could even be accused of acting with undue zeal. Another potential disadvantage is that putting in place such a system comes with a financial cost. Washington State, for instance, with a population of just under 6 million citizens, employs 25 people in its Public Disclosure Commission, which results in relatively high costs for a state of its size. In this regard, a cost–benefit analysis, encompassing what would likely occur in the absence of such regulations, is a possible way of justifying the existence of a commission of this size. However, such an analysis would be fraught with difficulties and strewn with counterfactuals. Lobbyists within such systems do not complain overtly about the level of red tape involved, but there can be little doubt that such a system places burdens on those who have to file regularly and also on the state, which is charged with maintaining such a system.

Our research also turned up some other interesting findings in what we referred to as 'positive kick-backs' (Chapter 5). That is, registration systems can provide some unexpected benefits for lobbyists themselves. By check-ing the registrar's online database, lobbyists can instantly see how much business any particular rival is engaged in. This can influence how they themselves behave and even, to some extent, promote the pursuit of 'best professional practice'. Thus, while legislation may be introduced to increase transparency and openness in government, lobbyists can use the register to advertise themselves to potential clients. By examining the register, citizens can come to see lobbyists as legitimate, policy-influencing actors. By stating that they are meeting with lobbyists, politicians can create the impression that everything they are doing is above board, thereby diminishing citizens' perceptions that anything untoward might be going on hidden from public view. The register can provide politicians with a means of defusing any public concern over how policy is being formulated. Consequently, lobby-ing regulations can affect lobbyists, politicians and citizens in ways other than those anticipated by their advocates.

Designing a system of lobbying regulation

As pointed out above, when contemplating designing a system of lobbying regulation, it is necessary to take into account the following: low-regulation systems in essence detail who is being paid to engage in lobbying government officials and elected representatives; medium-regulation systems report on what specific context lobbying takes place in, demand some limited spending disclosures, have a system for online registration, ensure public access to information and require a delay before politicians can jump into the world of lobbying after they leave office; high-regulation systems go still further, demanding to know the complete details of the lobbyist when registering, requiring full lobbyist and employer spending disclosures, ensuring all these details are open to public scrutiny on the web, having state agencies which can and do conduct mandatory reviews, and guaranteeing a cooling-off period.

Which is the best system to be enacted by those countries presently without lobbying laws? This question we cannot answer. Although we hope that the research presented here offers a foundation for actors in jurisdictions without lobbying rules to help frame their thoughts, they will inevitably have to come to their own conclusions. However, we do feel it is important to mention a few points which we believe are crucial to those seeking to design a regulatory system, by first reiterating some points made in the report from the British Committee on Standards in Public Life (Nolan Committee, 1995).

A central finding of the Committee was that if a register of lobbyists were established, lobbyists would attempt to persuade citizens that the best way to gain access to an elected representative would be through employing a lobbyist. While the findings of this book reject such a premise, there can be little doubt that in designing a system for regulating lobbyists it is crucial to write into the legislation why the establishment of a register is taking place and what it covers. It should also explicitly point out what it does not cover.

In all democracies, citizens need to be able to contact their representatives, and need to be able to know that in doing so they are not contravening any laws or regulations that pertain to the professional lobbying community. Putting in place a register of lobbyists need not affect the citizen–representative relationship. To suggest that citizens would feel that they needed to go through a lobbyist to speak to their elected representative on an issue which affects them would be, in many ways, to try to negate a century of western political culture. While lobbyists themselves might try to advocate such a scenario, to avoid having to register, or having regulations put in place at all, the reality is that any regulatory system of lobbyists needs to regulate only professional lobbyists. This should be explicitly written into any legislation.

The key point here is that lobbyists are different from ordinary citizens, as they are interacting with government officials and elected representatives and getting paid for doing so. Ordinary citizens do not. Lobbyists can be 'hired guns', advocating a cause based on nothing more than what their employer wants, whereas ordinary citizens are not. A senior legislative aide in Pennsylvania, intimately involved in ongoing attempts to write legislation regulating lobbyists in that state, commented to the authors that 'good regulation says what it is and what it's not'. This view was reiterated in several other elite interviews in the US and Canada. In that context, legislation should differentiate between paid lobbyists, ordinary citizens and representatives of sectoral interest groups such as farmers, trade unions and employers' organisations.

A comprehensive system of lobbying regulations should try to capture the information of who is accessing whom, what for, and what monies, if any, change hands. In principle, lobbyists should not be against having such a register and governments should want it, as it should keep transparent what is an entirely legal and even democratic process. In that context, what is being regulated is behaviour by interests who have the money to have their expectations potentially met by the access they enjoy. Registering lobbyists is not about regulating speech, but about preventing undue influence, including the potential abuse of a dominant financial position of some interest groups. The key here is to ensure that what is written into the regulation does not hinder average citizens from doing what they have always done, which is to lobby their respective representatives. The central point is to have a system that is as transparent as possible, and results in as much accountability as possible. Such a comprehensive system of regulation benefits the lobbyist, the legislator and the citizen. Regulation should be something that gives all stakeholders confidence in the system and in that context it must be kept simple initially, and not overburden lobbyists with legislation. The biggest complaint from lobbyists in relation to registers is the fact that in many jurisdictions they cannot register online. Any system that is currently being either contemplated or designed should have online registration facilities.

Finally, the enforcement of the legislation is crucial. Any such register should be controlled and monitored by an agency, preferably a completely independent agency. This, above all else, should both ensure and generate public confidence in the process.

Final words

This book constitutes a thorough comparative examination of extant lobbying regulations around the world. It has investigated the history of lobbying regulations, their origins and evolution, assessed the various laws currently in force, and examined attitudes towards lobbying regulations in both regulated and unregulated jurisdictions. While it took over 100 years for four political systems to regulate lobbying, it took just eight years for that number to more than double, to nine. Still more countries are in the process of either considering, or actually introducing, lobbying regulations, including Chile, the Czech Republic, Ireland and the UK.[1] Thus, the regulation of lobbyists, an idea that spent almost 100 years developing exclusively within the US, is gradually becoming an accepted notion across the democratic world. The more countries that have lobbying regulations, the more likely it is that other states will take notice of these, resulting in a possible snowball effect. In fact, it is conceivable that the regulation of lobbying could become a twenty-first century democratic phenomenon, as ease of access to registers of lobbyists is facilitated by the ever-expanding internet. Thus, the online registration and recording of lobbyists constitutes a potent example of one aspect of the greater democratisation and transparency of society promised by the information technology age. Our examination of current lobbying legislation suggests that it helps in fostering transparency, accountability and good governance in democratic societies.

Note

1 For example, the House of Commons Public Administration Select Committee recently produced a report on lobbying and influence in Whitehall (Public Administration Select Committee, 2009).

Appendix A

Sample calculations of CPI scores

Example 1: CPI score for Washington State

Question	Comment	Score
Definition of lobbyist		
1 In addition to legislative lobbyists, does the definition recognise executive branch lobbyists?	Yes	3
2 How much does an individual have to make/spend to qualify as a lobbyist or to prompt registration as a lobbyist, according to the definition?	$0	4
Individual registration		
3 Is a lobbyist required to file a registration form?	Yes	3
4 How many days can lobbying take place on before registration is required?	0	4
5 Is the subject matter or bill number to be addressed by a lobbyist required on registration forms?	Subj mat	1
6 How often is registration by a lobbyist required?	Biannl	1
7 Within how many days must a lobbyist notify the oversight agency of changes in registration?	6–10	2
8 Is a lobbyist required to submit a photograph with registration?	Yes	1
9 Is a lobbyist required to identify by name each employer on the registration form?	Yes	1
10 Is a lobbyist required to clearly identify on the registration form any additional information about the type of their lobbying work (i.e. compensated or non-compensated/contract or salaried)?	Yes	1
Individual spending disclosure		
11 Is a lobbyist required to file a spending report?	Yes	3
12 How often during each two-year cycle is a lobbyist required to report spending?	10+	3

13	Is compensation/salary required to be reported by a lobbyist on spending reports?	Yes	2
14	Are summaries (totals) of spending classified by category types (i.e. gifts, entertainment, postage, etc.)?	Yes	2
15	What spending must be itemised?	All	4
16	Is the lobbyist employer/principal on whose behalf the itemised expenditure was made required to be identified?	Yes	1
17	Is the recipient of the itemised expenditure required to be identified?	Yes	1
18	Is the date of the itemised expenditure required to be reported?	Yes	1
19	Is a description of the itemised expenditure required to be reported?	Yes	1
20	Is the subject matter or bill number to be addressed by a lobbyist required on spending reports?	Subj mat	1
21	Is spending on household members of public officials by a lobbyist required to be reported?	Yes	1
22	Is a lobbyist required to disclose direct business associations with public officials, candidates or members of their households?	No	0
23	What is the statutory provision for a lobbyist giving/ reporting gifts?	Gifts reported	2
24	What is the statutory provision for a lobbyist giving/ reporting campaign contributions?	All disclosed	1
25	Is a lobbyist who has done no spending during a filing period required to make a report of no activity?	Yes	1

Employer spending disclosure

26	Is an employer/principal of a lobbyist required to file a spending report?	Yes	3
27	Is compensation/salary required to be reported on employer/principal spending reports?	Yes	2

Electronic filing

28	Does the oversight agency provide lobbyists/employers with electronic/online registration?	Yes	1
29	Does the oversight agency provide lobbyists/employers with electronic/online spending reporting?	Yes	1
30	Does the oversight agency provide training about how to file registrations/spending reports electronically?	Yes	1

Public access

31	Location/format of registration or active lobbyist directory	Search database	3
32	Location/format of spending reports	Search database	3
33	Cost of copies	Free	1

34	Are sample registration forms/spending reports available on the web?	Yes	1
35	Does the agency provide an overall lobbying spending total by year?	Yes	2
36	Does the agency provide an overall lobbying spending total by spending report deadlines?	Yes	2
37	Does the agency provide an overall lobbying spending total by industries lobbyists represent?	Yes	2
38	How often are lobby lists updated?	Daily	4

Enforcement

39	Does the agency have statutory auditing authority?	Yes	2
40	Does the agency conduct mandatory reviews or audits?	Yes	2
41	Is there a statutory penalty for late filing of a lobby registration form?	Yes	1
42	Is there a statutory penalty for late filing of a lobby spending report?	Yes	1
43	When was a penalty for late filing of a lobby spending report last levied?	0–1 year	3
44	Is there a statutory penalty for incomplete filing of a lobby registration form?	Yes	1
45	Is there a statutory penalty for incomplete filing of a lobby spending report?	Yes	1
46	When was a penalty for incomplete filing of a lobby spending report last levied?	0–1 year	3
47	Does the state publish a list of delinquent filers either on the web or in a printed document?	No	0

Revolving-door provisions

48	Is a 'cooling off' period required before legislators can register as lobbyists?	Yes	2

Total CPI score		87

Source: Center for Public Integrity.

Example 2: Comparative CPI scores for countries with the longest history of lobbying regulations

Question	US, federal, 2007		Canada, federal, 2008		Germany		EU Parliament	
Definition of lobbyist								
1 In addition to legislative lobbyists, does the definition recognise executive branch lobbyists?	Yes	3	Yes	3	No	0	No	0
2 How much does an individual have to make/ spend to qualify as a lobbyist or to prompt registration as a lobbyist, according to the definition?	$500+	0	$0	4	$0	4	$0	4
Individual registration								
3 Is a lobbyist required to file a registration form?	Yes	3	Yes	3	Yes	3	Yes	3
4 How many days can lobbying take place on before registration is required?	16+	0	1–10	2	16+	0	16+	0
5 Is the subject matter or bill number to be addressed by a lobbyist required on registration forms?	Bill no. required	3	Bill no. Subject matter	3	Subject matter	1	No	0
6 How often is registration by a lobbyist required?	Quart	2	Monthly	2	Annual	2	Annual	2
7 Within how many days must a lobbyist notify the oversight agency of changes in registration?	16+	0	10	2	16+	0	16+	0
8 Is a lobbyist required to submit a photograph with registration?	No	0	No	0	No	0	Yes	1
9 Is a lobbyist required to identify by name each employer on the registration form?	Yes	1	Yes	1	Yes	1	No	0

10 Is a lobbyist required to clearly identify on the registration form any additional information about the type of their lobbying work (i.e. compensated or non-compensated/contract or salaried)?	Yes	1	Yes	1	Yes	1	No	0

Individual spending disclosure

11 Is a lobbyist required to file a spending report?	Yes	3	No	0	No	0	No	0
12 How often during each two-year cycle is a lobbyist required to report spending?	4–6	1	Never	0	Never	0	Never	0
13 Is compensation/salary required to be reported by a lobbyist on spending reports?	Yes	2	No	0	No	0	No	0
14 Are summaries (totals) of spending classified by category types (i.e. gifts, entertainment, postage, etc.)?	Yes	2	No	0	No	0	No	0
15 What spending must be itemised?	$100+	1	None	0	None	0	None	0
16 Is the lobbyist employer/ principal on whose behalf the itemised expenditure was made required to be identified?	Yes	1	No	0	No	0	No	0
17 Is the recipient of the itemised expenditure required to be identified?	Yes	1	No	0	No	0	No	0
18 Is the date of the itemised expenditure required to be reported?	Yes	1	No	0	No	0	No	0
19 Is a description of the itemised expenditure required to be reported?	Yes	1	No	0	No	0	No	0
20 Is the subject matter or bill number to be addressed by a lobbyist required on spending reports?	Subj mat	1	Bill no.	3	No	0	No	0

21	Is spending on house-hold members of public officials by a lobbyist required to be reported?	No	0	No	0	No	0	No	0
22	Is a lobbyist required to disclose direct business associations with public officials, candidates or members of their households?	No	0	No	0	No	0	No	0
23	What is the statutory provision for a lobbyist giving/reporting gifts?	Prohib	3	Prohib	3	None	0	None	0
24	What is the statutory provision for a lobbyist giving/reporting campaign contributions?	Dis-closed if $200+	1	All dis-closed	1	None	0	None	0
25	Is a lobbyist who has done no spending during a filing period required to make a report of no activity?	Yes	1	No	0	No	0	No	0

Employer spending disclosure

26	Is an employer/principal of a lobbyist required to file a spending report?	No	0	No	0	No	0	No	0
27	Is compensation/salary required to be reported on employer/principal spending reports?	No	0	No	0	No	0	No	0

Electronic filing

28	Does the oversight agency provide lobbyists/employ-ers with electronic/online registration?	Yes	1	Yes	1	No	0	No	0
29	Does the oversight agency provide lobbyists/employ-ers with electronic/online spending reporting?	Yes	1	Yes	1	No	0	No	0
30	Does the oversight agency provide training about how to file registra-tions/spending reports electronically?	Yes	1	Yes	1	No	0	No	0

Public access

31	Location/format of registration or active lobbyist directory	Databse dwnable	4	Databse dwnable	4	Search database	3	Search database	3
32	Location/format of spending reports	Databse dwnable	4	N/A	0	N/A	0	N/A	0
33	Cost of copies	Free	1	Free	1	Free	1	Free	1
34	Are sample registration forms/spending reports available on the web?	Yes	1	Yes	1	No	0	No	0
35	Does the agency provide an overall lobbying spending total by year?	No	0	No	0	No	0	No	0
36	Does the agency provide an overall lobbying spending total by spending report deadlines?	No	0	No	0	No	0	No	0
37	Does the agency provide an overall lobbying spending total by industries lobbyists represent?	No	0	No	0	No	0	No	0
38	How often are lobby lists updated?	Daily	4	Daily	4	Annual	1	Annual	1

Enforcement

39	Does the agency have statutory auditing authority?	Yes	2	Yes	2	No	0	No	0
40	Does the agency conduct mandatory reviews or audits?	Yes	2	Yes	2	No	0	No	0
41	Is there a statutory penalty for late filing of a lobby registration form?	Yes	1	Yes	1	No	0	No	0
42	Is there a statutory penalty for late filing of a lobby spending report?	Yes	1	No	0	No	0	No	0
43	When was a penalty for late filing of a lobby spending report last levied?	N/A	0	N/A	0	N/A	0	N/A	0
44	Is there a statutory penalty for incomplete filing of a lobby registration form?	Yes	1	Yes	1	No	0	No	0

45	Is there a statutory penalty for incomplete filing of a lobby spending report?	Yes	1	No	0	No	0	No	0
46	When was a penalty for incomplete filing of a lobby spending report last levied?	0–1 year	3	N/A	0	N/A	0	N/A	0
47	Does the state publish a list of delinquent filers either on the web or in a printed document?	No	0	Yes	1	No	0	No	0

Revolving-door provisions

48	Is a 'cooling off' period required before legislators can register as lobbyists?	Yes	2	Yes	2	No	0	No	0

Total CPI scores	62	50	17	15

Source: Chari *et al*. (2007) and authors' calculations.

Example 3: Comparative CPI scores for the US and Canada based on previous iterations of their lobbying regulations legislation

Question	US, federal, 1995		Canada, federal, 2003		Canada, federal, 1989	
Definition of lobbyist						
1 In addition to legislative lobbyists, does the definition recognise executive branch lobbyists?	Yes	3	Yes	3	Yes	3
2 How much does an individual have to make/spend to qualify as a lobbyist or to prompt registration as a lobbyist, according to the definition?	$500+	0	$0	4	$0	4
Individual registration						
3 Is a lobbyist required to file a registration form?	Yes	3	Yes	3	Yes	3
4 How many days can lobbying take place on before registration is required?	16+	0	1–10 days	2	1–10 days	2
5 Is the subject matter or bill number to be addressed by a lobbyist required on registration forms?	Bill no. subject matter	3	Bill no. subject matter	3	Bill no. subject matter	3
6 How often is registration by a lobbyist required?	Once	0	Annual	2	Annual	2
7 Within how many days must a lobbyist notify the oversight agency of changes in registration?	16+	0	16+	0	16+	0
8 Is a lobbyist required to submit a photograph with registration?	No	0	No	0	No	0
9 Is a lobbyist required to identify by name each employer on the registration form?	Yes	1	Yes	1	Yes	1
10 Is a lobbyist required to clearly identify on the registration form any additional information about the type of their lobbying work (i.e. compensated or non-compensated/contract or salaried)?	No	0	Yes	1	Yes	1
Individual spending disclosure						
11 Is a lobbyist required to file a spending report?	Yes	3	No	0	No	0
12 How often during each two-year cycle is a lobbyist required to report spending?	4–6	1	Never	0	Never	0
13 Is compensation/salary required to be reported by a lobbyist on spending reports?	Yes	2	No	0	No	0

14	Are summaries (totals) of spending classified by category types (i.e. gifts, entertainment, postage, etc.)?	No	0	No	0	No	0
15	What spending must be itemised?	None	0	None	0	None	0
16	Is the lobbyist employer/principal on whose behalf the itemised expenditure was made required to be identified?	No	0	No	0	No	0
17	Is the recipient of the itemised expenditure required to be identified?	No	0	No	0	No	0
18	Is the date of the itemised expenditure required to be reported?	No	0	No	0	No	0
19	Is a description of the itemised expenditure required to be reported?	No	0	No	0	No	0
20	Is the subject matter or bill number to be addressed by a lobbyist required on spending reports?	Bill no.	3	Bill no.	3	No	0
21	Is spending on household members of public officials by a lobbyist required to be reported?	No	0	No	0	No	0
22	Is a lobbyist required to disclose direct business associations with public officials, candidates or members of their households?	No	0	No	0	No	0
23	What is the statutory provision for a lobbyist giving/reporting gifts?	None	0	Gifts prohib	3	Gifts prohib	3
24	What is the statutory provision for a lobbyist giving/reporting campaign contributions?	None	0	Reported	1	Reported	1
25	Is a lobbyist who has done no spending during a filing period required to make a report of no activity?	Yes	1	No	0	No	0

Employer spending disclosure

26	Is an employer/principal of a lobbyist required to file a spending report?	No	0	No	0	No	0
27	Is compensation/salary required to be reported on employer/principal spending reports?	No	0	No	0	No	0

Electronic filing

28	Does the oversight agency provide lobbyists/employers with electronic/online registration?	No	0	Yes	1	No	0
29	Does the oversight agency provide lobbyists/employers with electronic/online spending reporting?	Yes	1	Yes	1	No	0
30	Does the oversight agency provide training about how to file registrations/spending reports electronically?	Yes	1	Yes	1	No	0

Public access

31	Location/format of registration or active lobbyist directory	Search database	3	Databse dwnable	4	P/copy	1
32	Location/format of spending reports	PDF on web	2	No	0	No	0
33	Cost of copies	Free	1	$1/pg	0	N/A	0
34	Are sample registration forms/spending reports available on the web?	Yes	1	No	0	No	0
35	Does the agency provide an overall lobbying spending total by year?	No	0	No	0	No	0
36	Does the agency provide an overall lobbying spending total by spending report deadlines?	No	0	No	0	No	0
37	Does the agency provide an overall lobbying spending total by industries lobbyists represent?	No	0	No	0	No	0
38	How often are lobby lists updated?	Semi-annually	1	Daily	4	N/A	0

Enforcement

39	Does the agency have statutory auditing authority?	No	0	Yes	2	Yes	2
40	Does the agency conduct mandatory reviews or audits?	No	0	Yes	2	Yes	2
41	Is there a statutory penalty for late filing of a lobby registration form?	Yes	1	Yes	1	Yes	1
42	Is there a statutory penalty for late filing of a lobby spending report?	Yes	1	No	0	No	0
43	When was a penalty for late filing of a lobby spending report last levied?	N/A	0	N/A	0	N/A	0
44	Is there a statutory penalty for incomplete filing of a lobby registration form?	Yes	1	Yes	1	Yes	1
45	Is there a statutory penalty for incomplete filing of a lobby spending report?	Yes	1	No	0	No	0
46	When was a penalty for incomplete filing of a lobby spending report last levied?	N/A	0	N/A	0	N/A	0
47	Does the state publish a list of delinquent filers either on the web or in a printed document?	No	0	No	0	No	0

Revolving-door provisions

48	Is a 'cooling off' period required before legislators can register as lobbyists?	Yes	2	Yes	2	Yes	2

Total CPI scores	36	45	32

Source: Center for Public Integrity, Chari *et al.* (2007) and authors' calculations.

Example 4: Comparative CPI scores for countries with the shortest history of lobbying regulations

Question	Lithuania		Poland		Hungary		Taiwan		Australia	
Definition of lobbyist										
1 In addition to legislative lobbyists, does the definition recognise executive branch lobbyists?	No	0	No	0	Yes	3	Yes	3	Yes	3
2 How much does an individual have to make/spend to qualify as a lobbyist or to prompt registration as a lobbyist, according to the definition?	$0	4	$0	4	$0	4	$0	4	$0	4
Individual registration										
3 Is a lobbyist required to file a registration form?	Yes	3	Yes	3	Yes	3	Yes	3	Yes	3
4 How many days can lobbying take place on before registration is required?	0	4	0	4	1–4	4	0	4	0	4
5 Is the subject matter or bill number to be addressed by a lobbyist required on registration forms?	Bill no.	3	Yes	3	Yes	3	Yes	3	No	0
6 How often is registration by a lobbyist required?	Annual	2	Once	0	Quart	2	Annual	2	Annual	2
7 Within how many days must a lobbyist notify the oversight agency of changes in registration?	6–10	2	7	2	11–15	1	5	3	6–10	2
8 Is a lobbyist required to submit a photograph with registration?	No	0	No	0	Yes	1	No	0	No	0

9 Is a lobbyist required to identify by name each employer on the registration form?	Yes	1	Yes	1	Yes	1	No	0	Yes	1
10 Is a lobbyist required to clearly identify on the registration form any additional information about the type of their lobbying work (i.e. compensated or non-compensated/contract or salaried)?	Yes	0	Yes	1	Yes	1	Yes	1	No	0

Individual spending disclosure

11 Is a lobbyist required to file a spending report?	Yes	3	No	0	No	0	Yes	3	No	0
12 How often during each two-year cycle is a lobbyist required to report spending?	Annually	0	Never	0	Never	0	Annually	0	Never	0
13 Is compensation/salary required to be reported by a lobbyist on spending reports?	Yes	2	No	0	No	0	Yes	2	No	0
14 Are summaries (totals) of spending classified by category types (i.e. gifts, entertainment, postage, etc.)?	No	0	No	0	No	0	No	0	No	0
15 What spending must be itemised?	None	0	None	0	None	0	None	0	None	0
16 Is the lobbyist employer/principal on whose behalf the itemised expenditure was made required to be identified?	No	0	No	0	No			0	No	0
17 Is the recipient of the itemised expenditure required to be identified?	No	0	No	0	No	0	Yes	1	No	0

18 Is the date of the itemised expenditure required to be reported?	No	0	No	0	No	0	No	0	No	0
19 Is a description of the itemised expenditure required to be reported?	No	0	No	0	No	0	No	0	No	0
20 Is the subject matter or bill number to be addressed by a lobbyist required on spending reports?	No	0	No	0	No	0	No	0	No	0
21 Is spending on household members of public officials by a lobbyist required to be reported?	No	0	No	0	No	0	No	0	No	0
22 Is a lobbyist required to disclose direct business associations with public officials, candidates or members of their households?	No	0	No	0	No	0	No	0	No	0
23 What is the statutory provision for a lobbyist giving/reporting gifts?	None	0	None	0	Limited	2	None	0	None	0
24 What is the statutory provision for a lobbyist giving/reporting campaign contributions?	None	0	None	0	Prohib	2	None	0	None	0
25 Is a lobbyist who has done no spending during a filing period required to make a report of no activity?	Yes	1	No	0	No	0	No	0	No	0

Employer spending disclosure

26 Is an employer/ principal of a lobbyist required to file a spending report?	No	0	No	0	No	0	No	0	No	0

27	Is compensation/ salary required to be reported on employer/principal spending reports?	No	0	No	0	No	0	No	0	No	0

Electronic filing

28	Does the oversight agency provide lobbyists/ employers with electronic/online registration?	Yes	1	Yes	1	Yes	1	No	0	Yes	1
29	Does the oversight agency provide lobbyists/employers with electronic/ online spending reporting?	No	0	No	0	No	0	No	0	No	0
30	Does the oversight agency provide training about how to file registrations/ spending reports electronically?	Yes	1	Yes	1	Yes	1	No	0	Yes	1

Public access

31	Location/format of registration or active lobbyist directory	Search database	3	Search database	3	Database dwnable	4	None	0	Search database	3
32	Location/format of spending reports	Search database	3	N/A	0	N/A	0	N/A	0	N/A	0
33	Cost of copies	Free	1	Free	1	Free	1	N/A	0	Free	1
34	Are sample registration forms/ spending reports available on the web?	Yes	1	Yes	1	Yes	1	No	0	Yes	1
35	Does the agency provide an overall lobbying spending total by year?	No	0	No	0	No	0	No	0	No	0
36	Does the agency provide an overall lobbying spending total by spending report deadlines?	No	0	No	0	No	0	No	0	No	0

37 Does the agency provide an overall lobbying spending total by industries lobbyists represent?	No	0	No	0	No	0	No	0	No	0
38 How often are lobby lists updated?	Quarterly	1	N/A	0	Weekly	3	N/A	0	Daily	4

Enforcement

39 Does the agency have statutory auditing authority?	Yes	2	Yes	2	Yes	2	Yes	2	No	0
40 Does the agency conduct mandatory reviews or audits?	Yes	2	No	0	Yes	2	Yes	2	No	0
41 Is there a statutory penalty for late filing of a lobby registration form?	Yes	1	Yes	0	Yes	1	Yes	1	Yes	1
42 Is there a statutory penalty for late filing of a lobby spending report?	No	0	No	0	No	0	No	0	No	0
43 When was a penalty for late filing of a lobby spending report last levied?	N/A	0	N/A	0	N/A	0	N/A	0	N/A	0
44 Is there a statutory penalty for incomplete filing of a lobby registration form?	Yes	1	Yes	0	Yes	1	Yes	1	No	0
45 Is there a statutory penalty for incomplete filing of a lobby spending report?	No	0	No	0	No	0	Yes	1	No	0
46 When was a penalty for incomplete filing of a lobby spending report last levied?	N/A	0	N/A	0	N/A	0	N/A	0	N/A	0
47 Does the state publish a list of delinquent filers either on the web or in a printed document?	Yes	0	No	0	Yes	1	No	0	No	0

Revolving-door provisions

48	Is a 'cooling off' period required before legislators can register as lobbyists?	Yes	2	No	0	No	0	Yes	2	Yes	2

Total CPI scores	44	27	45	38	33

Source: Authors' calculations.

Appendix B

Survey instruments

Survey 1. Survey sent to elected officials, civil servants and lobbyists in jurisdictions with lobbying regulations (in the US, Canada, Germany and the EP) (results presented in Chapter 5)

If you are an *elected representative*, please answer questions 1 and 2 and then go to question 6.

1. Which constituency do you represent?

2. In which ministry do you work?

If you are a *public sector administrator*, please answer question 3 and then go to question 6.

3. In which area do you work?

If you are a *representative of a lobby group/interest organisation*, please answer questions 4 and 5, then go to question 6.

4. At which level of government does your organisation predominately operate: federal or provincial?

5. What type of lobby group would best describe your activity?
   - Business
   - Labour
   - Professional
   - Single interest (please specify)

Questions

6. You consider yourself to be knowledgeable about the relevant legislation pertaining to the regulation of lobbyists at the federal level.
   - Strongly agree
   - Agree
   - Neutral
   - Disagree
   - Strongly disagree

7. In your view, the overall regulations help ensure accountability in your political system.
   - Strongly agree
   - Agree
   - Neutral
   - Disagree
   - Strongly disagree

8. Specific rules surrounding individual spending disclosures help ensure transparency.
   - Strongly agree
   - Agree
   - Neutral
   - Disagree
   - Strongly disagree

9.
a) Details of all political party campaign contributions by a lobbyist should be available to the public.
   - Strongly agree
   - Agree
   - Neutral
   - Disagree
   - Strongly disagree

b) There are loopholes in the system that allow individual lobbyists to give/receive 'gifts' regardless of the legislation in force.
   - Strongly agree
   - Agree
   - Neutral
   - Disagree
   - Strongly disagree

c) If you have answered 'Strongly agree' or 'Agree', in b) above, please elaborate on what the loopholes are and what the 'gifts' may consist of.

10. In your view, a register of lobbyists makes ordinary citizens feel inhibited about approaching their local representatives alone.
   - Strongly agree
   - Agree
   - Neutral
   - Disagree
   - Strongly disagree

11. Public access to an official list of lobbyists is freely available.
   - Yes
   - No

12.
a) Public access to an official list of lobbyists ensures accountability.
   - Strongly agree
   - Agree
   - Neutral
   - Disagree
   - Strongly disagree

b) If you have answered 'Disagree' or 'Strongly disagree', please elaborate why you feel that accountability has not been achieved.

13.
a) Reviews or audits by state agencies of lobbyists are effective in ensuring accountability.
   - Strongly agree
   - Agree
   - Neutral
   - Disagree
   - Strongly disagree

b) If you have answered 'Disagree' or 'Strongly disagree', please explain why you feel that this is the case.

14. In your view, how could the regulation be improved in order to ensure better transparency, accountability and effectiveness (please elaborate in the space below)?

15. Are there any other comments you wish to make?

Thank you for completing the questionnaire.

This section relates to follow-up interviews and the results of the survey

Please tick as appropriate
- I would like to receive a copy of the data collected.
- I would like to receive a copy of the data collected and am available to be interviewed

Name:
Address:
Email:

Thank you again for your time.

Survey 2. Survey sent to elected officials, civil servants and lobbyists in jurisdictions without lobbying regulations (results presented in Chapter 6)

If you are an *elected representative*, please answer questions 1 and 2 and then go to question 6.

1. Which provincial constituency do you represent?

2. In which ministry do you work?

If you are a *public sector administrator*, please answer question 3 and then go to question 6.

3. In which province do you work?

If you are a *representative of a lobby group/interest organisation*, please answer questions 4 and 5, then go to question 6.

4. In which province does your organisation predominately operate?

5. What type of lobby group would best describe your activity?
- Business
- Labour
- Professional
- Single interest (please specify)

Questions:

6. As you know, in your province there is no legislation regulating lobbying activity. In your view, what is the main reason for this lack of legislation (please tick):
  - Political actors are opposed to it.
  - Lobby groups are opposed to it.
  - 'Self-regulation' is considered sufficient.
  - There is no need to have legislation because lobbying activity is minimal
  - Other (please specify)

7. Lobbyists should be required to register when lobbying public officials.
  - Strongly agree
  - Agree
  - Neutral
  - Disagree
  - Strongly disagree

8. A lobbyist should be required to file spending reports at the following intervals in order to ensure transparency:
  - Weekly
  - Monthly
  - Quarterly
  - Bi-annually
  - Annually
  - Never

9. Details of all political party campaign contributions by a lobbyist should be available to the public.
  - Strongly agree
  - Agree
  - Neutral
  - Disagree
  - Strongly disagree

10. A list of all lobbyists (and the amount they have spent on their lobbying activity) should be freely available to the public:
  - By law, at all times, for example on a centralised website
  - By law, upon request to the state or a lobby group
  - On a voluntary basis as the state or lobby group sees appropriate
  - Never

11. In your view, a register of lobbyists makes ordinary citizens feel inhibited about approaching their local representatives alone.
  - Strongly agree
  - Agree
  - Neutral
  - Disagree
  - Strongly disagree

12. Should an independent agency have the power to pursue mandatory reviews or audits of lobbyists?
  - Always
  - Only when it is deemed necessary by the independent agency
  - Never

13. Penalising unprofessional lobbying behaviour (such as excessive campaign contributions or incomplete filing of reports) acts as a deterrent against such behaviour.
  - Strongly agree
  - Agree
  - Neutral
  - Disagree
  - Strongly disagree

14. If legislation regulating lobbying activity were implemented, then transparency, accountability and effectiveness in public policy making would be improved.
  - Strongly agree
  - Agree
  - Neutral
  - Disagree
  - Strongly disagree

Please feel free to elaborate your answer:

15. Are there any other comments you wish to make?

This section relates to follow-up interviews and the results of the survey
Please tick as appropriate
  - I only wish to receive a copy of the data collected.
  - I wish to receive a copy of the data collected and am available to be interviewed.

Name:
Address:
Email:

Thank you again for your time.

Bibliography

Ainsworth, Scott H. 1993. 'Regulating Lobbyists and Interest Group Influence', *Journal of Politics*, Vol. 55, No. 1, pp. 41–56.

Ainsworth, Scott H. 1997. 'The Role of Legislators in the Determination of Interest Group Influence', *Legislative Studies Quarterly*, Vol. 22, No. 4, pp. 517–533.

Almond Gabriel, A. 1956. 'Comparing Political Systems', *Journal of Politics*, Vol. 18, No. 2, pp. 391–409.

Antal, Zsuzsanna. 2005. 'Introduction to Hungarian Law Research', Hauser Global Law School Program, New York University School of Law, www.nyulawglobal.org/globalex/Hungary.htm.

Baumgartner, Frank R. and Leech, Beth L. 1998. *Basic Interests: The Importance of Groups on Politics and in Political Science*, Princeton, NJ: Princeton University Press.

Baumgartner, Frank R. and Leech, Beth L. 2001. 'Interest Niches and Policy Bandwagons: Patterns of Interest Group Involvement in National Politics', *Journal of Politics*, Vol. 63, No. 4, pp. 1191–1212.

Bentley, Arthur F. 1908. *The Process of Government*, Chicago: University of Chicago Press.

Bertók, János. 2008. *Lobbyists, Governments and Public Trust: Building a Legislative Framework for Enhancing Transparency and Accountability in Lobbying*, Paris: OECD, www.oecd.org/dataoecd/5/41/41074615.pdf.

Blondel, Jean. 1995. *Comparative Government: An Introduction* (2nd edition), New York: Harvester Wheatsheaf.

Bouwen, P. 2003. 'A Theoretical and Empirical Study of Corporate Lobbying in the European Parliament', *European Integration Online Papers (EIoP)*, Vol. 7, No. 11, www.eiop.or.at/eiop/texte/2003-011a.htm.

Brinig, Margaret F., Holcombe, Randall G. and Schwartzstein, Linda. 1993. 'The Regulation of Lobbyists', *Public Choice*, Vol. 77, No. 2, pp. 377–384.

Broz, J. L. 2002. 'Political System Transparency and Monetary Commitment Regimes', *International Organisation*, Vol. 56, No. 4, pp. 861–887.

Burson-Marsteller. 2005. *The Definitive Guide to Lobbying the European Institutions – Based on a Survey of the European Parliament, the Council and the European Commission*, Brussels: Burson-Marsteller, www.euractiv.com/29/images/The Definitive Guide to Lobbying the European Institutions (Spring 2005)_tcm29-140977.pdf.

Campos, Nauro F. and Giovannoni, Francesco. 2006. *Lobbying, Corruption and Political Influence*, IZA Discussion Paper No. 2313, http://ssrn.com/abstract=934356.

Chambers, S. 2003. 'Deliberative Democratic Theory', *Annual Review of Political Science*, Vol. 6, No. 1, pp. 307–326.

Chari, Raj. 1998. 'Spanish Socialists, Privatising the Right Way?', *West European Politics*, Vol. 21, No. 4, pp. 163–179.

Chari, Raj. 2008. *Why Did the Irish Reject Lisbon? An Analysis of Referendum Results*, Madrid: Real Instituto Elcano.

Chari, Raj and Cavatorta, Francesco. 2002. 'Economic Actors' Political Activity on "Overlap Issues": Privatisation and EU State Aid Control', *West European Politics*, Vol. 25, No. 4, pp. 119–142.

Chari, Raj and Kritzinger, Sylvia. 2006. *Understanding EU Policy Making*, London: Pluto.

Chari, Raj, Murphy, Gary and Hogan, John, 2007. 'Regulating Lobbyists: A Comparative Analysis of the USA, Canada, Germany and the European Union', *Political Quarterly*, Vol. 78, No. 3, pp. 422–438.

Chatterjee, Pratap. 2007. 'Sunshine Laws to Track European Lobbyists', *Spectrezine*, 7 November, www.spectrezine.org/europe/chatterjee.htm.

Christiansen, Thomas and Piattoni, Simona. 2004. *Informal Governance in the EU*, London: Edward Elgar.

Citizens' Conference on State Legislatures. 1971. *State Legislatures: An Evaluation of Their Effectiveness*, New York: Praeger.

COEC (Chief Official Ethics Commission, of the Republic of Lithuania). 2007. Presentation to the OECD symposium 'Lobbying: Enhancing Transparency and Accountability', June.

Coen, David. 1997. 'The Evolution of the Large Firm as a Political Actor in the European Union', *Journal European Public Policy*, Vol. 4, No. 1, pp. 91–108.

Coen, David. 1998. 'The European Business Interest and the Nation State: Large Firm Lobbying in the European Union and Member States', *Journal of Public Policy*, Vol. 18, No. 1, pp. 75–100.

Collier, David. 1997. 'Comparative Method in the 1990s', *APSA-CP: Newsletter of the APSA Organized Section in Comparative Politics*, Vol. 9, No. 1, pp. 1–5.

Corporate European Observatory (CEO). 2005. *Brussels: The EU Quarter* (3rd edition), Amsterdam: CEO.

Cowles, Maria Green. 1996. 'The EU Committee of AmCham: The Powerful Voice of American Firms in Brussels', *Journal of European Public Policy*, Vol. 3, No. 3, pp. 339–358.

Cronenberg, Elke. 2006. 'An Insider in Brussels: Lobbyists Reshape the European Union', 18 September, www.corpwatch.org/article.php?id=14119.

CPI (Center for Public Integrity). 2007. Discussion of the 'Hired Guns' methodology behind the CPI index, www.publicintegrity.org/hiredguns/default.aspx?act=methodology.

Curtin, D. 2006. 'Framing Public Deliberation and Democratic Legitimacy in the European Union', in S. Besson and J. Luis Marti (eds), *Deliberative Democracy and Its Discontents*, pp. 133–158. Aldershot: Ashgate.

Dabertrand, Fanny. 1999. *Les Institutions Communautaires face au lobbying: une comparaison entre l'attitude de la Commission et du Parlement Europeen*, Memoire de fin d'etudes, Institut D'Etudes Europeennes, Universite Libre de Bruxelles.

Dahl, Robert. 1961. *Who Governs? Democracy and Power in an American City*, New Haven, CN: Yale University Press.

Davies, Norman. 2005. *God's Playground: A History of Poland in Two Volumes*, Oxford: Oxford University Press.

de Kort, J. 1999. 'Foreign Direct Investment in Hungary: Lessons for Central and Eastern Europe', *Journal of East–West Business*, Vol. 5, No. 3, pp. 81–94, http://media.leidenuniv.nl/legacy/JdK1999.05.pdf.

Dinan, William. 2006. 'Learning Lessons? The Registration of Lobbyists at the Scottish Parliament', *Journal of Communication Management*, Vol. 10, No. 1, pp. 55–66.

Domanski, H. 2005. 'Legitymizacja systemu politycznego w dwudziestu jeden krajach' [Legitimization of Political System in Twenty-One Countries], *Studia Socjologiczne*, Vol. 177, No. 2, pp. 5–39.

Dryzek, John. 2000. *Democracy and Beyond*, Oxford: Oxford University Press.

Dyck, Rand. 2004. *Canadian Politics, Critical Approaches* (4th edition), Toronto: Thomson Nelson.

Easton, D. 1957. 'An Approach to the Study of Political Systems', *World Politics*, Vol. 9, No. 5, pp. 383–400.

Elster, Jon. 1998. *Deliberative Democracy*, Cambridge: Cambridge University Press.

Emmerson, Russell. 2009. 'Lobbyist Register Likely To Fail', *Advertiser* (Adelaide), 22 July, www.news.com.au/adelaidenow/story/0,22606,25817445-2682,00.html.

Esping-Anderson, Gosta. 1990. *Three Worlds of Welfare Capitalism*, Cambridge: Polity Press.

European Commission. 1992. *Communication from the Commission: An Open and Structured Dialogue with Special Interest Groups*, Brussels: European Commission.

European Commission. 2001. *European Governance: A White Paper*, COM (2001), 428 Final, Brussels: European Commission.

European Commission. 2006. *Green Paper: European Transparency Initiative*, Brussels: European Commission.

European Parliament, DG for Research. 2003. *Lobbying in the European Union: Current Rules and Practices*, Luxembourg: European Parliament.

Finkelstein, Neal D. 2000. 'Introduction: Transparency in Public Policy', in Neal D. Finkelstein (ed.), *Transparency in Public Policy*, pp. 1–9, Basingstoke: Macmillan.

Fisher, Roger, Ury, William and Patton, Bruce. 1999. *Getting to Yes: Negotiating an Agreement Without Giving In* (2nd edition), London: Random House.

Francis, J. C. 1993. *The Politics of Regulation: A Comparative Perspective*, London: Blackwell.

Galkowski, Juliusz. 2008. 'Poland's Experience of Developing and Implementing the Act on Legislative and Regulatory Lobbying', in *Lobbyists, Government and Public Trust*, pp. 127–158, Paris: OECD.

Gallagher, Michael, Laver, Michael and Mair, Peter. 2006. *Representative Government in Modern Europe: Institutions, Parties and Governments* (4th edition), New York: McGraw-Hill.

Garziano, Luigi. 2001. *Lobbying, Pluralism and Democracy*, London: Palgrave.

Geraats, P. M. 2002. 'Central Bank Transparency', *Economics Journal*, Vol. 112, No. 483, pp. 532–565.

Giorno, Guy. 2006a. *Canadian Lobbyist Registration Law: Overview and Comparison*, Toronto: unpublished manuscript given to authors.

Giorno, Guy. 2006b. 'Staying on the Right Side of the Law', paper presented at the 3rd Annual Government Relations Summit, Ottawa, Ontario, February.

Gordon, Neil. 2005. 'State Lobbyists Near the $1 Billion Mark. Laws in Flux for 19 States', 10 August, Center for Public Integrity, www.publicintegrity.org/hiredguns/report.aspx?aid=728.

Government of Canada. 2008. *The Lobbying Act – A Summary of New Requirements*, Ottawa: Office of the Registrar of Lobbyists, www.ocl-cal.gc.ca/eic/site/lobbyist-lobbyiste1.nsf/vwapj/Info_booklet_Eng.pdf/$FILE/Info_booklet_Eng.pdf.

Gray, Virginia and Lowery, David. 1998. 'State Lobbying Regulations and Their Enforcement: Implications for the Diversity of Interest Communities', *State and Local Government Review*, Vol. 30, No. 2, pp. 78–91.

Greenwood, Justin. 1998. 'Regulating Lobbying in the European Union', *Parliamentary Affairs*, Vol. 51, No. 4, pp. 587–599.

Greenwood, Justin. 2007. *Interest Representation in the EU*, Basingstoke: Palgrave.

Greenwood, Justin and Thomas, Clive S. 1998. 'Regulating Lobbying in the Western World', *Parliamentary Affairs*, Vol. 51, No. 4, pp. 487–499.

Griffith, Gareth. 2008. *The Regulation of Lobbying*, Briefing Paper No. 5/08, Sydney: NSW Parliamentary Library Research Service, www.parliament.nsw.gov.au/prod/parlment/publications.nsf/key/TheRegulationofLobbying.

Groseclose, Tim and McCarty, Nolan. 2001. 'The Politics of Blame: Bargaining Before an Audience', *American Journal of Political Science*, Vol. 45, No. 1, pp. 100–120.

Gutmann, Amy and Thompson, Dennis. 1996. *Democracy and Disagreement*, Cambridge, MA: Belknap Press of Harvard University Press.

Gutmann, Amy and Thompson, Dennis. 2004. *Why Deliberative Democracy?*, Princeton, NJ: Princeton University Press.

Harvard Law Review. 2002. 'The Political Activity of Think Tanks: The Case for

Mandatory Contributor Disclosure', *Harvard Law Review*, Vol. 115, No. 5, pp. 1502–1524.

Héritier, Adrienne. 1999. 'Elements of Democratic Legitimation in Europe: An Alternative Perspective', *Journal of European Public Policy*, Vol. 6, No. 2, pp. 269–282.

Hix, Simon. 2002. 'Constitutional Agenda Setting Through Discretion in Rule Interpretations: Why the European Parliament Won at Amsterdam', *British Journal of Political Science*, Vol. 32, No. 2, pp. 259–280.

Hix, Simon. 2005. *The Political System of the European Union* (2nd edition), London: Palgrave.

Hogan, John, Murphy, Gary and Chari, Raj. 2008. 'Next Door They Have Regulation But Not Here...: Assessing the Opinions of Actors in the Opaque World of Unregulated Lobbying', *Canadian Political Science Review*, Vol. 2, No. 3, pp. 125–151.

Holman, Craig. 2008. 'Lobbying Reform in the United States and the European Union: Progress on Two Continents', paper presented at the Conference of the American Political Science Association, Boston, MA, 31 August.

Holman, Craig. 2009. 'Lobbying Reform in the United States and the European Union: Progress on Two Continents', in Conor McGrath (ed.), *Interest Groups and Lobbying: Volume 1 – The United States, and Comparative Studies*, pp. 267–296, Lewiston, NY: Edwin Mellen Press.

Howlett, Michael and Ramesh, M. 2003. *Studying Public Policy: Policy Cycles and Policy Subsystems*, Oxford: Oxford University Press.

Hrebenar, Ronald J. 1997. *Interest Group Politics in America* (3rd edition), New York: M. E. Sharpe.

Hrebenar, Ronald J., Nakainura, Akira and Nakamura, Akio. 1998. 'Lobbying Regulation in the Japanese Diet', *Parliamentary Affairs*, Vol. 51, No. 4, pp. 551–558.

Hunter, Kennith G., Wilson, Laura Ann and Brunk, Gregory G. 1991. 'Societal Complexity and Interest-Group Lobbying in the American States', *Journal of Politics*, Vol. 53, No. 2, pp. 488–503.

James, Michael, Blamires, Cyprian and Pease-Watkin, Catherine (eds). 1999. *Political Tactics: The Collected Works of Jeremy Bentham*, Oxford: Oxford University Press.

Jasiecki, Krzysztof. 2006. 'Regulating Lobbying in Poland: Background, Scope and Expectations', Brussels: Council of Europe, www.coe.int/t/dg1/legalcooperation/ economiccrime/cybercrime/cy%20activity%20Interface2006/143%20_2006_-if-rep%20jasie.pdf.

Johnson, C. 1982. *MJTI and the Japanese Miracle: The Growth of Industrial Policy, 1925–1975*, Stanford, CA: Stanford University Press.

Jordan, Grant. 1991. *The Commercial Lobbyists*, Aberdeen: Aberdeen University Press.

Jordan, Grant. 1998. 'Towards Regulation in the UK: From "General Good Sense" to "Formalised Rules"', *Parliamentary Affairs*, Vol. 51, No. 4, pp. 524–537.

Kallas, Siim. 2007. 'The European Transparency Initiative: An Issue for Berlin', speech to the Zukunftskolloquium Politikberatung (de'ge'pol), Berlin, 19 October, http:// ec.europa.eu/commission_barroso/kallas/doc/ 20071019_berlin_en.pdf.

Kalniš, Valts. 2005. *Parliamentary Lobbying: Between Civil Rights and Corruption*, Riga: Nordik Publishing House.

Keane, Bernard. 2008. 'Why Faulkner's Lobbyist Register won't work', *Crikey*, 3 April, www.crikey.com.au/2008/04/03/why-faulkners-lobbyist-register-wont-work.

Keohane, Robert O. and Nye, Joseph. 2003. 'Redefining Accountability for Global Governance', in M. Kahler and D. Lake (eds), *Governance in a Global Economy: Political Authority in Transition*, pp. 386–411, Princeton, NJ: Princeton University Press.

Kernell, S. and Jacobson, Gary C. 2003. *The Logic of American Politics* (2nd edition), Washington, DC: CQ Press.

Klemencic, Goran. 2006. *A Review of the Compliance of the Lithuania Legal and Institutional Framework Against Corruption*, Vilnius: United Nations Development Programme, Lithuania Office, www.transparency.lt/new/images/ti_lithuania_uncac. pdf.

Koen, Vincent. 2006. 'The "Soaring Eagle": Poland's Economic Performance and Challenges', Paris: OECD, www.oecd.org/dataoecd/29/0/37737384.pdf.

Kolko, Gabriel. 1965. *The Triumph of Conservatism: A Reinterpretation of American History, 1900–1916*. Princeton, NJ: Princeton University Press.

Korkut, Umar. 2005. 'The Relationship Between Democratization and Invigoration of Civil Society: The Case of Hungary and Poland', *East European Quarterly*, Vol. 39, No. 2, pp. 149–177.

Kovács, Balázs and Villányi, Viktória. 2006. 'Country Report: Hungary (2006)', Washington, DC: Freedom House, www.freedomhouse.org/template.cfm?page=47&nit=403&year=2006.

Kovács, Balázs and Villányi, Viktória. 2007. 'Hungary', in *Nations in Transit 2007*, pp. 299–323, Washington, DC: Freedom House, www.freedomhouse.hu//images/fdh_galleries/NIT2007final/nit-hungary-web.pdf.

Krajewski, Andrzej. 2006. 'Country Report: Poland (2006)', Washington, DC: Freedom House, www.freedomhouse.org/template.cfm?page=47&nit=405& year=2006.

Krajewski, Andrzej. 2008. 'Poland', in *Nations in Transit 2008*, pp. 447–466, Washington, DC: Freedom House, www.freedomhouse.hu/images/fdh_galleries/NIT2008/NT-Poland-final.pdf.

Krishnakumar, Anita S. 2006. 'Towards an Interest-Group-Based Approach to Lobbying Regulation', bepress Legal Series Paper 1091, Berkeley Electronic Press, http://law.bepress.com/expresso/eps/1091.

Largerlof, Johan and Frisell, Lars. 2004. 'Lobbying, Information Transmission and Unequal Representation', *Centre for Economic Policy Research*, No. 4313, pp. 1–27.

Lékó, Zoltan. 2007. 'How Much Disclosure Is Enough? Lobby Registration System in Hungary', presented at an OECD seminar, 8 June.

Lindblom, Charles. 1977. *Politics and Markets: The World's Political–Economic Systems*, New York: Basic Books.

Lindstedt, C. and Naurin, D. 2006. 'Transparency Against Corruption: A Cross-country Study', paper presented at the IPSA 20th World Congress, Fuhuoka, Japan, 9–13 July.

Lloyd, C. 1990. 'Political Lobbying: Dynamiting or Gentle Persuasion?', in P. Cullen (ed.), *No Is Not an Answer: Lobbying for Success*, Sydney: Allen and Unwin.

Lord, Christopher. 2004. *A Democratic Audit of the European Union*, Basingstoke: Palgrave.

Mackenzie, G. C. 2002. *Scandal Proof: Do Ethics Laws Make Government Ethical?*, Washington, DC: Brookings.

Mahler, Gregory S. 1995. *Comparative Politics: An Institutional and Cross-national Approach* (2nd edition), Englewood Cliffs, NJ: Prentice Hall.

Mahoney, Christine. 2004. 'The Power of Institutions: State and Interest Group Activity in the EU', *European Union Politics*, Vol. 5, No. 4, pp. 441–466.

Mahoney, Christine. 2007. 'Lobbying Success in the US and the EU', *Journal of Public Policy*, Vol. 27, No. 1, pp. 44–45.

Malone, Mary, 2004. *Regulation of Lobbyists in Developed Countries*, Dublin: Institute of Public Administration.

Marsh, Ian. 2004. 'Political Integration and the Outlook for the Australian Party System: Party Adaption or Regime Change?', in Paul Boreham, Geoffrey Stokes and Richard Hall (eds), *The Politics of Australian Society*, pp. 119–140. Frenchs Forest, NSW: Pearson.

Martin, Albro. 1971. *Enterprise Denied: Origins of the Decline of American Railroads, 1897–1917*, New York: Columbia University Press.

Mayer, Lawrence C., Burnett, John H. and Ogden, Suzanne. 1993. *Comparative Politics: Nations and Theories in a Changing World*, Englewood Cliffs, NJ: Prentice Hall.

McCubbins, M., Noll, R. and Weingast, B. 1987. 'Administrative Procedures as Instruments of Political Control', *Journal of Law, Economics, and Organization*, Vol. 3, No. 2, pp. 243–277.

McGrath, Conor. 2005. *Lobbying in Washington, London, and Brussels: The Persuasive Communication of Political Issues*, Lewiston, NY: Edwin Mellen Press.

McGrath, Conor. 2008. 'The Development and Regulation of Lobbying in the New Member States of the European Union', *Journal of Public Affairs*, Vol. 8, Nos 1–2, pp. 15–32.

McGrath, Conor (ed.). 2009. *Interest Groups and Lobbying: Volume 1 – The United States, and Comparative Studies*, Lewiston, NY: Edwin Mellen Press.

Michalowitz, Irina. 2006. 'The European Platform of Women Scientists and Potential Obstacles and Dangers of Civil Society Participation in Multi-level Governance Systems', paper presented at the Institute for International Integration Studies, Trinity College Dublin.

Miliband, Ralph. 1969. *The State in Capitalist Society*, London: Weidenfeld and Nicolson.

Moncrieffe, J. M. 1998. 'Reconceptualizing Political Accountability', *International Political Science Review*, Vol. 19, No. 4, pp. 387–406.

Moran, Michael. 2007. *The British Regulatory State: High Modernism and Hyper-innovation*, Oxford: Oxford University Press.

Moravscik, Andrew. 1993. 'Preferences and Power in the European Community: A Liberal Intergovernmentalist Approach', *Journal of Common Market Studies*, Vol. 31, No. 4, pp. 473–524.

Murphy, Gary. 2004. 'Interest Groups in the Policy Process', in John Coakley and Michael Gallagher (eds), *Politics in the Republic of Ireland* (4th edition), pp. 352–383, London: Routledge.

Murphy, Gary, Hogan, John and Chari, Raj. 2009. 'The Politics of Regulating Lobbyists: Assessing the Attitudes of Actors in the World of Regulated Lobbying', in Conor McGrath (ed.), *Interest Groups and Lobbying: Volume 1 – The United States, and Comparative Studies*, pp. 297–328, Lewiston: Edwin Mellen Press.

National Conference of State Legislatures. 2008. 'Ethics: How States Define "Lobbying" and "Lobbyist"', www.ncsl.org/programs/ethics/lobbyingdefinitions.htm.

Naurin, Daniel. 2006. 'Transparency, Publicity, Accountability – The Missing Links', *Swiss Political Science Review*, Vol. 12, No. 3, pp. 90–98.

Naurin, Daniel. 2007. 'Backstage Behaviour? Lobbyists in Public and Private Settings in Sweden and the European Union', *Comparative Politics*, Vol. 39, No. 2, pp. 209–228.

Nelson, Michael. 2007. Presentation to the symposium 'Lobbying: Enhancing Transparency and Accountability', Organisation for Economic Co-operation and Development, 8 June.

Newmark, Adam J. 2009. 'Personal Relationships and Information as Lobbying Strategies: Adaptation in the Context of the American States', in Conor McGrath (ed.), *Interest Groups and Lobbying: Volume 1 – The United States, and Comparative Studies*, pp. 75–102, Lewiston, NY: Edwin Mellen Press.

Nolan Committee. 1995. *First Report of the Committee on Standards in Public Life*, Cm 2850-I, London: HMSO, www.archive.official-documents.co.uk/document/cm28/2850/2850.htm

Nownes, Anthony J. 2006. *Total Lobbying: What Lobbyists Want (and How They Try to Get It)*, Cambridge: Cambridge University Press.

O'Flynn, I. 2006. *Deliberative Democracy and Divided Societies*, Edinburgh: Edinburgh University Press.

Opheim, Cynthia. 1991. 'Explaining the Differences in State Lobby Regulations', *Western Political Quarterly*, Vol. 44, No. 2, pp. 405–421.

Pateman, Carol. 1976. *Participation and Democratic Theory*, Cambridge: Cambridge University Press.

Piasecka, Aneta. 2005. 'Country Report: Lithuania (2005)', Washington, DC: Freedom House, www.freedomhouse.org/template.cfm?page=47&nit=371&year=2005.

Piasecka, Aneta. 2006. 'Country Report: Lithuania (2006)', Washington, DC: Freedom House, www.freedomhouse.org/template.cfm?page=47&nit=394&year=2006.

Piasecka, Aneta. 2007. 'Country Report: Lithuania (2007)', Washington, DC: Freedom House, www.freedomhouse.org/template.cfm?page=47&nit=428&year=2007.

Piasecka, Aneta. 2008. 'Lithuania', in *Nations in Transit 2008*, pp. 363–385, Washington,

DC: Freedom House, www.freedomhouse.hu/images/fdh_galleries/NIT2008/NT-Lithuania-final.pdf.

Popper, Karl. 1963. *Conjectures and Refutations: The Growth of Scientific Knowledge*, London: Routledge.

Public Administration Select Committee. 2009. *Lobbying: Access and Influence in Whitehall*, London: The Stationery Office, www.parliament.the-stationery-office.com/pa/cm200809/cmselect/cmpubadm/36/36i.pdf.

Public Disclosure Commission. 2008. 'Washington Continues to Lead Nation in Campaign Finance Disclosure', press release, 17 September, www.pdc.wa.gov/archive/mediareleases/pdf/NationalRanking2008.pdf.

Pulzer, Peter. 1995. *German Politics, 1945–1995*, Oxford: Oxford University Press.

Putnam, Robert D. 1988. 'Diplomacy and Domestic Politics: The Logic of Two-Level Games', *International Organization*, Vol. 42, No. 3, pp. 427–460.

Rakowski, Piotr and Rybicki, Robert. 2000. 'Features – An Overview of Polish Law', Law and Technology Resources for Legal Professionals, www.llrx.com/features/polish.htm.

Rechtman, Rene. 1998. 'Regulation of Lobbyists in Scandinavia – A Danish Perspective', *Parliamentary Affairs*, Vol. 51, No. 4, pp. 579–586.

Regulski, Jerzy. 2003. *Local Government Reform in Poland: An Insider's Story*, Budapest: Open Society Institute.

Risse, Thomas. 2000. '"Let's Argue!" Communicative Action in World Politics', *International Organization*, Vol. 54, No. 1, pp. 1–39.

Rogers, R. E. 1969. *Max Weber's Ideal Type Theory*, New York: Philosophical Library.

Ronit, Karsten and Schneider, Volker. 1998. 'The Strange Case of Regulating Lobbying in Germany', *Parliamentary Affairs*, Vol. 51, No. 4, pp. 559–567.

Roper, Steven D. 2002. 'Are All Semipresidential Regimes the Same? A Comparison of Premier–Presidential Regimes', *Comparative Politics*, Vol. 34, No. 3 (April), pp. 253–272.

Rosenthal, A. 2001. *The Third House: Lobbyists and Lobbying in the States*, Washington, DC: Congressional Quarterly.

Ross, Robert. 2000. 'The 1995–1996 Taiwan Strait Confrontation: Coercion, Credibility, and Use of Force', *International Security*, Vol. 25, No. 2, pp. 87–123.

Rush, Michael. 1998. 'The Canadian Experience: The Lobbyists Registration Act', *Parliamentary Affairs*, Vol. 51, No. 4, pp. 516–523.

Ryan, S. 2008. 'MPs Escape Scrutiny by Lobbyist Code', *The Australian*, 3 April.

Scharpf, Fritz W. 2006. *Problem Solving Effectiveness and Democratic Accountability in the EU*, IHS Political Science Series No. 107, Vienna: Institut für Höhere Studien (IHS; Institute for Advanced Studies).

Schedler, Andreas. 1999. 'Conceptualising Accountability', in Andreas Schedler, Larry Diamond and Marc F. Plattner (eds), *The Self-restraining State: Power and Accountability in New Democracies*, pp. 13–29, London: Lynne Rienner.

Scott, Colin. 2000. 'Accountability in the Regulatory State', *Journal of Law and Society*, Vol. 27, No. 1, pp. 38–60.

Sekuless, P. 1991. *Lobbying Canberra in the Nineties*, Sydney: Allen and Unwin.

Serrill, Michael S. 1990. 'Soviet Union War of Nerves', *Time International*, 2 April.

Siaroff, Alan. 1999. 'Corporatism in 24 Industrial Democracies: Meaning and Measurement', *European Journal of Political Research*, Vol. 36, No. 6, pp. 175–205.

SME Support Project. 2006. *Government Relations in Georgia: A Guide for Business Associations*, Washington, DC: US Agency for International Development (USAID), www.iesc.ge/files/guidebookreduced.pdf.

Smyth, Jamie. 2006. 'EU Proposes Voluntary Registration for Lobbyists', *Irish Times*, 4 May.

Standing Committee on Finance and Public Administration. 2008. *Knock, Knock... Who's There? The Lobbying Code of Conduct*, Canberra: Senate Printing Unit, Parliament House, www.aph.gov.au/Senate/committee/fapa_ctte/lobbying_code/report/report.pdf.

Stark, A. 1992. 'Political Discourse Analysis and the Debate Over Canada's Lobbying Legislation', *Canadian Journal of Political Science*, Vol. 25, No. 3, pp. 513–534.

Stasavage, David. 2003. 'Transparency, Democratic Accountability, and the Economic Consequences of Monetary Institutions', *American Journal of Political Science*, Vol. 47, No. 3, pp. 389–403.

Stasavage, David. 2004. 'Open-Door or Closed-Door? Transparency in Domestic and International Bargaining', *International Organization*, Vol. 58, No. 4, pp. 667–703.

Subramaniam, V. 1983. 'Public Accountability: Context, Career and Confusion of a Concept', *Indian Journal of Public Administration*, Vol. 29, No. 3, pp. 446–456.

Thomas, Clive S. 1998. 'Interest Group Regulation Across the United States: Rationale, Development and Consequences', *Parliamentary Affairs*, Vol. 51, No. 4, pp. 500–515.

Thomas, Clive S. 2004. 'Lobbying in the United States: An Overview for Students, Scholars and Practitioner', in Phil Harris and Craig S. Fleischer (eds), *The Handbook of Public Affairs*, pp. 281–303, London: Sage.

Thomas, Clive S. and Hrebenar, Ronald. 1996. 'Regulating Interest Groups in the United States: National, State and Local Experiences', paper prepared for presentation at the annual meeting of the American Political Science Association, San Francisco, CA, 5–8 September.

Transparency International. 2006. *Report on the Transparency International Global Corruption Barometer 2006*, Berlin: International Secretariat, Transparency International, www.tikenya.org/documents/GCB_2006.pdf.

Trommer, S. and Chari, R. 2006. 'The Council of Europe: Interest Groups and Ideological Missions?', *West European Politics*, Vol. 29, No. 4, pp. 665–686.

Tusinski Berg, Kati. 2009. 'Lobbying as Advocacy Public Relations and Its "Unspoken" Code of Ethics', in Conor McGrath (ed.), *Interest Groups and Lobbying: Volume 1 – The United States, and Comparative Studies,* pp. 135–156, Lewiston, NY: Edwin Mellen Press.

United Nations Development Programme. 2005. *Institutional Arrangements to Combat Corruption: A Comparative Study*, Bangkok: Democratic Governance Practice Team, UNDP Regional Centre in Bangkok, http://regionalcentrebangkok.undp.or.th/practices/governance/documents/Corruption_Comparative_Study-200512.pdf.

Vleugels, Roger. 2008. 'Overview of All 86 FOIA Countries', www.freedominfo.org/features/FOIA_overview_vleugels.pdf.

Ward, Alan J. 1999. 'Australian Parliamentary Orthodoxy: A Foreign Perspective on Australian Constitutional Reform', lecture in the Senate Occasional Lecture Series at Parliament House on 18 June, www.aph.gov.au/SEnate/pubs/pops/pop35/c04.htm.

Warhurst, John. 1998. 'Locating the Target: Regulating Lobbying in Australia', *Parliamentary Affairs*, Vol. 51, No. 4, pp. 538–550.

Warhurst, John. 2008. *The Lobbying Code of Conduct: An Appraisal*, Democratic Audit Discussion Paper 4/08, Hawthorn, Victoria: Democratic Audit of Australia (Institute for Social Research, Swinburne University of Technology), http://democraticaudit.org.au/?page_id=15.

Watson, R. and Shackleton, M. 2003. 'Organized Interests and Lobbying in the EU', in Elizabeth Bomberg and Alexander Stubb (eds), *The EU: How Does It Work?*, pp. 88–107, Oxford: Oxford University Press.

Weber, Max. 1904. *The Methodology of the Social Sciences*, translated by E. A. Shils and H. A. Finch, New York; Free Press (1949).

Weller, Patrick and Fleming, Jenny. 2003. 'The Commonwealth', in Jeremy Moon and Campbell Sharman (eds), pp. 12–40, *Australian Politics and Government*, Cambridge: Cambridge University Press.

Wolpe, Bruce C. and Levine, Bertram J. 1996. *Lobbying Congress: How the System Works*, Washington, DC: CQ Press.

Wyrzykowski, Miroslaw and Cielen, Agnieszka. 2006. 'Presidential Elements in Government Poland – Semi-presidentialism or "Rationalised Parliamentarianism?', *European Constitutional Law Review*, Vol. 2, No. 2, pp. 253–267.

Yoder, Jennifer. 2007. 'Leading the Way to Regionalization in Post-Communist Europe: An Examination of the Process and Outcomes of Regional Reform in Poland', *East European Politics and Society*, Vol. 21, No. 3, pp. 424–446.

Young, I. M. 2002. *Inclusion and Democracy*, Oxford: Oxford University Press.

Zeller, B. 1958. 'Regulation of Pressure Groups and Lobbyists', *Annals of the American Academy of Political and Social Sciences*, Vol. 319, No. 1, pp. 94–103.

Žiliukaite, Ruta, Ramonaite, Aiste, Nevinskaite, Laima, Beresnevičiute, Vida and Vinogradnaite, Inga. 2006. *Neatrasta galia: Lietuvos pilietines visuomenes žemelapis* [*Undiscovered Power: Map of the Civil Society in Lithuania*], Vilnius: Civil Society Institute (conclusion section available in English at www.civitas.lt/files/Project_MapOfCivilSociety_Conclusiosns.pdf [*sic*]).

Index

CPSIA information can be obtained at www.ICGtesting.com
Printed in the USA
237188LV00002B/1/P